Neighbourhood

MANAGING THE TRAI[N
Putting the basics into practice

Service
Training.

Latest titles in the McGraw-Hill Training Series

TOTAL QUALITY TRAINING
The Quality Culture and Quality Trainer
Brian Thomas   ISBN 0-07-707472-6

CAREER DEVELOPMENT AND PLANNING
A Guide for Managers, Trainers and Personnel Staff
Malcolm Peel   ISBN 0-07-707554-4

SALES TRAINING
A Guide to Developing Effective Salespeople
Frank S. Salisbury   ISBN 0-07-707458-0

CLIENT-CENTRED CONSULTING
A Practical Guide for Internal Advisers and Trainers
Peter Cockman, Bill Evans
and Peter Reynolds   ISBN 0-07-707685-0

TRAINING TO MEET THE TECHNOLOGY CHALLENGE
Trevor Bentley   ISBN 0-07-707589-7

IMAGINATIVE EVENTS Volumes I & II
Ken Jones   ISBN 0-07-707679-6 Volume I
                   ISBN 0-07-707680-X Volume II
                   ISBN 0-07-707681-8 for set of Volumes I & II

LEARNING THROUGH SIMULATIONS
A Guide to the Design and Use of Simulations in Business and Education
John Fripp   ISBN 0-07-707588-9

MEETINGS MANAGEMENT
A Manual of Effective Training Material
Leslie Rae   ISBN 0-07-707782-2

WORKSHOPS THAT WORK
100 Ideas to Make Your Training Event More Effective
Tom Bourner, Vivien Martin
and Phil Race   ISBN 0-07-707800-4

TRAINING FOR PROFIT
A Guide to the Integration of Training
Philip Darling   ISBN 0-07-707785-7

THE HANDBOOK FOR ORGANIZATIONAL CHANGE
Strategy and Skill for Trainers and Developers
Carol A. O'Connor   ISBN 0-07-707693-1

DEVELOPING DIRECTORS
Building an Effective Boardroom Team
Colin Coulson-Thomas ISBN 0-07-707590-9

Details of these and other titles in the series are available from:

The Product Manager, Professional Books, McGraw-Hill Book Company Europe,
Shoppenhangers Road, Maidenhead, Berkshire SL6 2QL, United Kingdom.
Telephone: 0628 23432. Fax: 0628 770224

Managing the training process

Putting the basics into practice

Mike Wills

McGRAW-HILL BOOK COMPANY

London · New York · St Louis · San Francisco · Auckland
Bogotá · Caracas · Lisbon · Madrid · Mexico · Milan
Montreal · New Delhi · Panama · Paris · San Juan · São Paulo
Singapore · Sydney · Tokyo · Toronto

Published by
McGRAW-HILL Book Company Europe
Shoppenhangers Road, Maidenhead, Berkshire SL6 2QL, England.
Telephone: 0628 23432
Fax: 0628 770224

British Library Cataloguing in Publication Data
Wills, Mike
   Managing the Training Process: Putting
   the Basics into Practice. – (McGraw-Hill
   Training Series)
   I. Title II. Series
   658.3124

   ISBN 0-07-707806-3

Library of Congress Cataloging-in-Publication Data
Wills, Mike,
   Managing the training process: putting the basics into practice /
   Mike Wills.
      p. cm. — (The McGraw-Hill training series)
   Includes bibliographical references and index.
   ISBN 0-07-707806-3
   1. Employees—Training of—Management. I. Title. II. Series.
HF5549.5.T7W4934 1993
   658.3'124—dc20

93-22669
CIP

1234 CL 96543

Typeset by Book Ens Limited, Baldock, Herts
Printed and bound in Great Britain by Clays Ltd, St Ives plc

Contents

Acknowledgements

The problem with acknowledgements is that it is nearly impossible to list everybody who has influenced the writing of a book. Even if I were to try, I am sure I would miss out some of my most important influences.

So, rather than attempt the impossible, I would like to dedicate this book to all the people I have ever taught, and to all my colleagues who have influenced me by way of suggestions, discussion, argument, or demonstration of good training practice. Thank you all.

Series preface

Training and development are now firmly centre stage in most organizations, if not all. Nothing unusual in that—for some organizations. They have always seen training and development as part of the heart of their businesses—but more and more must see it the same way.

The demographic trends through the 'nineties will inject into the marketplace severe competition for good people who will need good training. Young people without conventional qualifications, skilled workers in redundant crafts, people out of work, women wishing to return to work—all will require excellent training to fit them to meet the job demands of the 'nineties and beyond.

But excellent training does not spring from what we have done well in the past. T&D specialists are in a new ball game. 'Maintenance' training—training to keep up skill levels to do what we have always done—will be less in demand. Rather, organization, work, and market change training are now much more important and will remain so for some time. Changing organizations and people is no easy task, requiring special skills and expertise which, sadly, many T&D specialists do not possess.

To work as a 'change' specialist requires us to get to centre stage—to the heart of the company's business. This means we have to ask about future goals and strategies, and even be involved in their development, at least as far as T&D policies are concerned.

This demands excellent communication skills, political expertise, negotiating ability, diagnostic skills—indeed, all the skills a good internal consultant requires.

The implications for T&D specialists are considerable. It is not enough merely to be skilled in the basics of training, we must also begin to act like business people and to think in business terms and talk the language of business. We must be able to resource training not just from within but by using the vast array of external resources. We must be able to manage our activities as well as any other manager. We must share in the creation and communication of the company's vision. We must never let the goals of the company out of our sight.

In short, we may have to grow and change with the business. It will be hard. We shall not only have to demonstrate relevance but also value for money and achievement of results. We shall be our own boss, as accountable for results as any other line manager, and we shall have to deal with fewer internal resources.

The challenge is on, as many T&D specialists have demonstrated to me over the past few years. We need to be capable of meeting that challenge. This is why McGraw-Hill Book Company Europe have planned and launched this major new training series—to help us meet that challenge.

The series covers all aspects of T&D and provides the knowledge base from which we can develop plans to meet the challenge. They are practical books for the professional person. They are a starting point for planning our journey to the twenty-first century.

Use them well. Don't just read them. Highlight key ideas, thoughts, action pointers or whatever, and have a go at doing something with them. Through experimentation we evolve; through stagnation we die.

I know that all the authors in the McGraw-Hill Training Series would want me to wish you good luck. Have a great journey into the twenty-first century.

ROGER BENNETT
Series Editor

About the series editor

Roger Bennett has over 20 years' experience in training, management education, research and consulting. He has long been involved with trainer training. He has carried out research into trainer effectiveness, and conducted workshops, seminars, and conferences on the subject around the world. He has written extensively on the subject including the book *Improving Trainer Effectiveness* (Gower). His work has taken him all over the world, and has involved directors of companies as well as managers and trainers.

Roger Bennett has worked in engineering, several business schools (including the International Management Centre, where he launched the UK's first masters degree in T&D), and has been a board director of two companies. He is the editor of the *Journal of European Industrial Training*, and was series editor of the ITD's *Get In There* workbook and video package for the managers of training departments. He now runs his own business called The Management Development Consultancy.

Introduction

'Training and education are now being given the prominence and priority that they deserve throughout business and industry.'

Well, perhaps such an optimistic statement might be a headline from a future newspaper, but recently I have been getting the impression that many companies have been putting, and keeping, training on the agenda.

The reason for this is not altruism, but a growing realization that companies which are successful take the training of their people very seriously. Of course this is not a simple cause-and-effect relationship. Good training doesn't guarantee spectacular results, otherwise we could simply sink vast amounts of money into training and immediately have highly profitable companies. It sounds too easy and it is too easy.

The relationship between training and business results is a very complex one. This is because results are affected by many differing and varying influences. Economic influences are some of the most prevalent.

For example, in 1973 many companies had a spectacularly successful year and managing directors congratulated themselves on how well they had managed their companies. What they had failed to realize was that VAT was introduced on 1 April 1973. The increase in revenue was due to the demand for equipment and services that would help cope with the introduction of the new tax.

Identifying training's contribution to a business would involve the training department in the immensely difficult task of filtering out the effects of all these other influences. Although it is doubtful whether this calculation could ever be done with any sort of accuracy, this situation is one training managers often find themselves in—simply because they are asked to justify their current training curriculum.

Another approach is to regularly assess the business needs. The skills required are then identified and a training plan is developed to eliminate the skills deficiencies. In this way training becomes an essential and integral part of the business strategy and plans.

Even though training makes an essential contribution to the business, it should be remembered that training does not provide the complete solution for the development of a company's employees. I estimate that putting people on to training courses probably accounts for about 10 per cent of their development, with experience accounting for the remaining 90 per cent. Sometimes people are surprised at how low this estimate is—especially coming from a training manager! However, I would maintain that this is a vital 10 per cent. Unless people have the skills, knowledge, and theoretical framework to make sense of what is going on around them, how can they make the right decisions and take the right actions?

Total Quality Management is an example of a business strategy that cannot succeed without a huge investment in training. The Quality principles were first put forward by Deming and Juran, taken up with shattering success by the Japanese, and now being used by increasing numbers of Western companies.

Quality is defined as meeting customer requirements. This can only be achieved by every single person in the organization taking individual responsibility for the quality of their work.

People cannot take responsibility for their own quality if they are not able to use the new Quality processes and technologies. A once-off injection of training is not enough because Quality means continually improving business processes. Improved processes require new skills and knowledge.

Additionally, skills can quickly go out of date because customer requirements are becoming more stringent by the day. Competition is becoming fiercer, and the pace of change is ever accelerating. If this isn't bad enough, the older style of organization is just not responsive enough to cope with today's changing environment because no one in the organization dares to make a move until decisions have been made and received from the people at top of the hierarchy.

Organizations are also getting flatter, with technology helping people to take on more work and greater spans of control. This kind of structure can be very cost effective. However, the flatter organization can only be effective, flexible, and responsive if the work force is highly motivated, trained, and educated.

Another effect of flatter organizations is that responsibility for training gets fragmented throughout the organization. Different processes and standards start to emerge, and there is a consequent fall in quality coupled with a waste of meagre training resources. Often, exactly the same training need is met by different courses in different parts of the company. For example, it is said that one large multinational once had 37 different courses on 'presentation skills' running throughout the world. Apart from wasting resources this approach leads to confusion and poor communication because people from different parts of the company end up using different processes and terminology.

The instinctive reaction to this situation is to heavily centralize the training operation, but this approach can create an inflexible and unresponsive bureaucracy.

In 1990 my own organization had realized that work needed to be done on coordinating our training effort. This was a problem that was further aggravated by language differences and geographically dispersed locations (UK, France, The Netherlands, and Spain).

Training and human resource development (HRD) representatives for the three main sites met to define and solve the problem.

The situation that we had found ourselves in was that demands for training were coming from a wide range of diverse sources. This resulted in us having:

- no overall training plan for the organization;
- no agreed training process;
- poorly understood roles and responsibilities;
- a sub-optimal use of the slim training resource.

What we had to do was to:

- integrate the training into the business;
- set agreed standards for training;
- be able to measure the level of training delivered.

The solutions that the group proposed were to:

- develop a process for managing the organization's training;
- establish a training forum to integrate training plans and resources;
- establish roles and responsibilities.

I then developed a 'strawman' training process that the group of training and human resource managers further refined. The advantage of this approach was that instead of having to force and then 'police' the process from the centre, all the HRD and training managers reached consensus on the process. In this way we had defined the standards that we would all be working to, while at the same time giving the local training departments the flexibility to meet their own local needs.

While we were developing this process I was approached by McGraw-Hill to see whether I would be interested in writing a book on 'managing the training process'. So, the process described in this book arose out of a real need. In fact, writing the book helped us to further refine our process.

The first draft was a training process with elements that all our training and human resource managers recognized. Although all the steps were familiar, very few of us had seen the entire process put together on one sheet. The power of this was that we could quickly and easily see where our current processes fell short of this benchmark.

Having a benchmark process only solved part of the problem; the process still had to be locked into the organization's business cycle, and responsibilities for each step of the process had to be assigned.

The development of the process and the writing of this book then proceeded together—the one feeding off the other.

The way that this book has been structured means that it can be used as:

- a checklist for training professionals;
- a guide for people, such as directors, human resource managers, and line managers, who need to understand how the training process is managed;
- a detailed explanation for those such as training managers, trainers, and training administrators, whose job it is to make the process work.

The purpose of this book is to provide a guide to managing the training process which meets the needs of today's organizations. The emphasis throughout the book is one of practicality. This does not mean to say that the theoretical basis of training, which has been covered in detail by other books in this series, has been ignored. Rather, this book concentrates on what you have to *do* when you are identifying the need, bringing on new trainers, sourcing new courses, and deciding how you are going to integrate the many demands that are cascaded down from corporate, head office, or the board.

Of course there are no easy answers to all of this, but this book offers some practical approaches you can take to help you through the training jungle.

The structure of the book is driven from a series of flow charts. Chapter 1 describes the top level process. The subsequent chapters take one or more steps from the top level process and describe them in more detail. Each of these steps has its own process and flow chart.

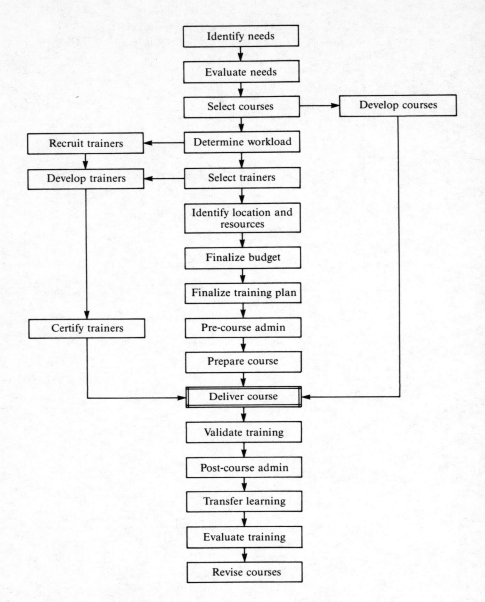

Figure 1.1   *Top level flow chart of the training process*

1 The process of training

When people talk about the training process they usually mean the day-to-day activities that make up the annual training cycle. Concentrating on the process is the best place to start if you want a quick and significant improvement in training efficiency. Indeed, the greater part of this book is devoted to describing this basic training process.

There are, however, several dangers in considering the training process in isolation. The most obvious is that the training provided will have little or no relevance either to business requirements, or to the development needs of the people. Another danger is that maintaining the process can become an end in itself. Then training becomes inflexible and insensitive to change.

It is very easy to say that effective training has to be aligned with a company's business directions and values; that the training department has to provide courses which support the company's goals; and that anyone who is involved in managing the training process has to have a clear idea of where the business is going.

All this assumes that those involved in running the business have a clear idea of where they are going. Unfortunately, this is not always the case and proactive training managers will often find themselves involved with senior management in getting the basics right. If this foundation is not firm, no training process can successfully support the business objectives.

As well as giving an overview of the training process this chapter also describes how successful companies define their businesses and how they clarify their attitudes towards training.

Getting the basics right

Not every company uses the same method to ensure the business is built on firm foundations, but the following is a summary of current thinking on the subject. Much of this thinking comes from Japan. If you are interested in reading about the Japanese approach in more detail, Masaaki Imai's book *Kaizen: The Key to Japan's Competitive Success* gives a detailed account.

Alignment

The key to getting the basics right is making sure everybody has the same understanding of the current situation and that everyone is pulling in the same direction for the future.

Figure 1.2   *Misalignment of company organizations*

Figure 1.3   *Alignment of company organizations*

The large arrow in Fig. 1.2 represents the company's intended business direction. The small arrows show the directions of the individual organizations. Each department is pursuing its own interests, and spends more time on in-fighting than fighting the company's competitors.

Without the alignment shown in Fig. 1.3 no company can make progress; no training department could provide efficient and effective training. Training provided for one organization would not be suitable for another, and little of the training would align with the company's business direction.

Philosophy   A philosophy is a statement of what the company stands for. It is a set of values and beliefs by which actions can be judged. A philosophy makes it clear which behaviours are appropriate—and which are unacceptable. Fig. 1.4 is an example of a typical company philosophy. It is based on Xerox's core values.

Missions   A mission is a statement of what a company or organization is here to do today. It is the reason for their existence. A mission should describe what is done for whom in such a way that it could not be confused with

> We succeed through satisfied customers
>
> We value our employees
>
> We aspire to deliver quality and excellence in all that we do
>
> We require premium return on assets
>
> We use technology to deliver market leadership
>
> We are responsible members of society

Figure 1.4   *Example of a company philosophy*

anybody else's mission. An example of a mission for a training department might be: 'To provide sales training for XYZ's UK-based sales staff.'

Communicating the mission to every employee ensures everybody knows what business they are in. It also helps to highlight any duplication or gaps in a company's structure.

If you think a company's mission is so obvious that it hardly warrants the effort of defining it, be prepared to shock yourself. Try asking a selection of people what they think their department's mission is.

> A company had just embarked on the development of a new product. The design team was brought together to define their mission.
>
> Half of the team thought their mission was to look after the product from 'cradle to grave'. The other half of the team thought they were there to 'caretake' until the *real* design team was formed.

Assessment   The mission is about maintaining today's processes, but training and surviving in today's business environment is also about encompassing and loving change. Change always has its roots in the past and has to start in the present.

There is not much point in deciding where you are going if you do not know where you are starting from. Assessment is very much about understanding where the company is today, and determining the reasons for both success and failure.

Visions   A vision is a 'picture' of where the organization wants to be in the future. By describing the future in emotional rather than measurable terms, a vision can exert a strong pulling force which helps keep the organization aligned.

Examples of visions are: 'There will be a time when generations of people have lived, died and been born on Mars' and 'Every household will have their own wind-driven generator'.

Describing events in pictorial terms, and from a future viewpoint where success has already been achieved, greatly enhances the probability of a vision coming to fruition.

Like the philosophy, a vision provides a basis for deciding which actions should be taken.

Goals Goals are quantitative figures, such as sales, profit, and market share, that are established by top management. Goals put the flesh on to the vision. Without goals the vision will only remain a dream.

Policies A policy is a medium to long-range course of action comprising a goal and a strategy. A strategy is the means of achieving the goal. Without the means a policy is only a slogan like 'Work harder' or 'Think smarter'. Imploring people to improve without providing the means cannot, and does not, work.

Be careful of how the word 'policy' is used, as it is often used interchangeably with 'philosophy', which is quite a different meaning of the word.

Policy deployment Policy deployment is the process of ensuring that the company's policies for quality, cost, and delivery (QCD) are understood from the highest to the lowest levels in the company.

The way the system works in practice is that the policy is communicated across the organization as well as being cascaded down through the line managers.

Cross-functional communication of the policies is very important because it binds the functions together in pursuit of the company goals. It helps functions cooperate instead of selfishly pursuing their own objectives at the expense of others. It is this subtle but important distinction that separates policy deployment from managing by objectives (MBO).

As a policy cascades down, line managers are expected to discuss and agree their goals with their managers. They then interpret the policy in the light of their own responsibilities, and identify the necessary strategies to achieve the goals.

Policy deployment is a cyclical process. Progress against the goals should be checked, the reasons for any deviations (both positive and negative) diagnosed, and the policies modified in the light of the diagnosis.

Making change happen There are two basic approaches to bringing change about. The first is through innovation and the second is through continuous improvement. Western cultures concentrate on innovation, but Eastern cultures put more importance on continuous improvement. In Japan the word for continuous improvement is *kaizen*.

Innovation causes leaps in efficiency and productivity, but competitors can copy the innovation and the competitive advantage is soon whittled away. Innovation is often dramatic and causes resistance to change.

Continuous improvement helps you keep ahead of the competition until your competitors introduce an unexpected innovation. The most successful companies get the best of both worlds by both innovating and continuously improving.

Change is occurring far more rapidly than ever before. Companies have to adapt to change or become extinct. Resistance to change has to be overcome.

The single most important factor for successful management of change is the leadership shown by the people at the top of an organization. A company's employees rarely do what management exhorts them to do. Instead, they follow the lead given by successful managers. If leaders do not model the new behaviours and attitudes, their followers cannot be expected to change.

Successful leaders provide vision and direction. They understand their people. They understand the factors that are working for them and those that are working against them.

Making change happen in an organization is like trying to light a bonfire. Although change cannot happen unless the 'logs' catch fire, you would not dream of lighting a fire by holding a match to the logs. You light the paper, add more fuel, and fan the flames until the logs are consumed in the blaze.

Training plays a vital role in making change happen. Skills that once lasted for generations are now redundant. New skills have to be identified and trained.

Work processes

In the end a company has to produce something, whether it be goods or services, that customers are willing to buy. No sales means no income and no company. Although much work has to be done to determine which products meet the customers' requirements, it is the work processes that ensure those requirements are met every time. So, an essential part of getting the basics right is to identify the critical work processes and constantly strive to improve them.

The company's attitude towards training

So far we have talked about the company getting its own house in order. A company that has already gone to this amount of trouble is very likely to be committed to training. However, it would be a mistake to take this commitment for granted. Commitment that is taken for granted often turns to apathy or resistance. It is not worth going any further without obtaining a high level of commitment to training. Senior management's actions and behaviours are crucial to the success of any venture.

Senior management commitment to training is not enough by itself. The training department has to get its own house in order and the organization has to be aware of the importance that is attached to training.

Getting the training function's house in order

The process for getting the basics right for any department is the same as for the whole company. This is no less true for the training function.

Training function alignment

As previously stated, training has to be aligned with the business direction of the company. If the company has got its basics sorted out, and communicated them effectively, the training function should be in no doubt as to which business directions and values should be supported.

In most companies, whether they be large or small, it is very rare for all training to be delivered by one department. This gives ample opportunity for fragmentation and misalignment of the training effort. It would not be unknown for several different versions of the same course to exist within the same organization. One multinational corporation was said to have had 37 different 'effective presentation' courses!

Variability in the training process, as with other processes, increases the chances of poor quality products. The answer to this is to ensure that all the key players within the training community agree on:

- the missions of the various training departments,
- a training philosophy,
- a training policy,
- training standards,
- definition of training,
- the training process, and
- accountability and responsibilities.

The training forum

In our own organization we tackled this problem by forming a training forum which comprised the following key players:

- Total Quality Manager,
- Human Resource Director,
- Site Human Resource Managers,
- Group Training Manager, and
- Site Training Managers.

The forum first met to reach consensus on the basics. Once these had been established, the forum then met twice a year to ensure continuing alignment on business direction and training needs.

Obviously, the composition of a forum will depend on how the company is organized.

Training department's mission

Where there is more than one training organization within a company it becomes imperative that the 'coverage' provided by each training department is understood and well defined. This helps to avoid duplication and prevents training needs falling between the cracks. An example of a training department's mission could be: 'To provide sales and customer care training for all the sales representatives who work in the corporation's telecommunications division'.

Notice that this mission states what types of training are provided for which population of students. It can be inferred from the statement that this training department does not do technical training, but provides sales and customer training for telecommunications staff wherever they are located. If this is not true then the mission statement would have to be modified. For example, in a large multinational corporation the end of the statement might be modified to: '. . . who *are based in France* and work in the corporation's telecommunications division'.

Training philosophy

The training philosophy is a statement of a company's or organization's attitude towards training. It has to define clearly the importance that is attached to training. It has to be communicated, with conviction, to every employee. If the philosophy is just a set of words without the backing of real and practical commitment, the authors of the policy will soon be 'found out' and the damage will, perhaps, be irreparable. The first paragraph of the following statement on training is a typical example of a training philosophy.

Education and Training Philosophy and Policies

1. We are committed to having a workforce prepared to meet current and future business objectives by providing our employees, at all levels, with appropriate education and training opportunities.

2. We are committed to defining clearly the minimum training requirements which are related to the job holder's role, responsibilities, and needs, including *Leadership Through Quality* and customer satisfaction.

3. All new employees will be oriented in the philosophy, ethics, values, principles, and business priorities of the company, including Total Quality Management and induction into their own organization, within three months of their employment.

4. Employees will only take up new job assignments when they have completed the minimum level of training specified for that job.

5. All newly hired or first-time people managers will successfully complete specified supervisory training within four months of appointment.

6. Managers will successfully complete functional knowledge and skills training to properly coach, inspect, and reinforce the work of their employees.

Figure 1.5 An example of a training philosophy and policies

Training policy

In the same way that a business policy has a goal and the means to attain the goal, a training policy should also have targets and measures.

For example, having all employees oriented to the company's philosophy, ethics, values, principles, and business priorities is a goal. Having new employees attend induction and Quality training within three months of joining the company is the measure that will achieve the goal.

Following the principles of policy deployment, these measures now become the goals of the new employees' managers and for the training department. The managers will have to provide the means for releasing new employees for training within three months. The training department has to take measures to ensure the availability of training.

Training standards

The training policy will incorporate many of the training standards such as:

- hours of functional training per employee,
- additional hours of training for managers,
- minimum level of training before starting a new job, and
- the amount and timing of induction training.

There are many other standards that have to be agreed and met, for the training process to run smoothly. The following are just a selection:

- trainer-to-student ratio,
- trainer training,
- trainer accreditation,
- face-to-face percentage,
- delivery-to-preparation ratio,
- cost per student-day,
- cost per trainer-day,
- classroom standards,
- administrative standards, and
- course development standards.

These standards will be dealt with in detail in the rest of this book.

Definition of training

While it is essential to have a training philosophy, policy, and standards, it is impossible to judge whether our training is in accordance with these if there is not a clear definition of training.

For example, a company might have a target to give each of its employees five days of training every year. Depending on what is considered to be training, one company might say they are providing three days of training, and another company might claim nine days—even though both company's employees have actually received exactly the same amount of training and development!

There are an amazing number of activities that might be considered as training. The following is just a selection:

- classroom (trainer led),
- distance learning,
- computer-based training,
- on-the-job training,
- external courses,
- large-scale workshops,
- attendance at seminars,
- attending exhibitions,
- attending conferences,
- attending communications meetings,
- evening classes,
- further education,
- assignments,
- participating in Quality circles, and
- reading articles and books.

Some of the above activities, such as classroom training and computer-based training, would always be considered as training. Activities such as exhibitions, conferences, assignments, and reading would not usually be classified as training.

Clearly, on-the-job training should be considered as training, but surely not be considered to be training because the prime purpose of a Quality 'hours of training'. The conclusion we came to was that the time spent on producing usable output should not be included in the training time.

In Europe, and the USA, participating in Quality circles would probably not be considered to be training because the prime purpose of a quality circle is thought to be solving the company's problems. Any learning that comes about would be thought to be secondary. In fact this is another indication of how Western culture has misunderstood Japan's Quality revolution, because one of Japan's main aims in starting Quality circle activities was to enable factory workers to study together and teach themselves Quality control.

This is a fairly subjective method of deciding whether an activity should be recognized as training, and it still leaves a number of activities that could fall into either camp.

To make this task less subjective a definition of training is required. The working definition of training that we use in our organization is: 'Training is the transfer of defined and measurable knowledge or skills'.

From this definition it can be seen that training activities should have objectives and a method for checking whether these objectives have been met.

Training, defined in this way, deals only with changes in behaviour and knowledge. Some definitions include changes of attitude as part of training. We do not include attitude change within the definition because, apart from being incredibly difficult to measure, it is the environment and culture of a business that primarily determines attitude. Training has an important part to play in this, and can help to create the environment in which attitudes can change, but training alone will not change anybody's long-term attitude.

Many different attempts have been made to define what constitutes a training activity, and these all vary, depending on the definition of training that is used. Agreeing *one* definition is more important than choosing the *best* of the many good definitions of training. This allows you to be aligned within your own company, and to make sensible comparisons with other companies.

If you have not already done so, this would probably be a good time to consider which of the activities in your company should be considered as training.

For example, the French Ministry of Work, Employment, and Professional Training considers that training activities are those activities which are paid for by employers and take place in accordance with a programme which:

- has predetermined objectives,
- specifies the teaching methods,
- specifies the personnel to be used,
- has an implementation plan,
- assesses the results,
- is given in premises separate from the production area, unless it includes practical training, and
- can include correspondence courses, safety, and security training, and training outside of work hours.

The French ministry specifies no set minimum duration for a training activity and a course of any duration can be included in the minimum statutory time per worker (1.2 per cent), if the training agency agrees. However, in practice, the French authorities do not often allow a training activity lasting less than a day to be included.

Training as part of the business

A useful approach for understanding the training process is to consider the process to be a system whose boundaries interact with the rest of the business (see Fig. 1.6). Training needs are identified, training is provided to meet the needs, the output is compared to the requirements, and any necessary changes are made to the system to obtain the desired output.

While this approach helps you to understand how training processes operate, it does put training at the centre of the universe. The effect of this training-centred approach is that the business will see training as either a panacea for all problems or as having no direct relevance to the business. Neither of these impressions will help you manage the training process effectively.

A better approach is to extend the boundaries of the system so training is an integral part of the business (Fig. 1.7).

Figure 1.6 *Training as a system whose boundaries interact with the business*

Figure 1.7 *Training as part of the business system*

The training process

Having established where training really fits into the business we can now take a look at the training process itself. The fundamental elements of any process are:

- accountability (ownership),
- identification of stakeholders,
- definition and documentation of the process,
- checkpoints,
- responsibility for the steps of the process, and
- continuous improvement of the process.

Accountability and responsibility

No process will work efficiently unless somebody 'owns' or is accountable for the process. The accountable person is the person whose telephone rings when something goes wrong with any part of the process. This person is like the captain of a ship, ultimately accountable for everything that happens on board even though the crew are responsible for carrying out most of the tasks. Although the captain holds individual crew members accountable for their responsibilities, the captain's own accountability cannot be abdicated. The difference between an ordinary organization and a 'Quality' organization is that in a 'Quality' organization people *feel* accountable for their own responsibilities.

The training manager is the 'owner' of the training process. This makes the training manager accountable for every step as well as the entire training process. Being accountable for every step is tough because the responsibility for carrying out many of the individual steps lies with other people. It is the training manager who has to make sure nothing falls down the cracks between the steps of the process.

Identifying the stakeholders

A stakeholder is a person who has a vested interest in the outcome of the process. Stakeholders often have a positive or negative impact on the outcome of a process even though they might not take a direct part. This is especially true if the process involves 'treading on their turf'.

This makes it vital for you to involve stakeholders during the early stages of process design. Managing directors, heads of departments, and human resource managers are all stakeholders in the training process.

Defining and documenting the training process

Definition of a process involves establishing the boundaries of the process. In theory, any process could be traced back to the 'Big Bang' or projected forwards to 'the End of the Universe'. In practice, this make the process too large and cumbersome to handle so you need to define the beginning and end points of your process. Although defining the boundaries is, to some extent, arbitrary, the following guidelines should help you decide:

- the beginning of your process is where you take over control from someone else;
- the end of your process is where you hand over control to another person.

The easiest way of documenting a process is to tape some sheets of flip chart paper together and use Post-its to represent the steps of the process. You already have the beginning and end points, so these can be stuck on to the sheets straight away. Stick additional steps on to the sheets until you have a series of related steps that connect the end point to the beginning point.

Make sure you use a verb and a noun to describe each step in the process. This clarifies what is involved in each step and separates one step from another. 'Select course' is different to 'Develop course', which in turn is different to 'Deliver course'.

The flow chart (Fig. 1.1) shown at the beginning of this chapter is an overview of the overall training process. Subsequent chapters in this book will expand on this 'level 1' process by describing a 'level 2' process for one or more of the steps. In the interests of clarity and simplicity, checkpoints, decision boxes, and feedback loops have been left out at this stage.

A brief overview of the steps of the training process follows.

> Identify needs

The process starts off by identifying the business needs and turning these needs into training requirements.

> Evaluate needs

A check is made to ensure that the requested, or mandated, training is suitable for the people concerned. A check is also made to make sure training can meet the identified need.

In the cases where training is not a suitable approach the need has to be analysed further so that alternatives to training can be suggested.

> Select courses

Given that the business need is one where training can make a contribution, the next step is to identify suitable courses. The choice will be between:

- using an existing company course;
- buying-in an external course;
- developing a new course.

> Develop courses

If no suitable courses are available, new courses have to be developed and piloted.

> Determine workload

At this stage you should be able to make your first estimate of the resources you will require to meet the training need.

> Recruit trainers

If you do not have sufficient trainers to meet the expected workload, you will need to start the process of recruiting new trainers. It often takes three months or more to recruit a new trainer so you will need to start this step as early as possible.

> Select trainers

Before a course can be delivered suitable trainers need to be identified.

> Develop trainers

It is likely that the trainers you select to run new courses will need further development of their own skills and knowledge. It is even more likely that trainers recruited from outside will require development.

If you are developing people to be trainers, you will need to put them through a programme of training and experiences before you allow them to train unassisted. Depending on the level and frequency of the courses, this could take from three months to a year.

> Certify trainers

If a course is new to the trainers, they should undergo a programme of observation and practice to ensure that they reach the required standard before they are allowed to deliver the course by themselves.

> Identify location and resources

Before advertising the dates of the proposed courses make sure that appropriate locations and resources are available.

> Finalize budget

By this stage you should have enough information to know how much it is going to cost to meet the training need.

Negotiations over the actual budget are started.

> Finalize training plan

After budget negotiations are complete you will need to make adjustments to the training plan.

Often there will be more demand for a course than there are places available so it will be necessary to prioritize the candidates. Prioritizing should still be done even if sufficient places are available, so the people most in need of the course will still get trained if budgets are cut later in the year.

The training plan is built up throughout the early steps of the training process and it is at this stage that the finalized plan can be put together ready for presentation to senior management.

> Pre-course admin

Once the training plan has been concurred the course administrator has to ensure that the identified people get to the right course, at the right time.

> Prepare course

Before the courses can be delivered the trainers need to prepare themselves, the materials, and the training rooms. The trainees also need to prepare themselves for the course.

Deliver course

Although course delivery is the manifestation of all the efforts that have been put into the previous steps, it should be remembered that, as far as the rest of the organization is concerned, this is only the start of the change process.

Validate training

Validation is the process of ensuring that the course meets and continues to meet its stated objectives. Tests, observations, and student feedback are all data which have to be analysed to determine whether the objectives are being met.

Post-course admin

As soon as the training has been completed attendance should be noted on the students' training records.

Transfer learning

The students then have to use the knowledge and practise the skills to ensure that the learning is transferred into the business.

Evaluate training

As with any process, the training process should have a method of ensuring that the process has had the desired effect.

Revise courses

The courses then need to be revised to incorporate the changes identified during evaluation.

Establishing checkpoints

You need to establish checkpoints to keep the process on track, under control, and producing the required outputs. Checkpoints can occur at the beginning, during, and at the end of the process. Checks at the beginning answer the question of whether the correct outputs *will* be produced. Checks during the process answer the question of whether the correct outputs *are* being produced. Checks at the end answer the question of whether the correct outputs *have* been produced. Deviations that you detect early on in the process are easier and cheaper to correct than those found at the end of the process.

The major checkpoints of the training process shown in Fig. 1.1 are:

- needs analysis and evaluation;
- pilot courses (within course development);
- trainer certification;

- finalize budget;
- finalize training plan;
- course preparation;
- validate training;
- evaluation.

The most important checkpoint is evaluating the needs. If we identify the needs incorrectly, all else that follows is built on sand. Each process step has its own checkpoints and these will be discussed in the following chapters.

Responsibility for the steps of the process

The training manager should identify, by name, the people responsible for carrying out each task or step in the process. Attaching a person's name to a responsibility is a sure way of flushing out conflicting responsibilities, gaps, and potential overloading.

If more than one person is involved in a process step, one of the people should be given the prime responsibility so that nobody can ever say: 'I thought it was somebody else's responsibility to make sure that the task was completed.'

Table 1.1 shows how responsibilities could be allocated for the steps in the training process. This table gives job titles in the responsibility column. In practice you would also identify the people's names.

Additional responsibility matrices should be drawn up if there is more than one training organization in the company. The additional matrices should show clearly which courses or types of course are covered by the responsibilities.

Table 1.1　*Possible responsibilities for the steps in the training process*

Process: the training process
Process owner: training manager

Step	Responsibility
Identify needs	Training manager
Evaluate needs	Training administrator Training manager
Select courses	Training manager Training administrator
Develop courses	Course developers
Determine workload	Training manager
Recruit trainers	Training manager

Step	Responsibility
Select trainers	Training manager
Develop trainers	Training manager
Certify trainers	Course developers
Identify location and resources	Training manager Training administrator
Finalize budget	Training manager
Finalize training plan	Training manager Development committees
Pre-course admin	Training administrator
Prepare course	Trainers
Deliver course	Trainers
Validate training	Trainers
Post-course admin	Training administrator
Transfer learning	Participants Managers Trainers
Evaluate training	Trainers Training manager
Revise courses	Course developers Trainers

Improving the training process

We should always be looking for ways of continually improving the training process. There are two main ways of improving a process:

- reducing errors, and
- reducing cycle time (the time it takes to go from the beginning to the end of a process).

To do this you should take a close look at your process by documenting what actually happens at every step of the process.

When you design a new process it is very likely that you will have designed an ideal process. It won't show gaps, duplication, dead ends, confusing responsibilities, or activities that add no value to the end-product.

You can now compare your actual process with the ideal and make sure that gaps are plugged, duplication and dead ends eliminated, and responsibilities clarified. Activities that add no value to the end-product are:

- correcting errors,
- waiting time,
- storage, and
- transport time.

By reducing these activities to a minimum you will reduce the cost of, and the time for, providing training.

Training strategies

The training process is a cycle that you need to manage continuously. You respond to needs. You ensure that the training is aligned with the business. The process has a relatively short cycle time—usually no longer than a year. Managing the training process is essentially operational or tactical.

If we always manage training at this level we are in danger of being reactive rather than proactive; starting and stopping training programmes or perhaps even failing to deliver anything.

We need to have a clear idea of how we are going to deliver training over a longer period. Training needs analysis and training policies provide the 'what' and the 'how much'. A training strategy provides the long-term orientation.

To put a training strategy together you should have a 'vision' of what training in your organization should look like in, say, five years. You should then map out the years and the key milestones along the way. When you are putting a training strategy together you should ask yourself the following questions.

- How much training will you need to do each year?
- What type of courses will you need to provide?
- What types of people will you put on what type of course?
- What resources will you need in terms of space and trainers?
- Who will you use to do your training?
- Will you use full-time, part-time, or consultant trainers?
- What delivery methods will you use?
- How will changes in technology affect delivery methods?
- What business, social or environmental changes are likely to take place?

Every time you cycle through the training process you should re-examine your training strategy to see if it still holds up in the light of new training requirements and corporate policies. Try to make your strategy as robust as possible, and only change strategies when there are significant business, social or environmental changes. If your strategy is really robust you will find that you can respond to many changes by adjusting your tactics rather than throwing away your strategy.

It is difficult but essential to find the right balance between constantly chopping and changing strategies, and sticking with a useless and out-moded strategy.

Communicating the importance of training

Having a training philosophy and policy is the starting point for communicating the importance of training and it is very important that everybody is aware of them.

Posters, in-house magazines, staff briefings, and memos are all methods of putting the message across. But no matter how much effort is put into communicating through the usual channels there is still no getting away from the fact that the most powerful communication always occurs through the unwritten and unspoken channels:

- the amount of training that is done;
- the budget allocated to training;
- the status of training managers and staff;
- how often a training event has to be moved to another location to make room for another business activity;
- how often training is postponed or cancelled;
- the reasons managers give for pulling their people off courses;
- the standard of the training rooms;
- whether people are allowed to start a new job before they have been trained.

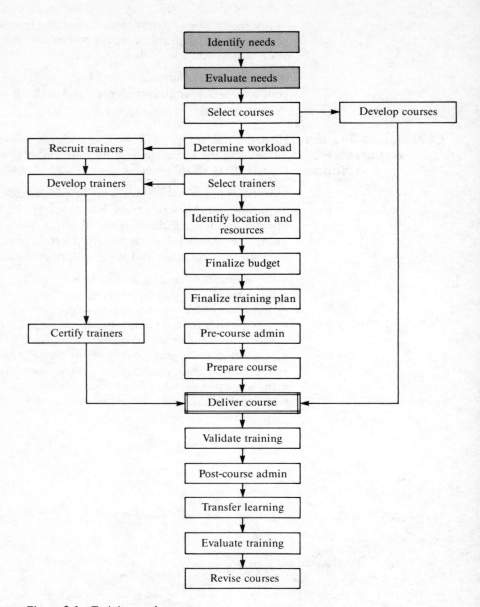

Figure 2.1   *Training needs*

2 Training needs

In this chapter we will be covering two steps (highlighted in Fig. 2.1) of the training process:

- identify needs, and
- evaluate needs.

Identifying training needs is the starting point for managing the training process. Yet this is often one of the last steps to be considered seriously—probably because a proper needs analysis is both difficult and time consuming.

Initially, it might be quicker and easier to forget about analysing the needs, and have your customers pick and choose from a catalogue, but this will ultimately lead to frustration and inefficiency.

Identifying training needs is not just a matter of finding the need and then simply satisfying it. There are often conflicting requirements from different interests within the company. The development needs of the individual have to be met while satisfying the skills requirements of the organization. These needs, once identified, have to be matched to appropriate training courses.

Sometimes there is a feeling that training will always be the solution for every identified development problem. However, there is no point in providing training if training is not an appropriate solution. When this is the case the training manager has to be brave enough to say that it is not appropriate—and creative enough to suggest alternative solutions.

Needs identification

Needs identification has to balance corporate demands, policies and strategies, as well as individual and organizational requirements. Fig. 2.2 outlines a process that balances these requirements. It shows that corporate policies and strategies should be the 'umbrella' under which individual and organizational training needs are identified. This helps to ensure alignment of training activities with the business direction.

Collect corporate policies and strategies

Corporate policies and strategies form the boundaries within which all training and development activities should take place.

Figure 2.2   Needs identification

There are two ways that corporate policies and strategies give rise to training needs. The first way is directly through mandatory training. The other is through indirect influence. When an organization puts its training plan together it should take account of both the business plan and individual development needs. This is where the process often breaks down and even the indirect influences shown in Fig. 2.2 start to disappear.

Policy deployment, which is a structured method of cascading corporate goals and strategies through the company, is a powerful method of ensuring that training needs are identified within the context of the company's business goals.

In Chapter 1 we discussed the importance of alignment and of getting the corporate basics right. If this has been done well, you will have no difficulty in collecting corporate policies and strategies. You will then be able to prepare a training plan that supports the direction of the business.

If your company is confused about its strategies, or does not communicate them effectively, you might as well miss this step out completely and be resigned to providing training that cannot completely support the business.

Start by reading your company's policies on training and development, reviewing the company's vision, and understanding the current goals and objectives.

> Identify
> mandatory
> training

Company policy dictates which employee groups are required to undergo prescribed courses. Some courses, such as 'Induction Training' and 'Total Quality Management', are an integral part of the company's culture, so all new employees have to attend this training.

Company strategy may also require all personnel to go through specified forms of training in a relatively short period.

Examples of this kind of training are:

- equal opportunities;
- empowerment;
- harassment;
- financial responsibility;
- new legal requirements.

Compulsory courses will usually be aligned with the company direction because they have been developed centrally for company-wide implementation.

> Identify business needs

Policy deployment and the training forum are two essential tools for identifying business needs. Policy deployment, and the training forum's role in defining the basics of the training process are both covered in Chapter 1 'The process of training'.

Policy deployment   Policy deployment is the process by which a company's strategies are communicated to its organizations. An organization then determines *what* it needs to achieve by understanding its part in the company's strategy. The 'what' should be measurable and take the form of goals or objectives.

Once an organization has determined *what* it has to achieve, it then has to decide *how* these objectives will be met. Once the 'how' has been identified it is possible to determine the skills and knowledge the organization will require.

Training forum's role   The training forum's role at this stage of the process is to:

- provide a 'forum' for identifying an organization's business needs;
- ensure that training plans are aligned with the company's direction;
- identify opportunities for sharing or exchanging resources.

Figure 2.3 *Schedule for training forum meetings*

The training forum comprises a group of training managers and other interested parties who meet to discuss training plans. They also identify opportunities for sharing resources. A forum is particularly useful when there are several, dispersed training organizations within a company.

The forum would normally need to meet twice a year: the first time to understand both corporate requirements and local issues; the second meeting to review draft training plans. Typical timings for the two training forum meetings are shown in Fig. 2.3.

Timing of these forum meetings is critical. The output of the second meeting needs to be available for inclusion in the annual business plan. Individual development plans should be completed before the draft training plans are put together.

Ideally, individual development plans should be available just after the first forum meeting. The training plans will be based on guesswork if the development plans are not available. If the development plans are available too early, the training plan could be out of time by up to six months. The following is a description of how the training forums work in practice.

1. Before the first meeting the Group Training Manager has a meeting with the organization's General Manager to understand the business direction and vision for the organization.

The Group Training Manager also collects general training requirements and demands from:

- functional heads,
- human resource managers, and
- corporate.

2. Preparation notes for the plan review meeting are issued (see Fig. 2.4) and the site training managers identify the following general training requirements and demands for their own areas:

- technical,
- induction and quality, and
- business.

Even a short statement from a general manager can have quite a profound effect on how the training plans are put together. For example, during preparation for their 1992 training plan, the director said: 'If we sell a product in Europe, we will manufacture it in Europe.'

The effect of this statement was to cause the training managers to reassess the skills that would be needed in their factories. A very different set of skills is needed to manufacture every machine that is sold rather than assemble small machines and pass the larger machines through a warehouse. The director said he wanted everybody to make themselves thoroughly familiar with the organization's mission and objectives which could be found in the recently published 'Blue Book'.

He also highlighted the shift in technology that will be required. In the past our business had been built on optical and mechanical technology. Today's and tomorrow's emphasis will be on digital technology. Flexibility will be key: flexible people and flexible manufacturing processes. He also had a concern about the plethora of training courses being produced within the corporation and expressed a hope that they would be properly prioritized and integrated. Another concern was the transfer of learning into the workplace.

It is amazing how much information this type of digging around can unearth. In preparation for the 1992 training plan, the finance community forewarned us that functional managers were to be made more responsible for financial and other process controls. This would generate additional training for functional managers and buying staff.

3. The training forum meets to understand overall requirements and issues, and to identify potential areas of cooperation. This is the pre-planning meeting. See Fig. 2.5 for the agenda of the meeting.

The first part of the meeting deals with general issues such as corporate business direction, human resource, quality issues, and management training. This is to ensure that the site training managers understand the context under which they will be developing their final plans.

During the second part of the meeting the site training managers present their draft plans. This gives an opportunity for resources to be shared and new ideas to be spread across the organization.

4. Preparation notes (Fig. 2.6) are issued and the site training managers then prepare the first draft of their training plans which include:

- the training needs that have been identified,
- what this would cost if the needs could be met fully,
- how many days of training per employee this would represent,
- how much of the above could be realistically provided during the coming training year,

---

TRAINING FORUM PRE-PLANNING MEETING
10 a.m.–4 p.m. Monday 22 April 1991

PURPOSE

To share information on the organization's business direction, challenges, and training requirements for 1992 so that the participants will be in a position to prepare proactive 1992 Training Plans for their organizations.

ATTENDEES

Total Quality Manager   Human Resource Director
Site human resource managers   Group Training Manager
Site training managers

PREPARATION

It is important to understand the challenges that we will be facing in 1992, so would the following people please prepare presentations on the following topics:

BUSINESS DIRECTION   Group Training Manager

1992 business and financial requirements and challenges.

TOTAL QUALITY MANAGEMENT   Total Quality Manager

The 1992 training requirements, challenges, and issues for total quality management—both locally and from corporate.

HUMAN RESOURCE MANAGEMENT   Human Resource Director

The 1992 human resource challenges, what skills deficiencies do we have, what new skills will we require?

MANAGEMENT TRAINING   Group Training Manager

The 1992 Management training requirements, challenges, and issues—both locally and for corporate.

SITES   Site training managers

The sites' 1992 training requirements, challenges, and issues.

Figure 2.4 *Preparation for training forum pre-planning meeting*

PRE-PLANNING MEETING AGENDA

Time	Topic
10.00	REVIEW OF PURPOSE AND AGENDA (10 min)
10.10	BUSINESS DIRECTION (20 min)
10.30	TOTAL QUALITY MANAGEMENT (30 min)
11.00	Break (15 min)
11.15	HUMAN RESOURCE MANAGEMENT (30 min)
11.45	MANAGEMENT TRAINING AND FINANCE (30 min)
12.15	Lunch (45 min)
13.00	SITE PRESENTATIONS (1 hr 15 mins)
14.30	Break (15 mins)
14.45	NEXT STEPS (30 min)
15.15	NEXT FORUM MEETING (30 min)
15.45	MEETING REVIEW (15 min)
16.00	End

Figure 2.5 *Agenda for the pre-planning meeting*

In preparation for the 1992 plan, the Human Resource Director pointed out that the human resource challenges will have to be approached against a background of:

- resource constraints,
- flatter organizations,
- matrix management,
- new technical skills,
- population demographics,
- education levels,
- the European Community and 1992,
- workforce empowerment and flexibility,
- equal opportunities,
- the environment and recycling,
- the mix of permanent and contract staff, and
- health, safety, security, and export control.

The 1992 training plans will also have to take account of the 'Total Quality' initiatives —the main one being the company's application for the European Quality Award. Part of the application process will be 'self-certification' of the key business processes. It is anticipated that 'self-certification' will identify additional training needs.

PLAN REVIEW MEETING 10 a.m.–4 p.m. Monday 1 July 1991 Room GW94

PURPOSE

To share and process information on 1992 training plans so that the overall level and cost of training can be estimated. The forum also provides an opportunity for sharing ideas, approaches, concerns, and resources.

ATTENDEES

Human Resource Director   Site training managers
Site human resource managers   Group Training Manager
Business Effectiveness Manager   Total Quality Manager

PREPARATION

Would the manufacturing sites and group human resources please prepare presentations (30 minutes Information Sharing, 20 minutes Information Processing) to cover:

• the training needs that have been identified, and
• what this would cost if you were able to meet the need fully.

(Only show costs that are taken out of the training budget. Please indicate whether trainers' and trainees' salaries are part of the training budget.)

• How many days training per employee would this represent?
• Realistically, how much will you be able to provide during 1992?
• What does this represent in terms of cost and days per employee?

The above should be estimates. We appreciate that your training plans will be revised over the next few months. The next two items should be accurate as we need to start booking venues for next year's management training.

• How many places do you think you will need, during the 1992 calendar year, for the first level, middle, and senior management courses?
• How confident do you feel that you will be able to fill the remainder of your 1991 calendar year management training course allocations?

And finally, would you please estimate the following so that we can plan our strategy for the European Management Training Institute.

• How many people per year do you expect to be promoted to first, middle, and senior levels of management?
• How many, first, middle, and advanced level managers do you have?
• How many of your first, middle, and advanced level managers speak English well enough to participate in courses run in English and American English?

Figure 2.6   *Preparation notes for draft training plans*

```
AGENDA

Time        Topic

10.00       REVIEW OF PURPOSE AND AGENDA (10 min)

10.10       REVIEW ACTION ITEMS (15 min)

10.25       SITES info sharing and processing
            (2 hrs 55 min—including break)

13.20       Lunch (45 min)

14.05       GROUP (50 min)

14.55       Break (15 min)

15.10       ISSUES AND OPPORTUNITIES IDENTIFIED
            info processing (30 min)

15.40       NEXT STEPS AND ACTION ITEMS (15 min)

15.55       MEETING REVIEW (5 min)

16.00       End
```

Figure 2.7 *Agenda for plan review meeting*

- resources required,
- approximately when the training will be carried out, and
- what this realistic estimate represents in terms of days per employee and total cost.

5. The forum meets again to review the site training plans. The meeting's agenda is given in Fig. 2.7. The site training managers present their draft training plans and an estimate is made of the amount of training that is planned to be delivered, as well as the cost and the resources required.

6. The site training managers finalize their training plans.

7. Group Training Manager prepares an overall training plan for the organization.

8. Training plans are submitted as part of the organization's business plan.

> Identify individual needs

Identifying training needs via business requirements is a 'tops down' approach which satisfies the need for training to be in alignment with the business direction. If we were only to use this approach, the coverage would be too broad to pick up individual development requirements. We also need to consider 'bottoms up' training requests and to make sure both sources of training requirements complement each other. Individual training requirements come from either direct requests or as a result of appraisal discussions.

Requests If we were honest with ourselves, we would probably admit that the majority of training needs are identified through requests received from either the employee or the employee's manager. At its most basic these requests would be an informal approach to the training department with the prospective student or manager saying something like: 'Have you got a course on XYZ?' The training administrator would then look through the training catalogues and say, 'Well, there doesn't seem to be an XYZ course, but how about the PQR course in July?'

Appraisals Another route for identifying training needs is through the annual appraisal system. You know how it can go. The employee's salary is directly related to the outcome of the appraisal and the first hour-and-a-half can be spent discussing what the person did, or did not do, seven months ago. With ten minutes left to go they happen upon a 'Training Required' box at the bottom of the last page of the appraisal form.

'I've heard that the "Welding for Pleasure" course is pretty good,' suggests the appraisee.

'I think that "Photographing Dustbins" is a better course,' replies the manager.

'Well, perhaps I ought to do both courses.'

'That's a good idea,' agrees the manager. 'Let's put them both down and then we can wrap this up and get some coffee.'

These sketches might seem a bit extreme but they illustrate the point that the training requests received by the training department often have more to do with perceived demand than actual need. However, it has to be said that it is much better to be demand-led than place-led.

Being place-led is where the number of places on a training course has been previously fixed (usually by the size of the budget) and the training administrator has to search around to find people to fill the places.

Approaching needs analysis this way might, by chance, provide training which meets a need, but the odds of this aligning with the company's values and business directions are virtually non-existent.

The way to improve this situation is to take a developmental approach to training needs identification, and to have a broader view of where training needs originate.

A developmental approach to needs identification The whole idea behind a developmental approach to training needs identification is that a person's current skill level is established and compared with the skills, or competencies, required to do today's as well as tomorrow's job.

Some companies' training request forms have a section that asks what the development need is, and how the requested course would help the candidates do their jobs better. This gives the training administrator a much better chance of suggesting an appropriate course.

A good appraisal system can produce development-related training needs. However, the waters are muddied when the next promotion, or salary increase, is linked to the results of the appraisal.

It would be better if development could be entirely divorced from salary-related assessment. This, of course, would be difficult in companies that run performance-related salary schemes, but development planning and appraisal could still be two separate discussions. Even if no separation is possible, the appraisal can be improved by having the right balance of past performance and future development.

In too many appraisals too much time is spent looking backwards, and not enough time discussing future development. The past has gone and although it is valuable to see what lessons can be learnt, the past cannot be changed. Only the future can be changed.

Average appraisers spend only 12 per cent of the appraisal talking about the future; expert appraisers concentrate on future behaviour for 40 per cent of the time.

A developmental approach to appraisal and training would have the discussion centred around the employee's current strengths and weaknesses, and would put together a developmental plan to sustain the strengths and minimize the weaknesses. Notice that it is called a 'developmental plan' rather than a 'training plan'. This is quite deliberate because there is sometimes an immediate assumption that training is the answer to all development needs and performance problems.

Sometimes there is a confusion between personal development and career development. Personal development is all about improving people's skill and knowledge so that they can do today's job better. Career development is about preparing the person for the next career move.

It is very important to be clear on which type of development you are talking about when you are having discussions with your staff. Most people think that all development will give rise to better prospects and increased salaries. Given the current economic climate and the flatter, leaner nature of our organizations, these kinds of expectations are less likely to be fulfilled, and will ultimately lead to anger and frustration—especially if people think that attendance on a training course will automatically give them their next promotion.

Career development depends on opportunity, capability, and luck. Opportunity is simply the availability of a job at the next stage of a person's career development. Capability is the person's skill and knowledge level. Luck is being in the right place at the right time.

A person's capability can be improved through self-development. There is even something that can be done about luck. Determine the 'right place' and the 'right time', and position yourself accordingly.

Luck can be made, but unfortunately, the one thing that is almost impossible to influence is opportunity. The number of opportunities that are available in an organization are probably more to do with the general state of the economy and where the company is in its life cycle than anything the organization or individual can do.

Even if the discussions are centred around career development, be very careful about giving the impression that attendance at a particular training course is an automatic ticket to promotion. Careless selection of courses for people can also lead to false expectations. For example, sending people, who are not suited to being managers, on a management training course would give them the wrong impression of their prospects and abilities.

Even worse is the avoidance behaviour of sending people on courses in the hope that the course will do the 'dirty work' of revealing unsuitability for a particular kind of job.

Development is not something that can be done *to* someone. People have to take the responsibility for their own development. Having said that, the company should provide development opportunities and encourage development. These opportunities should be aligned with the business needs, even though it could be argued that any development of an individual is good for the business and should be encouraged. In reality resources are limited and priorities have to be made.

So, development is a shared responsibility between a person, the manager, and the company. Ideally, the individual should take prime responsibility, the manager should have the secondary responsibility, and training and personnel should be third in line. It really does have to be a combined effort.

This is all very well, but is it reasonable to expect the individual and the manager to understand the details and ramifications of all the courses that are available? Providing a training catalogue can help, but even with the best catalogue the manager does not have the background knowledge that is required to make the optimum choices.

Expert systems

What the managers and the individuals really need is an expert training adviser sitting beside them as the choices are made. Obviously this would not be a cost-effective prospect so it could be worth considering the use of artificial intelligence in the form of an expert system. An expert system is a computer program that can be given a set of rules which allow it to make the same decision as the expert. Even at its simplest level an expert system could be of great assistance to a manager.

For example, you might provide both an 'Effective Meetings' course and a more advanced 'Meeting Facilitator's Workshop'. A person who has completed the 'Meeting Facilitator's Workshop' would not need to attend 'Effective Meetings' because 'Effective Meetings' is basically the first day of the 'Meeting Facilitator's Workshop'.

Although the two courses are mutually exclusive it can be guaranteed that you will receive requests for people to attend both. Now it's no use complaining that the managers should have read the details in the training catalogue. Beating up already pressurized managers doesn't help anybody. An expert system could easily and unobtrusively avoid this problem. More advanced systems could take account of the person's job, training record, and career path.

Development open days

Expert systems involve a certain amount of expense and, although they can provide instant advice, it will probably be a long time before they can be as effective as discussions with professional advisers.

A way of meeting this need, which also increases the profile of training and development, is to hold a development open day. The day could be in the form of an exhibition with training and human resource professionals on hand to discuss development needs. Any member of staff would be able to attend the event, but it would be primarily designed for managers who want to understand what development opportunities are available for their people.

Frequency and timing of appraisals

Assuming that all the problems associated with running an appraisal session have been ironed out, there are still the questions of where the output from the appraisal fits into the overall planning cycle, and whether all the needs have been identified.

One of the problems of identifying needs through appraisal is that the training need is identified only once, or maybe twice, a year. In reality, new training needs can surface at any time of the year and unless the training department can react quickly to train new skills requirements in well under a year then a company's competitive advantage could be seriously eroded.

The timing of the appraisal is also important. Most companies start submitting their plans for the next financial year about three months before the end of the current financial year. If the appraisal occurs towards the end of the year then the needs analysis will not be done in time for the training plan to be included into the business plan. If the appraisal is done too early, over half of the training would need to have been completed before the business plan was approved.

Even if there were a perfect time to complete appraisals, the chances are that other important activities would need to be done at the same time.

Development plans

The answer to these difficulties is for each individual to have a development plan. A development plan is best produced as the output of a counselling session. Instead of being 'once-off' plans, they should be kept 'evergreen'—that is, they should be revised every time an old development need has been met or a new one identified.

Notice that the development plan shown in Fig. 2.8 includes activities other than training. This shows that the manager and employee who

ACTION PLAN

(BEHAVIOURS)

NAME __J. Ford__

DATE __15/3/93__

STRENGTHS	ACTIVITIES TO MAINTAIN	SCHEDULE/FOLLOW-UP DATE
1. Project Management	1. Run workshop on Project Management	1. 22/3/93, 25/3/93
2. Recognising people	2. Provide information on creative use of recognition and reward	2. 3/4/93, 15/4/93

IDENTIFIED NEEDS	ACTIVITIES TO DEVELOP	SCHEDULE/FOLLOW-UP
1. Problem solving	1. Use problem solving process at next staff meeting	1. 3/5/93, 17/5/93
2. Team building	2. Hold team building session with direct reports	2. 2/4/93, 16/4/93
3. Meeting skills	3. Attend meeting management workshop	3. 17/3/93, 3/4/93

Figure 2.8   An example of a development plan

put this plan together have a good idea of what can, and cannot, be achieved by training.

Because these development plans are always up to date, the training needs analysis can be done at any time of the year. The training administrator can request copies of the current development plan when the needs analysis has to be done.

> Identify
> departmental
> needs

So far we have seen how training departments can be aligned with each other and with the corporate business direction. We have also seen how individual development requirements can be identified. We now need to see how the detailed departmental training needs are identified.

The processes already described should ensure the department's training demands are based on corporate or company business needs and requirements. The individual requirements give us a picture of the demand within a department, but not necessarily the need.

In fact, the process for identifying departmental needs is very similar to the process for identifying need at the corporate level. Each department should assess where it is. The department should have a vision, a mission, and a strategy for realizing the vision.

> Identify skills and training required for each job

The department's mission, and the work processes the company uses, determine the jobs the department needs to produce its products. Each job has an associated set of skills. New jobs require new skills.

In its simplest form, identifying the training required for each job involves:

1. identifying the skills required to do a job;
2. comparing the required skills to the current skills level of the people who will be doing the job.

It is training's function to bridge the gap between current and required skills.

The skills and knowledge required for every job should be documented. You should also document the courses that a representative person will need to reach the required skill level. This makes it easier to select the correct courses. A representative person is the type of person you would normally employ to do the job.

The basis of identifying and documenting the required skills is the 'Job Description'. A job description should include the tasks that have to be performed and the outputs that have to be produced by the job holder. Outputs are products or services that are handed on to someone else. An output should have a standard or specification attached to it so the quality of the output can be measured.

For job descriptions which cover a large number of employees it is worth producing a 'Training Specification Matrix'. This matrix describes the training courses that correlate to the skills described in the person specification.

The next step is to prepare a 'Person Specification' from the job description. A person specification describes the ideal person to fill the job. It is a profile of the required personal skills and characteristics, also known as competencies.

You shouldn't be surprised if all this sounds rather familiar. It is exactly the same as the recruitment process—the only difference being that we are developing existing people to fit the person specification rather than recruiting the 'ideal' person.

If you are recruiting to fill a vacancy, you may not be able to find anybody who fits the person description. You might also want to give people, who do not yet meet the person specification, a chance to work at a higher level. In these cases you will need to provide additional training to bring these people to the required level.

```
Identify affected individuals
```

Arising out of your analysis of corporate policies, mandatory training, business needs, and job skill requirements you will be able to identify which groups of employees will need what training. For example, all new managers will need training on the basics of management, and all electronics assembly people will need training on electrostatic protection.

Effective training processes need to be managed at the level of the individual, so the next step is to identify those individuals who are part of the group who need the training. This task is made a lot simpler by computerized personnel and training records. If each person's job is given a job code, the computer can print out a report of the people who have a particular type of job and have yet to receive the required training.

This task is made even easier if the personnel and training records are part of the same database. If you have separate records, you will need to update the training database every time someone joins, leaves, or changes jobs.

```
Enter potential needs on training records
```

A training record should not only list the courses a person has attended, but it should also list the training a person needs. It is easier to prepare a training plan if the record also gives a range of dates for when the training is required. The potential need can either be in the form of a course or a skill.

It is important that the training record is a live reflection of current training requirements. It should be revised any time a new training requirement is identified. This can be after appraisal, when a training request form is received, or after an individual has attended an assessment centre. This means that an up-to-date training plan can be pulled off the system at any time of the year.

Produce training requirement reports

A training record shows the training that individuals have completed and the training they need to do. The next step is to sift through all the training requirements so you can evaluate the needs and estimate the amount of training that needs to be done. This can be done manually, but it is a lot quicker if you have computerized training records.

A computer can produce training requirement reports that list:

- all the people who have requested a particular course;
- all the people who need a particular skill;
- the amount and type of training requested by a particular organization.

Needs evaluation

All training requests need to be validated to ensure the training is both appropriate and necessary. The amount of effort and time that is required to validate the training requirements depends on the quality of the input received. The best time to evaluate training needs is when the needs are being identified. This is why it is worth spending the time to run development open days and to train managers in development needs analysis. In an ideal situation the training administrator should only need to perform a quick check when the training department receives the training requests. These checks are shown in Fig. 2.9.

Figure 2.9 *Process for evaluating training needs*

> Check individuals have not been previously trained

It is amazing how many requests for training involve people who have already been trained. Sometimes this is because the person has forgotten the name of the course. On other occasions it is because a nomination has been put forward without consulting the person concerned. Whatever the reason it is highly embarrassing when people turn up to courses they have already completed.

Usually this problem can be caught when the training request is entered on the training record. This is why it is absolutely essential to have accurate training records. If you forget to amend the training record when a person has completed a required training course, you could find that the person will be automatically renominated.

Even if the training records are not as accurate as they should be, many duplications can be identified by an experienced training administrator. As a further precaution it is worth while getting the trainers to review the training requirement reports.

> Check that training is an appropriate solution

Sometimes a business problem cannot be solved by a training solution. Where this is the case, it is the responsibility of the training department to make this known. However, if a training analyst says that a business problem cannot be solved by training, and does not suggest any alternatives, the organization will soon get the impression that the training department is being inflexible and not interested in the rest of the business.

If training is to be an integral part of a business's change process, it has the duty and responsibility to suggest alternative approaches when a training solution is not appropriate.

Many of the individual 'training' requests that the training department receives are unsuitable for the person concerned or are inappropriate performance problem solutions.

The training administrator and trainers should look through the training requirement reports to see whether any of the requirements seem to be inappropriate or unsuitable. This again underlines the value of having

> Some time ago I was observing a report writing course. One of the students came up to me and said that he had been on a 'Report Writing' course five times before. Being somewhat surprised by this I asked whether he really couldn't write reports. 'Oh, I can write all right', he said. 'I just *refuse* to write them!'

experienced trainers and training administrators who have extensive local knowledge.

```
┌─────────────────────────────────────────────┐
│         Check queries with managers         │
└─────────────────────────────────────────────┘
```

In their book *Analysing Performance Problems,* Mager and Pipe recognized the problem of training being an inappropriate solution to many performance problems and they produced an algorithm that was designed to help trainers and managers avoid this pitfall. Figure 2.10 is a development of the first part of their algorithm. Its purpose is to determine whether training is an appropriate solution or whether alternatives to training need to be found. The algorithm can form the basis of a discussion with a candidate's manager when it is suspected that training is not appropriate.

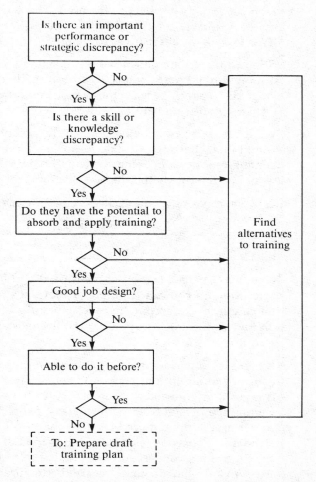

Figure 2.10 *An algorithm for determining whether training is an appropriate solution*
Source: adapted from Mager, R.F. and Pipe, P., © 1984 Lake Publishing Company, Belmont, CA, 94002, USA

Ideally a manager would go through this process before making a training request. The algorithm is also used to validate general as well as individual training requirements.

To demonstrate how this algorithm is used for performance problem analysis, let's take the example of the student who refused to write reports even though he had been on a report writing course five times before.

In answer to the first question: there is an important performance discrepancy. He is not writing reports, and he should be writing reports. I have used the word discrepancy rather than deficiency because not all training is aimed at making up deficiencies. Training should also be concerned about change and continuous improvement.

The second question asks whether there is a skill or knowledge discrepancy. The answer to this question is 'No' as we know he could write a report if a gun were held to his head. This tells us that training would not be a suitable solution for this performance discrepancy. We would have to look for alternatives to training.

Contrast this to the person who is unable to write reports. Again, there is an important performance discrepancy. There is also a skill or knowledge discrepancy because the person could not write a good report even if a gun were held to his head.

We would then ask whether he had the potential to be trained. We would then check whether there was anything about the job that is preventing reports from being written. The next thing we would check would be to see whether he was ever able to write reports.

Only after making all these checks could we say that training is a suitable solution.

Find alternatives to training

Figure 2.11 is an adaption of the second part of Mager and Pipe's algorithm. As you can see there are several alternatives to training, ranging from counselling to redesigning the job. The five entry points on this algorithm correspond to the five exit points on the previous algorithm.

If there is no performance or strategic discrepancy, there is no problem and we should not put people on courses just for the sake of it. If there is no skill or knowledge discrepancy, we have to look at what is preventing the person from performing. If people do not have the potential to perform at the required level, we have to look at our selection standards. Poor jobs need to be redesigned. If the person was able to do the job before, we may have to provide refresher training, but it is more likely that on-the-job coaching will be required.

In the case of the person who wouldn't write reports the entry point is 'No Skill or Knowledge Discrepancy'. If there is nothing in the environ-

Figure 2.11 *Algorithm for finding alternatives to training*
Source: adapted from Mager, R.F. and Pipe, P., © 1984 Lake Publishing
Company, Belmont, CA, 94002, USA

ment that is distasteful or punishing, if performance *does* matter, and if
there are no obstacles in the way, we would be led to the conclusion
that we are dealing with an attitude problem.

So, instead of sending this person on yet another report writing course,
a better answer would have been for this person to be have been
counselled by his manager. As you can see this is not a training
solution. If any training is required, it would be to send that
person's manager on a counselling course.

Counselling   Counselling is a critical skill for managers and it is especially important when training needs are being identified. The steps in the counselling process are:

1. set climate,
2. set expectations,
3. seek counsellee's views of strengths and weaknesses,
4. agree a development plan, and
5. summarize.

Chapter 4 deals with the counselling process in more detail. Although the process in Chapter 4 describes a training manager counselling a trainer, the techniques are just as applicable to appraisal and development discussions.

```
┌─────────────────────────────────────────────────┐
│            Prepare a draft training plan          │
└─────────────────────────────────────────────────┘
```

When you have validated the training requirements you are in a position to put a draft training plan together. This should include estimates of:

- the number of trainer-days you think you will have to provide,
- the spread of the training load over the year,
- the cost of the training, and
- the number of days of training per employee.

We cover how to put a detailed training plan together in Chapter 6.

```
┌─────────────────────────────────────────────────┐
│          Estimate impact of training load         │
└─────────────────────────────────────────────────┘
```

Take the draft training plan and consider its impact from two perspectives:

1. the impact on the training department, and
2. the impact on the organization.

The impact on the training department is really a question of whether you have the capability, space, budget, and resource to meet the demand. If you do not have the capability to deliver the demand, now is the time to signal that you may need more resources.

The impact on the organization is a little more subtle. Try asking yourself the following questions to help you understand the impact.

- What do the estimated hours of training per person mean in terms of people being away from the workplace?
- What are the expected short-term penalties, in increased production times and costs, compared with the long-term benefits?
- How many people can you afford to have absent from one department at the same time?
- What other claims are there on the budget you need to deliver the training plan?

```
┌─────────────────────────────────────────────┐
│   Discuss draft plan with organization heads  │
│        and human resources managers           │
└─────────────────────────────────────────────┘
```

Considering the impact of the training puts you in a good position for discussing the draft plan with senior management, departmental managers, and the human resource managers. The purpose of this step is to get 'buy-in' from the stakeholders before you go public with the final plan. It is far better to deal with 'fatal flaws' and objections at this stage than later on in the training cycle.

You can discuss what the demand and training load mean in order to avoid 'nasty surprises' later in the year. You can get agreement to the proposed budget. You can discuss issues. You can discuss whether all the requested training is appropriate.

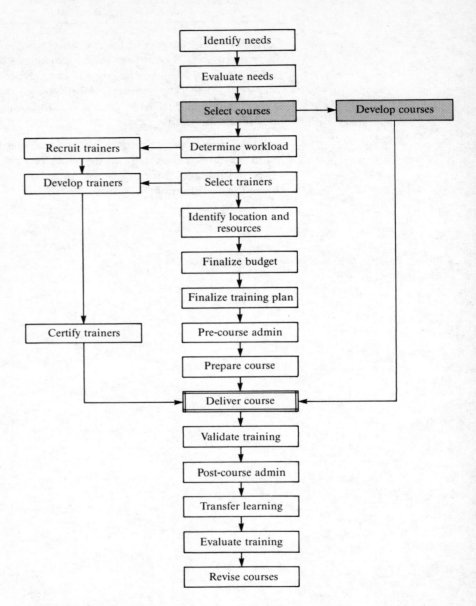

Figure 3.1 Training courses

3 Training courses

In this chapter we will be covering two more steps of the training process:

- select courses, and
- develop courses.

Having established that training is appropriate for the identified development needs, the next step is to find courses that meet the needs. We have to make choices about whether we buy or develop our courses. Developing a course from scratch can be both expensive and time consuming. Even purchasing a course that exactly matches all the requirements is not as easy as it sounds.

Course selection

When it comes to selecting courses you have the following options:

- using an existing course,
- modifying an existing course,
- buying or licensing an external course,
- developing your own course,
- using an 'in-house' course, and
- using a public course.

When you choose one of these options you need to consider the availability of existing material, and the urgency and demand for the course. Figure 3.2 is an algorithm that will help you make this decision.

| Consider |
| using company |
| course |

First, check whether a suitable course already exists within your own training department. If you're fortunate, and you have a good system for storing your materials, you will be able to find a course on the shelf that exactly fits the bill. If you are managing a new training department, the chances of you finding a suitable course on the shelf are considerably reduced.

If you work for a small company, your search may have to end there. However, don't give up too quickly if your first searches draw a blank. You'll be surprised how many courses are developed and run over the years. Tracking these courses down can be a bit like finding a needle in a haystack.

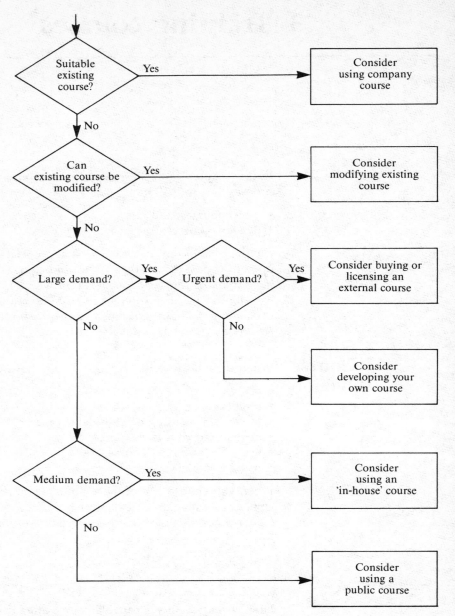

Figure 3.2 *An algorithm for selecting courses*

First try the personnel department—personnel often get called upon to run training courses. Also try asking supervisors and section managers—sometimes managers independently arrange training courses for their own people.

Did your company disband their training department some years ago? This can be a cyclical process. In good times training departments expand, and in difficult times training is often one of the first activities to be hit. If you are fortunate, the trainers may still be in the company but working in other departments. In these circumstances you will have to use all your powers of tact, persuasion, and diplomacy. Nurture these ex-trainers. Their cupboards, shelves, and filing cabinets are often gold-mines of training material.

If you work in a large or multinational company, you will have a much larger search area to contend with. Spend some time on the telephone to the other training departments within your company. Ask for copies of their training catalogues. Follow up items that you read about in the house magazines. Check out rumours you hear on the grapevine. It can take some time and persistence getting to the right person and the right training course, but it can be very rewarding.

Another approach is to form links with training managers in other companies in your area. This is always a good idea because it is very useful to exchange notes and compare methods of working. You may also find that, providing no proprietary material is involved, it will be mutually beneficial to exchange training material.

Despite all your efforts you may still not be able to find an existing course that will meet your needs. Even more frustrating will be the times when you are faced with the classic response of: 'I only threw that out last week—I didn't think that it would ever be needed again!'

```
+------------------------+
|        Consider        |
|   modifying existing   |
|         course         |
+------------------------+
```

Having exhausted all the possibilities for finding a suitable existing course the next step is to see whether any other course could be modified to meet the need.

How easy this will be depends on how the course was originally developed. Some courses are so tightly structured that it is impossible to remove parts of the course without destroying the structure of the whole, or losing the meaning of the individual parts. Any change in one part of this type of course will have a ripple effect throughout the entire course. You will find yourself entering into a major rewrite.

If the course has a modular structure, the tasks of modification and adaption become a lot easier. Parts can be added, removed, and rearranged until you have the course you require.

When you come to develop your own course you should consider using modular structures which are easy to adapt for future requirements. In some areas of training, such as management training, the content will remain constant over many years. Yes, the emphasis may change and some topics may be added or subtracted, but the basics will still be the same. Good management is still good management, whatever you like to call it. Good managers have been exhibiting the same skills over the centuries.

An introduction to management will nearly always have modules on:

- communication,
- motivation,
- leadership,
- the role of the manager,
- coaching and counselling,
- decision making,
- planning and organizing,
- meetings,
- delegating, and
- interviewing.

You also might want to throw in modules on time and stress management. To do all these topics justice would probably take about 60 hours. A menu of these modules, showing what is involved for each subject, will help you or your client prioritize and make decisions about the content. See Fig. 3.3 for an excerpt from a typical menu.

There is a lot of argument among trainers about the use of 'training menus' or 'training catalogues'. Many trainers feel uneasy about giving clients a menu because they feel the customers will just choose what they 'fancy'. You can avoid this danger by being present to provide advice when the customer is making a selection.

One of the main advantages of a menu is that you can quickly draw up a specification for a course which is based on your interpretation of the customer's requirements. Any misunderstanding is soon flushed out by presenting the specification back to the customer.

> Consider buying or
> licensing an
> external course

If you have a large and urgent demand, you will need to buy or license an external course.

Buying suitable courses

Even if you have a large budget, which few of us do, finding a suitable course can still be very difficult. Looking through the magazines and putting yourself on to mailing lists can be helpful, but be warned that you will have to spend some time wading through all the mail you will receive. You will also need a very good filing system to recover the relevant brochure when you need it. A small database on a computer will help you retrieve the information, but you will have to be very disciplined about inputting the data as you receive it.

Some courses come as a complete package with transparencies, lesson plans, student materials, and a video. Look very carefully at packages that come with a video as standard. Sometimes it seems that a video has been included because it is the 'thing to do' rather than being an essential part of the training.

Also, look out for whether you have been given the copyright to make

BASICS OF MANAGEMENT

A. Role of the Manager (3 hrs)

    1. Challenges of Management (0.5 hrs)
       a) Video: 'Role of the Supervisor'   0.3 hrs
       b) Discussion: Challenges Facing Participants   0.2 hrs

    2. Functions of Management (2.6 hrs)
       a) Exercise: 'Operation Land Deal'   1.3 hrs
       b) Case Study: 'Computer Systems Inc'   1.3 hrs

B. Decision Making and Problem Solving (4.5 hrs)

    1. Decision Making (2.5 hrs)
       a) Lecturette: What is Decision Making?   0.1 hrs
       b) Lecturette: Decisions and Problem Solving   0.2 hrs
       c) Lecturette: The Steps of Decision Making   0.5 hrs
       d) Example: 'Replacement Windows' Case Study 0.5 hrs
       e) Exercise: 'The New Cars' Case Study   1.0 hrs

    2. Problem Solving (2.0 hrs)
       a) Discussion: Review of Problem Solving   0.3 hrs
       b) Exercise: 'Carry the Torch' Case Study   1.7 hrs

C. Communication (2 hrs)

    1. Communication Principles
       a) Lecturette: Communications Model   0.2 hrs

    2. Communication Barriers
       a) Exercise: 'Silencers Ltd'   0.4 hrs
       b) Exercise: 'Chinese Whispers'   0.4 hrs

    3. Communication Helps
       a) Exercise: 'Feedback'   0.5 hrs
       c) Lecturette: Effective Communication   0.3 hrs

D. Understanding Finance (5 hrs)

    1. Budgetary Control (2.5 hrs)
       a) Lecturette: Budgeting Process   0.3 hrs
       b) Lecturette: Cash Forecasting   0.3 hrs
       c) Lecturette: The Profit and Loss Account   0.3 hrs
       d) Lecturette: The Balance Sheet   0.3 hrs
       e) Exercise: 'XYZ plc' Budgetary Planning   1.0 hrs

Figure 3.3 *Excerpt from a training menu*

photocopies of the student materials. Otherwise, you might find yourself with the unexpected cost of purchasing more student materials every time you run the course. Some of these materials are very professionally produced and you may want to use them to save yourself time and effort. This is fine if you do this knowingly when you buy the package.

You also might like to look at the support you get with these packages.

For example, there may be no trainer training supplied. This is all right if you have very experienced trainers, who have an in-depth understanding of the subject. Otherwise, you might find that you are leaving your trainers very exposed—especially with the more 'lively' classes.

Licensing courses   There is another approach you can take if you do not have enough time to develop your own course. This approach is to have your own trainers licensed to run a commercial course. You will have to pay to have your own trainers trained. Additionally, you may have to pay a fee to give you the rights to run the course, plus a licence fee every time a course is run. Licensing has a large initial cost, but the more people you put through the course, the more cost-effective this becomes. Another reason for needing a reasonable demand to make this approach viable is that it can take up to four courses to bring a trainer up to speed. (See the section on trainer certification in Chapter 4.)

Licensing is not commonly advertised but you may notice one or two advertisements in the training magazines. For instance, a train-the-trainer assertiveness course that includes lesson plans and handouts was advertised for £595 + VAT in a recent issue of *Training & Development*. Even though a training company may not advertise the licensing option you may find a surprising number will be willing to negotiate the licensing of their courses if you are likely to put some more business their way.

> Consider
> developing your
> own course

Even assuming that you have all the expertise and time, it is only economic to develop your own course if you have a large demand. You can either use the expertise of your own trainers or you can hire consultants to develop the course for you. The latter will prove more expensive than using your own staff to develop the course, so only follow this approach if the course is specific to your company, and there is a large and urgent demand for the course.

Developing your own courses is covered on page 70.

> Consider
> using an
> 'in-house' course

An 'in-house' course is one which a training company runs one of their courses on your premises. An 'in-house' course is a good solution when there is medium demand for a course that is not in your own repertoire. Using consultants continually over a long period is considerably more expensive than having your own staff.

If you have to use consultants over a long period, it is worth while negotiating the fees. Most consultants do not expect to have paid work every day of the year. They factor the time they spend selling into their daily fees. This means they might be willing to give you a discount in return for a guaranteed medium to long-term commission.

You are more likely to get a discount from one-person bands and small groups of consultants. Surprisingly, the big institutions stick to their standard rates even in times of recession. Don't let this put you off. Make sure that you negotiate with the head of the institution. If you still meet resistance over discounts, try talking in terms of free places.

Also, consider having the course run on your own premises as this keeps your travel costs low and the institutions usually charge less for this.

Some companies charge by the trainer-day and this can be very expensive when a course needs two trainers. If the course requires a lead trainer and a co-trainer, you can save some money by offering to supply your own trainer as the co-trainer. This is particularly appropriate when the co-trainer's role is to observe and give feedback.

> Consider
> using a
> public course

Where there is a small or individual demand the most cost-effective approach is to send people to an externally run public course. Judging the quality of external courses is difficult without going on all the courses yourself—which is perhaps not the best use of your time. This is especially true if you are only going to send one or two people on each course.

The reputation of the company and the experiences of other training managers can help here. Don't be afraid of asking for the names of companies that have used the course. When you telephone these companies you nearly always get an honest appraisal of the course.

Talk to the providers of the training and to the potential delegates. This also will help you form an opinion of the course's suitability. Some training companies hold open days where they present extracts from their courses. This will help you get a feeling for their style, content, and professionalism.

Developing your own courses

In many ways developing your own courses can be very satisfying even though it can be expensive and time consuming.

Course development is an extremely large subject. It is very important you understand what it involves because it is a vital and intrinsic part of the training process. Being such a large subject, the development process really requires its own dedicated book. However, the following description should give you a very good idea of what it is all about.

The process I use has evolved over the years. Like all the processes described in this book, developing your own training courses is a lot

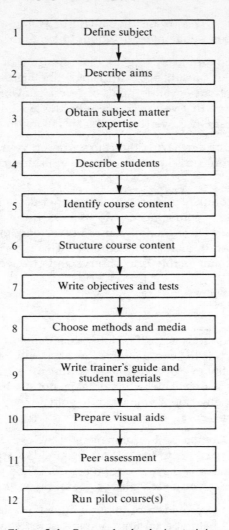

Figure 3.4 *Process for developing training courses*

messier than the neat, linear diagram shown in Fig. 3.4. Real life is usually a lot more circular and iterative.

Many people argue that the objectives should be precisely defined right at the beginning of the development process. In reality it is unlikely that the objectives can be defined precisely until the entire course has been written. This does not mean to say you should not have a clear picture of what you want to achieve. As Mager says, in *Preparing Instructional Objectives*: 'If you're not sure where you're going, you're liable to end up some place else.' The truth is that course development is a creative, organic process, as well as a structured endeavour.

The proposal, that there is very little that can be predetermined, has recently been recognized by both science and business schools.

Science has moved away from the determinism of Newton and is now embracing Chaos Theory. This theory says many systems are so sensitive to initial conditions that even infinitesimal changes to these conditions can significantly change the future behaviour of the system. This makes it impossible to determine the future with absolute precision. In a weather system this translates into what is only half-jokingly known as the Butterfly Effect—the idea that a butterfly fluttering its wings in Outer Mongolia today can cause storms over London next month. A good introduction to Chaos Theory is given by James Gleick in his book *Chaos*.

Similarly, business schools are putting less emphasis on decision trees, which attempt to determine the precise probability of a particular outcome, and are putting more emphasis on leadership, visions and strategic mapping that attempt to make the future happen rather than predicting what the future might be.

The other point that should be made is that this process is offered as one possible route for developing training material. It does not have to be followed slavishly. By all means explore some other routes for getting to your destination. Trying out alternative routes is not a sin as long as you are doing it knowingly and are not just straying absent-mindedly off the path. However, if you do get lost then you can use this process as a guide for getting back on track.

The process given here will help you produce excellent training materials, but it is no substitute for your own creativity. You could follow the process to the letter and still produce a deadly dull course.

An overall guideline, followed by Xerox in their development of their New Manager School, is the 'Seven M' strategy of design which means making the material:

- *m*otivational,
- *m*emorable,
- *m*eaningful, and
- *m*agical

through the appropriate use of:

- *m*etaphors,
- *m*odels, and
- *m*edia.

1 | Define subject |

The training needs analysis should have clearly defined the subject matter of the course. Do make sure that the training you think you have been asked to develop is what is really required.

Ambiguity is one the most common pitfalls. For example, you might have been requested to develop a course on planning and control. Seemingly simple, but is it 'Project Management' or 'Personal

Organization' that is required? 'Project Management' would cover subjects like critical path analysis and Gantt charts, whereas 'Personal Organization' would include topics such as time management and coping with paperwork.

Another example of this is the common request for 'Finance for Non-financial Managers'. Typically this course would cover balance sheets, profit and loss statements, and the common financial ratios. However, in large companies most managers would never have to deal with these. Although these subjects might be interesting, they would only be useful if the managers were to leave the company and set up their own businesses. What is really required is an explanation of how their departments' budgets are formed and controlled.

2
Describe aims

The aims of a course should be closely related to the business requirements that first generated the need for a new course. It is here that you describe what you want the people to know, or do, when they have left the course. You will also want to describe the effect the training will have on the business results or the business environment.

If you have carried out a good needs analysis, you will already know what you are trying to change or improve. If so, this step of the process should be comparatively easy. Also, think of this step as a checkpoint. After you have written down what you believe to be the aims of the course you should go back to your clients and check whether you have interpreted your clients' requirements correctly.

Do not fall into the trap of thinking that training is the complete solution. A course is usually only a solution to part of a much larger problem. Therefore, you should be very careful that the aims of the course describe which part of the problem the course will solve.

Identifying the aims of your training is essential for evaluating training effectiveness as well as developing the course. Aims are the indicators of what you are trying to achieve and allow you to 'complete the loop' as far as the training process is concerned. Chapter 12 covers evaluation in detail.

3
Obtain subject matter expertise

Having defined the subject, a source of subject matter expertise is next required. Many trainers become their own subject matter expert, but this can take a lot of time. You have to research many books to gather enough information to make a viable course.

It is one of the frustrating facts of developing training materials that one book will seldom produce enough information for more than 10 minutes of a training course.

All this amassed information has to be boiled down to the basic facts and concepts the students can take away with them. It is a lengthy task, but bear in mind that this amount of time is saved for every single student who takes the course. This reduces the time it takes to introduce new skills and knowledge into the business. It is one of the ways in which it can be proved that training increases business effectiveness.

If there is not enough time for the trainer to become a subject matter expert, other people need to be called upon to give the benefit of their knowledge.

There are many ways to get this kind of help. The easiest, of course, is to pay for their time. This arrangement gives more control over deadlines and expected results. Yet, in any company, subject matter experts are frequently other employees.

These people do not expect to be paid. It is part of their job. Unfortunately, very few companies have a system for sharing expertise, so trainers tend to use any means to beg, borrow, or steal their precious time. Figure 3.5 gives some guidelines for getting subject matter experts (SMEs) and keeping them happy.

---

1. Let SMEs know what is expected—in very specific terms (hours, products, deadlines). Ask them whether they can give what is wanted. (Be open, and do not try to sneak in a few major requirements at a later date. It is not fair to them and it risks losing their support—a high price to pay for a back-door approach.)

2. Do not worry about scaring off SMEs by asking for a lot of their time. Many people are motivated to volunteer because it enhances their credentials, they believe in the project or they have a stake in the final product.

3. Provide SMEs with an orientation to the project. Do not assume that they understand the training department's goals and work processes.

4. Keep SMEs informed about changes in the work plans or directions of the project—particularly changes that impact them. Volunteers like to be kept in the information loop. It makes them feel valued and increases their motivation.

5. Always follow through on commitments, respect their time. Do not expect them to make up the slack when you have missed your deadlines.

6. Provide meaningful recognition. It does not have to be gifts or money. People often place more value on intrinsic recognition—a pat on the back, a letter of appreciation sent to their manager, recognition of their peers. Do not assume a reward you value would satisfy your SMEs. Try asking if there is anything special that could be done for them. Then do it, if at all possible.

Figure 3.5 *Guidelines for using subject matter experts*
Adapted from: Marilyn Osborn, ITD Horizons, August 1991. Published by USCO Customer & Marketing Education IInstructional Technology (ITD) Group.

4 | Describe students |

As you might expect, a description of the students should include the students' current level of skill and knowledge. More surprisingly it also should describe the types of people you will be training, along with their attitudes, physical characteristics, what they enjoy, and what they dislike. The reason for going into all this detail is that it can make a tremendous difference to how you approach the development of the course.

> One technical training course required service engineers to read vast amounts of written material.
>
> If the course's authors had written a student description, they would have realized that service engineers are very practical people who spend little of their leisure time reading.
>
> The course developers would also have realized the engineers would find a text-based course boring and frustrating.

Physical characteristics should include hearing ability, sight, and strength. All these will influence the training methods, practical exercises, and the colour and size of the visual aids.

> I was once running a train-the-trainer course in Singapore and one of the trainees was having difficulty in choosing a suitable training project.
>
> As he was an engineer I suggested he teach the resistor colour code. (The resistor colour code is a numbering system where numbers are represented by coloured rings.)
>
> When I was coaching him on 'Describe the Students' I emphasized how important it is to describe the physical characteristics of the students—including colour blindness.
>
> I then heard laughter and chattering in Chinese from the rest of the class. When I asked what was causing the laughter, I was told that the student himself was colour blind. I had made the incorrect assumption that engineers would not be colour blind. There is nothing like being hoist by your own petard.

If the students come to training with a negative attitude about the course, you know you will have to allow extra time to diffuse these feelings. Learning cannot occur while grievances are being aired.

Above all, build up a mental picture of your students which will allow you to develop the course specifically for them. Novelists often use this technique. When they are writing the novel they imagine that they are telling the story to a typical reader who is sitting in front of them.

5 | Identify course content |

The content bridges the gap between the students' current competence and the level they should have after the learning experience. The second step of the development process (Describe Aims) identifies the desired state. The fourth step (Describe Students) determines the students' current level of skill and knowledge.

The use of the term 'learning experience' rather than 'course' is deliberate. Only part of the required behavioural change can develop during the short duration of a course. It is unrealistic to expect a course to do any more than develop an awareness of the required changes. A course also provides supervised practice of the new skills.

Whether the students use and become fluent in the skills depends far more on what happens after the course. Managing the transfer of learning from the classroom to the business is a vitally important part of the training process. Chapter 11 covers learning transfer in detail.

6 | Structure course content |

This is where you determine the structure and timing of the course. By now, you should be getting a feeling for the total length of the course.

There are two basic methods for determining the length of the course. The first is to estimate the durations of the individual components and simply add them up. The second is to start with a fixed time and see what you can fit in.

Starting with a fixed duration often arises from a training request that takes the form of: 'What we need is a one-day course on XYZ.'

Some trainers balk at being given a fixed time for a course. They respond with a statement like: 'I couldn't possibly train that in under five days!'

There is always something that can be usefully taught—no matter how little time we have. It is just a matter of being aware of the resulting limitations and consequences. You also should make sure that your client understands the limitations.

The effectiveness of a limited amount of training depends very much on the students' current state of knowledge. If there is no existing knowledge, any amount of training will make an improvement. Where knowledge is virtually non-existent, simply communicating 'three things that you need to know to get you out of trouble' can have a large and significant effect. As the students' knowledge and skill increase, the 'law of diminishing returns' starts to take over. The courses need to be correspondingly longer to achieve an appreciable improvement.

When there is a limited amount of time, or when you have to shorten a course to reduce costs, there are only two viable ways of doing this. The first is to look at the training methodology to see if there are more efficient ways of meeting the same objectives. For example, you might use the same exercise to give practice for both coaching and counselling, rather than having two separate exercises.

The other method is to take content out of the course. In this case the decisions you have to make are all about what you put in and what you leave out.

We shouldn't make the mistake of thinking that we can shorten a course by simply running faster or exerting very high pressure on the students. The effectiveness of the course will suffer. A training menu described earlier in this chapter is one method of helping the client prioritize what should be done in the available time.

When you have to make complex decisions it is better to analyse the content of the course very carefully against criteria. Agree the criteria with your client because you will be using them for including or rejecting course content. The actual criteria you use depend very much on your client's requirements, so it is very important that these criteria are determined very early on in the process.

> One of my clients once asked for all the content shown in the training menu to be taught in four days. A quick addition of the times soon revealed that it would take more than 60 hours to complete the training. Further discussions about the client's requirements and priorities resulted in 50 hours of training, spread over five days. To keep disruption to a minimum the course was split into two parts. The first part was to run for two days and the second, a three-day module, was to run from Thursday to Saturday.

A document called the 'Minimum Competency Statement' can then be written. This statement details the skills that the student will have at the end of the course. It is important that you get agreement to the statement before you start developing the course.

An example of how this method works for a real course is given on page 70.

The next step is to order the components of the course in a logical sequence. Some people can write down the right order straight away, but I find it easier to use Post-its.

Start by writing one of the course components (it does not matter which one) on a Post-it. Then stick the Post-it on to a sheet of flip chart paper and ask the following series of questions to help decide which components should come before or after.

- What has to be learnt before this component can be learnt? (i.e., What are the dependencies or prerequisites?)

- What else can be learnt now that this component has been learnt?
- What can be learnt at the same time?

The answers to these questions will suggest which components should be stuck on to the chart next.

Keep on asking these questions as each new Post-it is added to the sheet of flip chart paper. Draw lines to show the dependencies of the components and a network will be built up showing a logical sequence for the course.

The output of this step should be a course agenda or programme. If the course is short and uncomplicated the agenda will be like a meeting agenda (see Fig. 3.12). You would use the type of course programme shown in Fig. 3.6 when the course is longer and more complex.

	DAY 1	DAY 2		DAY 3	DAY 4	DAY 5
09 : 30 / : 00	Introduction	Motivation and leadership		Financial planning	Staff selection	Project management
10 : 30 / : 00	Role of the manager					
11 : 30 / : 00						
12 : 30 / : 00						
Lunch				Effective meetings		
14 : 30 / : 00	Communication	Managing time			Project management	Stress management
15 : 30 / : 00						
16 : 30 / : 00	Decision making			Coaching and counselling		
17 : 30 / : 00		Wrap-up				Wrap-up
18 : 00						
Evening	Desert survival exercise			The numbers game	Plan project	

Figure 3.6   An example of a course programme

7   Write objectives and tests

An objective is a statement of what the students should be able to do once they have completed a section of the course. It is an indicator of what learning has taken place. Notice that I said 'indicator' rather than 'measure'. Learning is what goes on inside a student's head and therefore cannot be directly measured. So while it is perfectly possible to have an objective of 'understanding interactive skills' it is not very useful for measuring the effectiveness of the training. The students could be asked whether they understand interactive skills, or the trainer could get a 'feeling' for how much has been understood by general questioning or observing body language.

Another approach is to use indirect indicators such as something the students should be able to do if learning has taken place. The skill in this approach is deciding what these indicators should be.

For example, a student who really understands interactive skills should be able to recognize and use all the different categories of verbal behaviour. Although a trainer can see the trainees using the verbal behaviours, checking whether somebody has recognized something is a little more difficult. One way round this would be to show a videotape of a number of different behaviours and have the student state the name of each behaviour.

The next question is how many of the responses would have to be correct to satisfy the trainer that the student had really understood interactive skills. Would it be 5, 20, 80 or 100 per cent?

Taking all this into account the objectives for 'understanding' interactive skills would look like this.

- Given a videotape showing 20 examples of verbal behaviour the student will be able to name correctly at least 18 of the behaviours.
- Given a list of 11 verbal behaviours the student should be able to give correct examples for a minimum of 10 of those behaviours.

A good objective has three components:

1. **Behaviour**: what the student will be expected to do.
2. **Conditions**: the conditions under which the behaviour has to occur.
3. **Standard**: the acceptable level of performance.

In the interactive skills example the behaviours are:

- 'naming behaviours';
- 'giving examples of behaviours'.

The conditions are:

- 'Given a videotape showing 20 examples of verbal behaviour';
- 'Given a list of 11 verbal behaviours'.

And the standards are:

- 'At least 18 out of 20 behaviours correctly named';
- 'A minimum of 10 correct examples of behaviours'.

Writing objectives is hard work, but the really neat thing is that if they are done to the above standard, writing the tests becomes very easy. As a good objective gives the standards and conditions under which the behaviour should occur, it also gives the conditions and standard for the test.

A test does not have to be an 'examination'. The minimum condition is that the trainer should be able to observe the desired behaviour so the standards can be checked to see whether the training has been effective.

Objectives are an essential tool for both presenters and developers of training material. Be careful of giving students the same detail of objective that you would use for developing a course. It would be confusing to have an objective that states: 'By the end of the module they will be able to identify the central processing unit, the random access memory, the read only memory, the video display unit, and the input/output interfaces.'

After all, if they already knew what these terms meant they would not have to attend the course.

A better objective might be: 'By the end of the module they will be able to identify all the major components of a microcomputer.'

Some objectives describe behaviours or conditions that can only exist in the classroom. Other objectives describe classroom activities like: '. . . will have participated in three simulations'.

It is much better to have objectives that describe behaviour and conditions that can be measured both inside and outside of the classroom. This allows you to monitor learning inside the classroom and monitor the transfer of learning to the business.

8
| Choose methods and media |

There are many different points-of-view about what are the 'best' training methods. The following is a summary of the most frequent arguments.

- Should courses be 'trainer led' or 'self-directed'?
- Should students be told the facts or be encouraged to go on a 'voyage of discovery'?
- Should you use a case study or should you use a real-life example?
- Should you start with a 'big-picture' overview and then work down to the details; or should you start with the basic 'building blocks' and develop the learning upwards from there?

Some trainers insist that the trainees be given freedom of choice. One method of doing this is to have a course map that has alternative routes through the course (see Fig. 3.7).

The students are allowed to take any of the routes through the course as long as they have completed the prerequisites. The prerequisite modules are the ones that are above, and on the same path as, the module the student wants to take.

But does this approach mean that the trainees have a real choice? Do they have enough information to come to sensible conclusions? It could be argued that if the students did have enough information to make rational rather than random choices, they wouldn't need to take the course anyway!

Proponents of any training method can be very persuasive with the arguments they bring forward to support their favourite approach. Training managers, personnel managers, and directors should be very

Figure 3.7   *An example of a course map*

careful of being seduced into spending huge amounts of money on new training technologies that are the 'only way to train'.

There are two other warnings to be given when it comes to training technology. The first is that the vision of what people want from the technology is often years in advance of what the technology is able to deliver today. The second, counterbalancing warning, is not to look at technology with a jaundiced eye, even though the last 20 demonstrations you attended were little more than gimmicks. One day you will miss that significant innovation you really need.

The truth is that there never will be one 'best' method or one 'best' medium for training people. Every student is different and every person learns in a different way. Some people have to know the detail first. Others couldn't possibly understand the detail until they have a mental framework to pin it on. Some people like facts and figures, others like a more inspirational approach to training.

There are many personality theories and questionnaires that claim to classify people into different types. Most of these seem to be based on the work of Jung and have four basic classifications. Each approach has its own names for the four types but usually the types fall into the following categories:

- logical people;
- people people;
- task-oriented people;
- intuitive/entrepreneurial people.

A recent version of this approach is Ned Herrmann's brain dominance theory. In this theory Herrmann builds on the 'split-brain' research of Nobel prize-winner Roger Sperry. According to Sperry the left side of the brain controls language, while the right looks after our visual and spatial skills. Extrapolating from this it is said that people with a dominant left-brain will be the more logical type of person, whereas intuitive and artistic people would have a dominant right-brain.

Herrmann is of the conviction that the brain is divided, not just into halves, but into four sections (see Fig. 3.8):

• upper left;
• lower left;
• upper right; and
• lower right.

The upper, 'cerebral' quadrants govern analytical intelligence, while the lower, 'limbic' regions control emotion and motivation.

Depending on our personality, some quadrants will be stronger than others. People with a strong leaning towards logic and statistics have a strong upper left sector, while the more conservative and cautious have dominant lower quadrants. Emotional, empathetic people are in the lower right, while the intuitive, idea generators have strong upper rights.

Given this understanding of how people are different, we can make better choices of which methods and media to use on our courses. Table 3.1 gives Herrmann's view on how people with different brain dominances learn. It also shows the types of learning activities that they respond to.

This again emphasizes the importance of having a good description of the students who will be attending your course.

If you have a homogeneous group of students, you will have a good idea of which types of methods and media that you should be using.

Figure 3.8   *Ned Herrmann's brain dominance theory*

Table 3.1 *Learning methods and media for different types*

	Learn by	Respond to
Upper left	Acquiring/quantifying facts Applying analysis and logic Thinking through ideas Building cases Forming theories	Formalized lecture Data-based content Technical case studies Text books Program learning
Lower left	Structuring content Sequencing content Evaluating/testing theories Practising skills Implementing content	Thorough planning Sequential order Organizational cases Text books Program learning Structure/Lectures
Upper right	Taking initiative Exploring possibilities Relying on intuition Self-discovery Constructing concepts Synthesizing content	Spontaneity/free flow Experiential activities Experimenting/playing Future oriented cases Visuals—aesthetics Individuality Involvement
Lower right	Listening and sharing ideas Integrating experiences Moving and feeling Harmonizing with content Emotional involvement Individuality	Experiential Sensory movement Music People-oriented cases Group interaction

For example, engineers would have a dominant upper left; accountants would have strong lower lefts; social workers dominant lower lefts; and musicians strong upper rights. Sales and marketing people would have their right sides predominating.

If you have a varied group of people to teach, the chances are that there will be a fairly even spread of the four different types. In this case it would probably be advisable to have a wide range of differing methods and media so that you can reach as many different types of people as possible.

This is not a new approach—have you ever wondered why there are four gospels in the Bible, each telling essentially the same story? Could it be that each is directed at a different type of person?

However, considering the learning preferences of the group is not all the story. Consideration should also be given as to which methods and media are the most suitable for each part of the course. The best courses have a wide range of media and learning experiences.

Table 3.2 *Advantages and disadvantages of different media*

Medium	Advantages	Disadvantages
Presenter	Relatively quick and inexpensive to produce, flexible response	Quality depends on the individual presenter
Flip chart	Inexpensive, flexible	Good handwriting required
Whiteboard	Clean, easy to alter	Difficult to clean if wrong pens used
Blackboard	Easy to alter	Dusty, reminiscent of school
Overhead transparencies	Easy and economic to produce, equipment widely available	Tendency to be overused
35 mm slides	High quality, standard format, equipment widely available	Equipment unreliable—slides prone to jam
35 mm slide/tape	Moderately easy and economic to produce	Unreliable synchronization of audio tape to slide projector
Videos	Wide range of videos available, reliable, widely available	Dear to buy, difficult to make, varying standards around the world
16 mm film	Good quality	Expensive and difficult to produce, unreliable, equipment obsolescent
Text	Fairly easy and economic to produce and revise	Not suitable for all students
Audio cassette	Fairly easy and economic to produce, equipment widely available, easily used outside classroom	Limited by lack of visual content

Medium	Advantages	Disadvantages
Text/Tape	Economic and easy to produce, good combination of sound and visuals	Student has to keep pace with audiotape
Computer-based training	Paced to student, wide range of programs available	Expensive and time consuming to produce
Interactive video	Paced to student, high-quality graphics	Expensive and time consuming to produce, very expensive equipment

Table 3.2 shows the range of media that are available, along with their advantages and disadvantages.

9 | Write trainer's guide and student materials |

In one of his *Lettres Provinciales*, Blaise Pascal wrote: 'I have written a long letter because I did not have time to write it shorter.' In the same way it is much easier and quicker to write a long course than a short one. It takes time to analyse what is essential and what could be left out. The virtue of writing at length is that you will probably include everything you need. The problem is that you will never know what you could have left out. Writing the materials as lean as possible has the advantage of producing succinct training and it will become obvious if anything has been left out.

Do make sure that the manuscripts are given a really good proofread. Although it seems unfair, you have to come to terms with the fact that some students judge the overall quality of the materials on their first impressions. Spelling and grammatical errors interfere with their learning. If the materials have been written on a word processor, you should put them through a spelling checker.

Some words of caution here. Only the very sophisticated spelling checkers, those that dabble in artificial intelligence, can do anything more than to tell you whether a particular word exists. Generally, spelling checkers cannot take any account of the grammar, context or meaning of the words. So, a sentence such as: 'Thee employees took there complained too their manger', would hardly cause a spelling checker to stutter.

There are also some grammar checkers on the market. Figure 3.9 shows what one of these made of the above example.

> Thee<<*__U3. ARCHAIC: Thee *>> employees took there complained too their<<*__S22. SHOULD too their BE two or to their? *>> manger.

Figure 3.9 *An example of a grammar checker*

The grammar checker caught some of the problems, but it didn't catch 'complained' instead of 'complaints', or 'manger' instead of 'manager'.

Also be very careful that you do not 'teach' the spelling checker to be a bad speller. When the spelling checker does not recognize a word it gives you the choice of skipping the word, correcting the word or adding the word to its dictionary. When you are working through a long document, pressing the 'add' button almost becomes a reflex reaction and, before you know it, another misspelt word is added to the computer's dictionary. Also, have a 'real' dictionary handy. Don't assume a word is not in the spelling checker's dictionary even when you are 'convinced' you know how to spell a word. After all you have been spelling the word this way for nearly all your life. For some unknown reason it is nearly always much easier to add than to remove a word from these electronic dictionaries.

Although there is no substitute for a thorough proofreading, a spelling checker is a very useful tool. It can spot many of errors that we overlook. A computer, unlike the human brain, does not see what it thinks should be there.

Trainer's guide

A good trainer's guide includes:

1. course objectives,
2. course programme,
3. course prerequisites,
4. course pre-work,
5. number of training and break-out rooms required,
6. list of student materials,
7. list of equipment required,
8. list of audio-visual materials (transparencies, posters, prepared flip charts, audiotapes and videotapes),
9. room layout,
10. preparation notes for each session,
11. lesson plans for each session, and
12. masters for the overhead transparencies.

Items 1 to 9, taken together, form the course specification which provides essential information for the course administrator. The order shown above reflects the structure of a trainer's guide—not necessarily the order you would write it in.

You would have already written the objectives in Step 7: 'Write Objectives and Tests'. You would also have determined the course programme in Step 6: 'Structure Course Content'.

The course prerequisites are determined by comparing the output from Step 5: 'Identify Course Content' with Step 4: 'Describe Students'. A prerequisite is a level of competence a student should have before attending a course. It could be attendance at another course, a certain level of education, or a particular skill.

You would normally identify the other components of the trainer's guide as you write the lesson plan. In fact, it is a good idea to have sheets of paper headed 'Student Materials', 'Videotapes', etc., so that you can note the requirements as you identify them.

Lesson plans   Writing a course is writing the lesson plan. It is a 'script' that not only provides you with your 'lines', but also describes detailed timings, structure, and activities.

There are many formats that you can use for a lesson plan. My preference is for a three-column format. The first column is for timings and type of activity such as: State, Ask, Stress, Action, and Exercise. The middle column is reserved for the actual statements, questions, and directions, and the third column lists the media. Figure 3.10 shows an example of this type of lesson plan. Notice that the timings are clock times. You have more than enough to do when you are running a course without adding up the times of the individual modules to see whether you are running to time.

10 | Prepare visual aids |

Preparing the visual aids is something that can be done at any time during the development of the student materials and lesson plan. My preference is to do this as I am writing the lesson plan.

As you develop the course, you should be constantly thinking whether a learning point could be better illustrated with a visual aid.

NEW COURSE		First Module
08.30	*FIRST MODULE* (1 hr 20 min)	
	Introduction	
State:	Welcome to the new course.	OHP 1
Ask:	How many people have been on a similar course to this?	
Action:	Count the number of people and write this on a flip chart.	FLIP CHART
Stress:	That this course builds on similar courses.	
Show:	'Attending Courses'.	VIDEO

Figure 3.10 *Example of a lesson plan format*

During this step of the process you should review the visual aids you have prepared so far, and create any additional visual aids that are required.

11 | Peer assessment |

Before you unleash your course on a group of unsuspecting students, it is a very good idea to have your colleagues review the materials. It is an even better idea to teach the course to your peers.

After all this time you will be too close to the course to notice even the more obvious mistakes. An experienced colleague will be able to spot the fatal flaws, annoying inconsistencies, and irritating errors.

12 | Run pilot course(s) |

Pilot courses are the 'test-flights' for your newly developed course. With a brand new course you will normally need to run two pilot courses. The first, sometimes called a developmental test, is run to get all the bugs and gremlins out of the course. It is not essential to have representative students on the developmental course, but it is risky to have stakeholders present. A stakeholder is person who has a vested interest in the course and could damage its reputation.

The reason for this is that the errors and the pauses will only serve to distort an observer's perception of the course. Reports of the 'disaster' will still be heard long after the course has established itself as a great success.

The second pilot course should have students who are representative of the target student population. This second course is a good time to invite some stakeholders along to observe and give some feedback. The course will be sufficiently developed to prevent annoying errors from getting in the way, but not so set in concrete that you would not be able to make changes based on the observers' feedback.

If the course is self-taught, you can take on the role of passive observer—only intervening if things start to go seriously wrong. It is much more difficult to be the passive observer when the course is trainer-led, and you are the only person who can run the course. You will be too involved to notice all the subtle, and not so subtle, reactions to the course. In this case you need to enlist the services of a colleague. Provide a copy of the lesson plan and student materials, and ask your colleague to do the observations for you.

If the course is large, and you are leading a team of training developers, you can either do all the observations yourself or take turns in making the observations.

When you are running a pilot course you must be extremely careful to avoid rationalizing away any negative reactions the students might have. It is all too easy to think that a problem was a chance occurrence. You might be persuaded that 'real' students wouldn't have the same difficulty. Always assume that minor difficulties, encountered on the pilot course, will become major problems if they are left uncorrected for the final version of the course.

Be a fly on the wall. Record any difficulty, hesitancy, or problem. Avoid coming up with solutions or rewriting the material at this stage because you might miss some of the other problems. Try not to interfere with the training.

Immediately after the training get the students to fill in a written feedback form. Then have general discussions about what went well and what could have gone better. Again, don't try to solve any of the problems at this stage. Don't try to explain why you wrote in a particular way. Above all, don't argue if you think their comments are wrong. Just record, without editing, all their comments on a flip chart. Some students will make suggestions for changing the course. These also should be recorded. This does not commit you to making those changes if you do not agree with them.

Always try to understand why the student wanted to have that change. Even if the suggested change is not a good idea, there is nearly always an underlying problem that needs to be addressed. Other students might just feel uncomfortable about something or feel that something is 'not quite right'. By all means ask some questions to help you understand what the problem might be but don't pressurize them to come up with explanations or solutions. After all, solving training problems is your job—not theirs.

When you have finished collecting information from the students, have a meeting with the trainers to get their feedback. Now you can work with the trainers to develop proposals on how the course should be changed, amended, or revised.

An example of course development

The following is an example of how a course was developed using this process. The chosen course is simple and straightforward, but it illustrates all the relevant points.

Defining the subject

A company had embarked on training all its full-time employees on Total Quality Management. As the culture and language of Total Quality started to embed itself into the fabric of the company it was realized that contract staff were becoming increasingly isolated from the rest of the company. They had no understanding of the language and the processes of Quality. It was not possible to justify the six days of training that full-time employees received. What was needed was a one-day overview that explained what Total Quality Management was all about.

Describing the aims

The aim of running a one-day introduction to Total Quality Management was to allow medium-term contractors to participate in Quality circles. They would not be expected to take a lead in the Quality circles.

They should not be confused when the company's permanent employees talk about Total Quality Management.

Obtaining subject matter expertise

In this case the training analyst assigned to the development of the one-day Total Quality Management had been training the full course for two years, so this person already had subject matter expertise. If the analyst had not had this previous experience, a considerable amount of time would have been needed to bring this person up to speed. Given the complexities of Total Quality Management, it could take about six months to gain sufficient subject matter experience and knowledge. Without this experience the analyst would not be able to determine the critical content that should be included in the course.

Describing the students

The students were to be medium-term contractors. They would want to know what Total Quality Management is all about. Contractors may have concerns about being treated differently from full-time staff. They also would be concerned whether there would be another contract after the current one expires. Medium-term contractors may not have the same loyalty to the company as full-time staff, but they have a professional approach and would be able to see how the concepts relate to their own businesses. In fact, it might be easier to communicate 'customer awareness' to these people than to permanent staff who very rarely see an external customer.

Most of them would be designers with electrical/electronic, software, or mechanical backgrounds. They would not appreciate a 'wordy' approach or put up with a significant amount of reading.

A significant minority would be translators with an arts background. Although English is not the mother tongue of many of the translators, the nature of their work obviously means that they would not have any language difficulties. Reading would not present any problems.

All the contractors identified for the course are in good health with normal hearing and sight. Colour vision would normally be good for engineering people, but this would not usually be a requirement for translators.

Although some of the contractors may have done business studies courses at university or polytechnic, the subject matter will be new to most of them.

Identifying the course content

Some people can write down the contents of the course in sequence by starting at the beginning, working through the middle and finishing at the end. Other people have 'grasshopper' minds and only feel comfortable if they are jumping from one topic to another and back again.

In his book *Use Your Head*, Tony Buzan describes a technique that he called 'Mind Mapping'. Mind Mapping is a creative method which is eminently suitable for those who prefer the 'grasshopper' approach. In fact, Buzan would argue that this method would be suitable for most people as it reflects the 'organic' way that the brain operates and stores

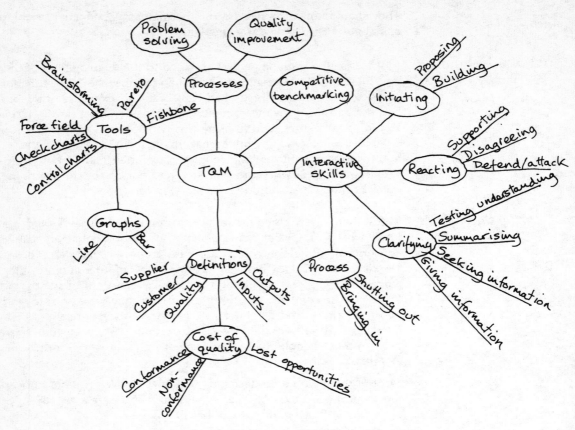

Figure 3.11 *A mind map for the TQM overview*

its information. These mental maps are also known as 'Spidergrams' or 'Bubble Diagrams'.

To apply this technique to the one-day 'Total Quality Management Overview' you would first draw a shape in the middle of a sheet of paper (see Fig. 3.11). In this shape you would write 'TQM' which is the subject of the course. Attached to branches radiating from this central shape are the main categories of topics that will make up the course. The categories come from thinking about the student description and the goals for this overview.

In this example the main categories were based on the questions the students would ask about Total Quality Management and what the company would expect them to be able to do after they had completed the training. You can then have the detailed topics radiating from the main category 'bubbles'. Although these detailed topics will form the content of the course, there are two other aspects that need to be considered before finalizing the content.

The first is to determine the level of the students' current knowledge. It will be a waste of time teaching topics that are already familiar to them.

These familiar topics can be crossed out on the mind map. In the case of the 'Total Quality Management Overview' all of the topics will be new to the vast majority of the contractors so no topics were omitted for this reason.

The other consideration is whether any of the topics are too advanced for the level of the course. In the example given in Fig. 3.11 statistical process control and the use of control charts were thought to be too advanced for a one-day overview.

Structuring the content   Although the detailed topics shown on the mind map form the content of the course, the larger bubbles will not necessarily be the course modules. The mind map is created while the training analyst is understanding the relationships between the detailed topics. This means that the structure that develops may not be the most efficient for learning the subject. The modules chosen for this course were as follows.

- Tools of the trade.
- Why did we introduce Total Quality Management?
- Quality is free?
- Who's the customer?
- What is Quality?

These major modules need to be put into an overall framework. A good framework for the structure of a course comes from the 'Army School of Training'.

- Tell 'em what you're goin' to tell 'em.
- Tell 'em.
- Tell 'em what you told 'em.

Or put another way:

- overview,
- body, and
- summary.

The major course modules are to be found in the body of the course. The body needs to be sequenced so that there is a logical flow from one module to another. The Post-it method described earlier in this chapter helps you to do this. A logical flow goes from:

- the simple to the complex,
- the general to the specific, and
- the known to the unknown.

The structure chosen for this course is given in the agenda that is shown in Fig. 3.12.

Choosing the methods   Given the potentially wide range of students we decided to base this
and media   introductory session on trainer presentations and student exercises. Short excerpts from existing videos would also be used.

We also had a tape/slide presentation put on to video. This was done to

```
AGENDA

Introduction                                    9:00
—Introductions
—Expectations
—Agenda

Why Total Quality Management?                    9:20
—The need
—Initial steps
—Quality gurus
—Birth of a strategy
—Key elements of the strategy

What is Quality?                                 9.40
—Definition
—Standard
—System
—Measurement

Quality is free?                                11:00
—Cost of Quality
—Conformance
—Non-conformance
—Lost opportunities

Who's the customer?                             11:20
—Suppliers
—Internal customers
—External customers

Tools of the trade                              12:00
—Problem-solving process
—Quality improvement process
—Process capability
—Fish-bone diagram
—Pareto analysis
—Force-field analysis
—Interactive skills

Where do we go from here?                       16:00

Review                                          16:30
```

Figure 3.12 Course agenda

increase reliability and to keep the number of different media down to a minimum.

Writing the objectives and tests

After each module the students should be able to do something they could not do before. Objectives are best written by considering what this change of behaviour should be. For example, after completing the 'Tools of the Trade' module the students should be able to: 'Describe the basic tools of Quality and their uses.'

> OBJECTIVES
>
> After completing today's session you will be able to:
>
> 1. State why the company introduced 'Total Quality Management'
> 2. Define Quality
> 3. Explain the basic concepts of Quality
> 4. Identify customers and suppliers in a given situation
> 5. Describe seven basic tools of Quality and their uses

Figure 3.13 *Objectives for TQM course*

You should keep the aims of the course in mind when you are writing the objectives. Although describing the tools and their uses would be a sufficient level for our target population, it would not be suitable for people who lead Quality circles. They would need to demonstrate competence at using the tools. Fig. 3.13 shows the objectives for the TQM overview.

Once the objectives have been written, tests become relatively easy to design. For example, the fourth objective is for the students to be able to identify customers and suppliers in a given situation. To test this we showed a video clip of a scene in a restaurant. There were four main characters:

- the paying customer,
- the waitress,
- the cook, and
- the owner.

Using the form shown in Fig. 3.14, the students were asked which of the four characters was the customer, and who was the supplier in the given situations. We developed the other tests in a similar manner.

Writing the trainer's guide and student materials

The trainer's guide and student materials were developed together. The student materials included a booklet which had a section for each of the modules. We also developed a set of cards that had objects, or pictures of larger products, glued to them. These cards were designed to help the students define Quality. They would have to decide whether they considered the product to be a Quality product. They would also have to give a reason for their decision.

Preparing the visual aids

Many of the visuals aids were developed as the trainer's guide and the student materials were being written. We saved some development time by using artwork we had prepared for the student's guide as masters for overhead transparencies. The videotapes were already available as they had been developed for the full-length course.

Peer assessment

The materials were given to a new trainer to review. It is a good idea to have one of your colleagues review the course at every stage of its

OUTPUT	SUPPLIER	CUSTOMER
• Order taken		
• Order delivered		
• Breakfast cooked		
• Breakfast served		
• Money taken		

Figure 3.14   *An example of a test based on a course objective*

development. The development of this course was also used to teach the new trainer the basics of course development.

Running the pilot course(s)

We decided to use a group of 12 'target population' students for the pilot course. The maximum number of students for this course was 18, but we decided to restrict the numbers for the pilot course. I conducted the course and the new trainer made observations of the training process and the students' reactions. We asked the students to complete the feedback forms and then we had a debriefing session.

Using criteria to determine the content of a course

The following is a description of the process we used when we were asked to reduce a technical training course from 15 to 5 days. At first sight this seems to be a particularly brutal reduction in course duration, but you have to bear in mind that this condensed course was needed for a different population of students.

We would use this shortened course to train maintenance engineers. Maintenance engineers were recruited at a lower skill level than service engineers. Their duties involved regular cleaning and maintenance of the machines, as well as repairing some of the more frequently occurring faults. It was always expected that these maintenance engineers would not be able to repair every single fault they come across. From time to time, they would have to call in a service engineer for assistance.

So, giving maintenance engineers the same training as the service engineers, with all the associated travel and accommodation costs, was not a good investment. Service engineers would always need to have the full three weeks of training.

The criteria we chose for selecting the tasks were:

- frequency (how often would the task have to be done?),
- difficulty (how hard was it to do the task?), and
- criticality (what is the impact of poor task performance?).

Frequency was the most important of the criteria because the strategy was to have the maintenance engineers performing the most commonly occurring tasks. The temptation might be to decide on the basis of frequency alone but this approach would lead to difficulties. For example, if we decided we would teach all tasks that occurred within a certain predetermined period (say six months) we would find we would also be teaching tasks that are so easy they need not be taught. Clearly, practising these tasks would be a waste of valuable teaching time.

Incorrect performance of other tasks, although infrequent, might lead to disastrous consequences. We would not want to take the risk of omitting them, even though the task is performed infrequently.

The criteria of difficulty and criticality were introduced to overcome these problems.

Table 3.3   Frequency ratings

Task interval (months)	Frequency rating
1–6	1
7–12	2
13–18	3

Having determined the decision criteria a method of rating the tasks against the criteria was required. We need an objective method for determining how frequent, difficult, or how critical a task is. Table 3.3, Table 3.4 and Table 3.5 show the ratings we used for our three criteria.

Another method of assessing the difficulty is to compare the time a freshly trained novice and a master performer take to complete the same task. The greater the difference, the more difficult the task.

The next step is to find a method of making a decision based on combinations of these criteria. One method would simply be to add up the frequency, difficulty, and criticality ratings for each task. If a task's total falls below a cut-off point, we would eliminate the task from the course. The problem with this approach is that it gives equal weighting to all the criteria.

To overcome this you can give more weighting to the more important criteria. However, getting the relative ratings correct starts to become a bit of a mathematical nightmare.

The approach we decided to take was to list every possible combination of the criteria (1 1 1, 1 1 2, 1 1 3, . . ., etc.). For each combination we

Table 3.4 *Difficulty ratings*

Difficulty rating	Definition
1	Without prior training, the maintenance engineer cannot or is not confident to perform the task without the assistance of a service engineer
2	Without prior training the maintenance engineer can perform the task correctly with the assistance of a service manual
3	Maintenance engineer can perform the task correctly without prior training, assistance of a service engineer or reference to a service manual

Table 3.5 *Criticality ratings*

Criticality rating	Definition
1	Incorrect completion of the task results in a safety hazard or catastrophic failure of the equipment
2	Incorrect completion of the task results in the equipment functioning at an unacceptable level
3	Incorrect completion of the task affects cosmetics only

Table 3.6 *'Train'—'Don't train' decision matrix*

Frequency	Difficulty	Criticality	Decision
1	1	1	Train
1	1	2	Train
1	1	3	Train
1	2	1	Train
1	2	2	Train
1	2	3	Border line
1	3	1	Don't train
1	3	2	Don't train
1	3	3	Don't train
2	1	1	Train
2	1	2	Train
2	1	3	Train
2	2	1	Don't train
2	2	2	Don't train
2	2	3	Don't train
2	3	1	Don't train
2	3	2	Don't train
2	3	3	Don't train
3	1	1	Don't train
3	1	2	Don't train
3	1	3	Don't train

Table 3.6   *(contd)*

Frequency	Difficulty	Criticality	Decision
3	2	1	Don't train
3	2	2	Don't train
3	2	3	Don't train
3	3	1	Don't train
3	3	2	Don't train
3	3	3	Don't train

used our experience to decide whether a task, with that combination of ratings, would normally be included in a course.

So, a task with a 1 1 1 combination of ratings (task encountered at least once every six months, very difficult to perform, and is a safety hazard if performed incorrectly) would definitely be included in the course. A task with a rating combination of 1 3 2 would not be trained. (The '3' difficulty rating signifies that the task can be performed correctly without any training.)

The decision matrix (Table 3.6) gives the 'train' or 'no-train' decisions for all these combinations of the frequency, difficulty, and criticality ratings. You should only use this matrix as a guide. You should give the training analysts the authority to make different decisions on the basis of their judgement and experiences, providing the reasons for those decisions are recorded.

Very experienced training analysts would probably not need to use the matrix in the normal course of their work, but it is an extremely powerful tool for communicating the rationale of training decisions to your clients. The matrix is also very useful for providing 'instant experience' to less experienced training analysts.

Notice that some of the ratings in the difficulty and criticality columns have been highlighted. These are to remind the analyst to make some checks before finally making a 'no-train' decision.

When the warning occurs in the criticality column the analysts should satisfy themselves that labels on the equipment and the service manual cover any safety hazard.

When the warning occurs in the difficulty column the analyst should be satisfied that field support is available or that there is detailed support in the service manual.

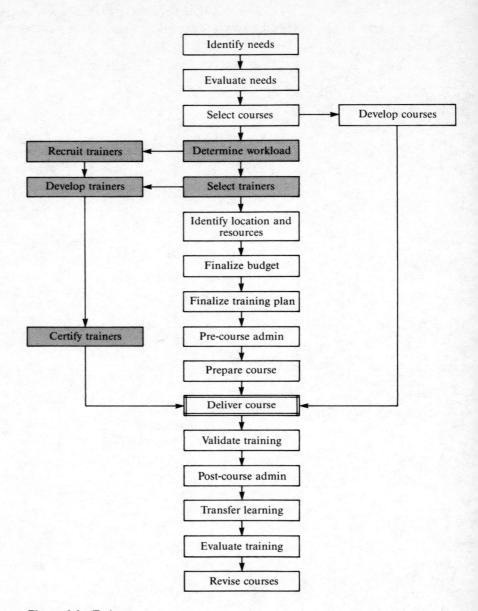

Figure 4.1   *Trainers*

4 Trainers

In this chapter we will be covering five more steps of the training process:

- determine workload,
- select trainers,
- recruit trainers,
- develop trainers, and
- certify trainers.

The first step is to determine the workload. If you have sufficient staff or contractors to meet the training needs, you can then select the most appropriate trainer(s) to run each of the identified courses. You also need to consider whether these trainers will need any further development.

If you cannot cover the load with your existing resources, you will need to recruit additional trainers or find more contractors. This will involve you in writing job descriptions and vacancy notices, as well as interviewing prospective trainers. If you are unable to find experienced trainers you will need to consider which people would make good trainers and what training these new trainers should receive.

Even if you recruit experienced trainers they may not have had experience of the type of training you will be asking them to provide. They will also need to undertake a programme of development. To do this you need to understand what skills and knowledge your trainers should have to train these courses.

Once the trainers have the basic skills and competencies needed to run these courses, you still need to plan how they will learn to train the new courses that you will be running. This is the process of certification.

Determining the workload

When you decide how many trainers will be required, you have to make an estimate of the work load each trainer can handle. The factors you have to take into account are:

- the number of courses,
- the duration of the courses,
- face-to-face ratio (the amount of time a trainer spends in front of a class),

- the number of trainers needed to run each course,
- how much time is spent in preparing courses,
- how much time is spent in developing courses,
- how much time is spent in other activities such as planning, supervising and evaluating, and
- the learning curve of new trainers.

Number and duration of courses

The number of courses you need to run depends on:

- the number of people you need to train;
- the number of people you can train per course.

The number of people you need to train comes from the needs analysis. The course specification will tell you the maximum number of people each course can accommodate, but don't base your estimates on this figure. It is unlikely you will be able to run with the maximum number on every course. The availability of people, as well as sickness and cancellations, will erode this figure. Always try to book the maximum number of people on to the course and you will probably find you will be running the course with the optimum number of students.

Rule of thumb: assume you will put people through the course at the rate of two-thirds of the maximum number.

If you find you can train people at a faster rate than this, nobody will complain if you finish a training programme ahead of time.

The course specification will give you the duration of the course.

Face-to-face ratio

The amount of time a trainer can spend in front of a class depends on many factors such as the difficulty of the course and the number of different courses that the trainer has to train.

It would be possible for trainers to spend 100 per cent of their time in the classroom if they have full administrative support and the courses always fill a complete week (it is difficult to schedule courses without any gaps between them).

Eventually, however, fatigue, with a corresponding decline in standards, will set in. If you have to support a massive training effort, and your trainers are committed to the programme, it is possible to sustain a face-to-face ratio of 80 per cent.

More realistically you would expect trainers to spend some of their time on preparation, administration, revision of existing materials, and development of new materials. The proportion of the times spent on these activities will vary depending where the trainers are on their career development. We will consider what these proportions might be when we look at developing trainers.

Rule of thumb: you would normally expect trainers to have a face-to-face ratio of 50 per cent.

This is supported by data from several benchmarking exercises carried out with other companies.

Number of trainers per course

The number of trainers you need to run a course depends on the complexity of the course and the number of students on the course. These are the factors you take into account when you plan the number of trainers required for a new course. The course specification should tell you how many trainers you need for existing courses.

The complexity of a course is driven by:

- the course logistics (the amount of preparation and 'scene shifting' that has to be done before each session);
- the amount of observation, facilitation, and coaching required;
- the amount of data processing that is required (e.g. running computer simulations or producing graphs and ratios from observation data).

It seems sensible to say that the more students you have, the more trainers you will need; and the more students each trainer has to deal with, the less effective the training becomes.

This would seem to be borne out by the constant argument about the size of classes in our schools. The problem of having a simple measure of effectiveness makes it difficult to put this hypothesis to the test. However, we had the opportunity to test out this hypothesis when we introduced Trainee Centred Learning (TCL).

The idea behind TCL is the same as that of self-paced learning, which is to say that students learn better at a pace which matches their own abilities; and do not move on to the next stage of learning until they have demonstrated competence at the previous stage. All the students have their own learning station and a set of training materials. Trainers are on hand to answer questions, demonstrate techniques, and to check the course objectives are being met. Using this approach it is intended that everybody leaves the course having reached a common standard, even though people may have taken different times to reach that standard.

Individually, the time taken to go through the course depends on the person's own learning pace and starting ability, but the average duration can be used as a measure of training effectiveness.

When the course durations were correlated to the 'student to trainer' ratio we found, as expected, that the course duration increased as the ratio went up from 6:1 to 10:1. Imagine our surprise when the course duration also increased as the ratio fell below 6:1 (see Fig. 4.2). While it is easy to explain the increase in duration with greater numbers of students in terms of longer waiting times, it is much harder to explain why the length of the course should increase when there are more trainers on hand.

We came to the conclusion that there must be an optimum level of trainer intervention. Too little contact from the trainer and the student

Figure 4.2 *The effect of student to trainer ratio on course effectiveness*

starts to flounder. Too much contact and the trainer starts to interrupt the learning process or, worse still, takes over the learning tasks from the student!

Another interesting result that came out of this exercise was the fact that a ratio of 20:2 is not the same as a ratio of 10:1. What this means is that 2 trainers spread over 20 students is not as effective as making each trainer primarily responsible for a sub-group of 10 students. With this approach the trainer only has to remember and monitor the progress of 10 trainees in detail rather than remembering the details of all 20 students.

So we concluded that the optimum student to trainer ratio for this type of training was in the region of 6:1. Of course this optimum is different for different types of training; in some cases such as tutoring or coaching 1:1 will be the optimum ratio. You should always consider the effect that this ratio will have on your training and not always assume 'the more, the better'.

Each course should have a course specification which specifies the number of trainers, observers, etc., that are needed to run the course. The student to trainer ratio should be expressed as two ranges: an optimum range, and a minimum to maximum range.

For example, an optimum range might be from 10:1 to 16:1. This means the course works best when there are between 10 and 16 students for every trainer. The minimum to maximum range for the same course might be from 8:1 to 18:1. This means the course is either unworkable outside this range, or effectiveness is seriously eroded above 18:1, or it is uneconomic to run the course with fewer than eight students.

Rule of thumb: generally speaking courses will work well up to the following student to trainer ratios.

Simple courses:	18:1
Complex courses:	12:1
Individual feedback:	6:1

Preparation time

The amount of time it takes to prepare for a course depends on the complexity of the course and the trainer's familiarity with the course. If a trainer is very unfamiliar with the material, it can take as much as a day of preparation for every hour of presentation time.

It can take a lot of time and effort to calculate the preparation times for courses of different complexity. Often the results are no more accurate than taking a 'broad-brush' approach. A useful guide for determining preparation time is given below.

Rule of thumb: on average, it takes one day of preparation for every three days of training.

This means trainers would normally spend a maximum of 75 per cent of their time in front of the class. This figure also takes interruptions into account (it is impossible to do a day's preparation without other business issues intervening).

Course development time

The time required to develop a new course is about as long as the proverbial piece of string. It depends on:

- the complexity of the course;
- how much material has to be produced;
- the standard of the materials;
- what is already available.

What is clear is that most people have no idea how long it takes to develop a course; and when they find out they are severely shocked.

Rule of thumb: Table 4.1 gives an estimated development-time to course-length ratios for different types of courses.

If you need to make a significant revision to an existing, complex, 5-day course, then you would need to plan 85 person-days to do the job. At first sight 85 days seems a very long time, so let's see where the time goes to.

The first thing to note is that the figure is a planning assumption—it assumes that very few days will pass without interruption and it is unlikely that development will take place in one block. The figures also assume the trainers are producing their own materials. Using a secretarial service will reduce the time by about 25 per cent, but it will also increase the costs.

Table 4.1   Development-time to course-length ratios for different courses

Type of course	Development time
Computer-based training	100:1
Complex/technical courses	40:1
Extensive restructuring/revision of an existing course	17:1
Moderate restructuring/revision of an existing course	11:1
Constructing a modular course from existing modules	6:1

A significant revision is one where every page of the lesson plan and the student materials needs to be changed and substantially retyped. A 5-day course could have 400 page-equivalents of lesson plans, students materials, handouts, posters, and slides. This means the trainer will have to research, revise, and restructure the course at the rate of five pages per day.

The same considerations apply when you are writing a new course, but you also have to add in a substantial amount of time for researching, learning, and condensing the subject matter.

Time spent on other activities

In addition to standing up in front of a class, trainers also need to spend time on planning, supervising, benchmarking. The proportion of time spent on these activities will vary depending on the individual. Generally, these activities will increase as a trainer progresses from instructor to training manager. We look at these issues in greater detail in the section on developing trainers.

Rule of thumb: the proportions of time spent in activities, other than preparing and training courses, are as follows.

Instructors: 30%
Trainers: 40%

Learning curve time

A trainer who is 'learning the ropes' will be less productive than an experienced trainer. You also have to allow time for experienced trainers to learn new courses. You can calculate the length of time based on the experience of the trainer and the number of new courses that have to be taught. The section on trainer development looks at this in more detail.

Rule of thumb: a new trainer will take about three months to become partially productive, and a year to become fully productive.

Rule of thumb: it will take an experienced trainer two courses to become familiar with a short, simple course, and four courses for a long, complex course.

Selecting trainers

In this step you match your existing trainers or consultants to the courses you need to run. There are only two factors to consider:

- experience, and
- availability.

Does the trainer have, or can the trainer acquire, the experience to run the course? Will the trainer be available to run the course when the client needs it?

When I discuss training needs with my clients I ask them whether it is possible for them to give me a 'window', or range, of dates for when they want a specified number of people trained. Matching trainers to a range of dates is much easier than matching them to fixed dates.

Full-time trainers or consultants?

Whether you use full-time trainers or external consultants depends on the criteria (such as cost and flexibility) you use for making your decision.

Rule of thumb: if the decision is made on the basis of cost, consultants start to become more expensive than full-time employees when you employ the same consultants for more than 50 per cent of their time.

Some training organizations prefer to use only external consultants for training. They enjoy the flexibility and the cross-fertilization they get from other companies. External consultants also specialize, which means that they are able to be experts in their field. Full-time trainers can only specialize if there is enough demand for their speciality to keep them fully utilized. Otherwise, the trainers will have to spread themselves thinly over a larger number of subject areas.

If you choose external consultants at random you will have the problem of ensuring consistency and quality. The answer is to have a core of consultants, or associates, to whom you have given your organization's seal of approval. External trainers and courses should be certified in the same way as you certify your own trainers and courses.

Using external consultants for delivery is expensive, but the cost is generally well understood. The cost of using external consultants for the development of materials can give you a heart attack. As we have said, the time required to develop a new course is about as long as the proverbial piece of string.

If you assume an average development time for a 5-day course is 10 days of development for every day of training, and a consultant day-rate of £400, the cost for developing this course would be £20 000. It would be far more cost-effective to buy a course off-the-shelf or to use one of your full-time employees to develop the course.

The problem arises out of applying a consultant's day-rate to the development of a course. As far as you are concerned you are not interested in how much time the consultant spends developing the course as long as it is ready by the time you need it. What is important is how much you think the finished product is worth to you.

If your application is a very specialized one, you may be prepared to pay a lot of money to have the course developed. If the course has wide applicability, you may feel you should not pay anything for the development—because the consultant can defray the development costs over a number of different customers. The situation is similar to buying a new car. If you were the first customer for a new model you would not expect to pay millions of pounds to cover the manufacturer's research and development costs. It is important to remember that the negotiating issue is not time but price.

External consultants will obviously not want to make a loss over the deal so, before taking on the contract, they will carefully consider the following.

- Whether they have existing materials which can be modified rather than developing the course from scratch.
- Whether they could charge less because of the prospect of having two months of continuous work (day rates are calculated on the basis of not being able to get work every day, a certain amount of personal preparation that is required before every course, and a certain amount of product development).
- How much they would expect to earn in a year, and what proportion of that expectation would be met by a fixed-price contract.
- Whether there are any costs or time associated with being away from base which would not be incurred during the development of the course.
- As it is not possible to work continually on course development (it is often more productive to give it a rest and work on something else for a while), are there any other money-making activities that could be worked on in parallel?
- What additional work could this project lead to? For example, is there a guaranteed minimum number of courses the consultant will be asked to run?
- Will the client be tied to the consultant for running future courses?
- Will the consultant be able to run the course for other clients and thus be able to defray the development costs over a larger number of courses?

Recruiting trainers

If you cannot cover the workload with your existing trainers or consultants you will need to recruit additional trainers.

Ideally you would want somebody who is currently very successful at doing the same kind of job—which unfortunately poses the questions: 'Where do "new-starters" get their experience?' and 'If someone is already doing this job—why would they want to come and work for our company?'

Internal or external recruitment? First see if there are experienced trainers in other parts of the company. Resist the temptation of always bringing-in 'new blood' from outside. New ideas and different experiences will always add richness to a training department, but don't underestimate the importance of company knowledge and experience. Avoid the 'grass is greener' trap. Internal candidates bring a record of achievements, failure, strengths, and weaknesses with them. Unless you probe very thoroughly external candidates will only tell you their strengths and achievements. The first time you get to find out about external candidates' failures and weaknesses may be after you have employed them!

If you have time you can develop somebody who does not have training experience, but has the desire and potential to be a trainer. Recruiting internally for someone who has no experience is a risk. Recruiting inexperienced people externally is an even greater risk. But how do you know whether somebody has the potential and the desire?

Training is an activity you have really got to want to do, so it is very likely that people with the desire to train will approach you. If a person has *always* wanted to do something, it is also very likely they have always done it. Not necessarily formal training, but they might have a history of successful presentations, or of coaching their colleagues.

As with all things it is a matter of getting the balance right. You need both experience and 'new blood'.

Rule of thumb: if you have a team of six trainers, you would probably want four existing trainers with company experience, one externally recruited trainer, and one 'apprentice' trainer.

There is really no difference between recruiting a permanent member of staff and finding a new consultant, except that you probably would not want to use an inexperienced consultant. The criteria for deciding whether you would recruit a new employee or find a new consultant are exactly the same as we discussed in the section on selecting trainers.

The recruitment process 'Recruitment is the process of finding and attracting a person who matches the requirements of the job.'

Recruiting trainers is much the same as recruiting for any other profession. Employers have to identify potential candidates and satisfy themselves as to which candidate is best able, and most willing, to do the job. Many interviewers concentrate on ability to the exclusion of willingness.

This matching process cannot start unless we understand what the job involves, and the type of person best suited to the job.

Job descriptions The job description tells you what the job entails. It is the basis on which you can decide the kind of person you need for the job.

The way to do this is to identify which tasks have to be completed to meet the requirements of the job. 'Developing a lesson plan' and 'analysing training needs' are examples of tasks. Note that both a verb and a noun are required to define the task.

Person specifications

The job description is the basis on which you can decide on the kind of person that you need to do the job. The best way of doing this is to analyse which competencies are needed to perform the tasks. Competencies are a combination of knowledge, skills, and behaviours.

So the person specification describes the ideal person to fill the job. It is a profile of the personal skills and characteristics you will look for in the recruitment and selection process.

The interview

The selection method that most companies put their trust in is the interview. The purpose of selection interviewing is 'to predict whether an applicant will fulfil the requirements of a particular job', and the interview attempts to do this by carrying out a comprehensive investigation to verify the facts of past achievement and failure, to assess the candidates' strengths and weaknesses, and to form perceptions.

Don't be misled by your perceptions—but don't ignore them either— they often serve as warning bells, indicating areas where you will need to dig up some more facts.

Being an interviewer is like being a detective. While intuition is useful; the final conclusion must be firmly based on facts and data.

Most jobs are filled through interviews, but the widespread reliance on this method is often based on assumptions which do not bear close examination. It cannot be automatically assumed that all experienced managers are good judges of an applicant's character and skills; being able to sum up an individual in an interview that often lasts for no more than an hour.

Even when the job lends itself to practical selection tests, or when companies are able to use extensive psychometric testing, the interview almost invariably forms the final selection process. (Psychometric tests are tests which measure ability, interest and personality.)

Given these limitations it is important that the interview is used effectively, and that those likely to be involved in interviewing are given training.

In any interview, the interviewer's task is to determine whether the candidate is both willing and able to do the job. Sometimes we concentrate on one of these to the exclusion of the other.

Checking a trainer's ability

Checking a candidate's ability is easier for training than for many other professions. It is relatively easy to simulate a training environment where you can observe a trainer's performance. A training session is the culmination of all the work and preparation the trainer has done. Most of the candidate's strengths and weaknesses will become apparent in a 40-minute session. The more accurately you can simulate the training environment, the better data you will get.

Many companies ask candidates to make a presentation when they come for a second interview. Unfortunately, the trainer will often try to do something 'special'. This, combined with performing in front of an interview panel, can give a distorted and misleading impression of the trainer's true abilities. Try to provide a natural environment for the presentation. Presenting to a single interviewer is very different to making a presentation to a large group.

Ideally, it would be better to observe trainers in their 'natural' environment such as a course they already had planned to run. Of course, this is very difficult if the person is currently working for another company. It is unlikely that a trainer's present employers would allow you to 'poach' on their own premises unless it was part of an 'out-placement' programme.

During the interview you will have established which courses the trainer is able to train. If there is a good match between the candidate and the job, it is more than likely that one of these courses will meet one of your training requirements. In this case you could invite the trainer to run a training session for a group of your own students.

If the prospective trainers are consultants, who want to take up full-time employment, it is relatively easy to get permission to observe them. You could even offer a fixed-term contract and observe the trainer in the environment they would be working in.

The observation form shown in Fig. 4.4, below, can be used as a checklist of points to look out for. Don't just observe the trainer; also look at the students to gauge their reaction.

Another good indicator of trainers' abilities are the lesson plans they have prepared. Ask prospective trainers to bring examples of lesson plans they have developed and use them as a basis for discussion. Examples of handouts and other student materials also give a lot of information about a trainer's ability.

One of the best predictors of future performance is past and present performance. During the interview get the candidate to talk about how they handled past situations. It is not a good idea to ask them how they would handle a hypothetical situation because they will either be stuck for words or they will describe how they feel the situation should be handled—not how they would actually perform.

Don't reject people just because they have been made redundant. There used to be a feeling that these people could not possibly be any good. In hard economic times you will find there are some very good people out on the street. The fact that a person is redundant is not as important as the reason for the redundancy. In any case you should always take up references and talk to people the candidates have worked for and to the students they have trained.

Experience may be related to age, but this can be a trap. There was once a person who claimed to have 15 years' experience, but this turned out to be one year's experience 15 times. Some companies have age blocks which are difficult to justify. An age block is even more difficult to justify for trainers because many trainers continue to work as consultants long after they have taken 'early retirement'.

You can easily check whether the person's education and training meets the requirements of the job, but be careful not to use education and qualifications as predictors for all the job requirements.

Physical qualities such as stamina are important for a trainer. Good hearing, vision (including colour vision where necessary), and clarity of voice are essential for communicating with the students. Boxes of training materials are surprisingly heavy, so a trainer also needs to be physically fit. Don't make assumptions on the basis of physical stature or disability. Small people can have immense strength, and physically disabled people learn to be enormously resourceful. The only way you can be sure the person is physically able to do the job is to observe them prepare and run a training session.

Appearance can be a trap for the unwary. It is unreliable to assess a person on the basis of appearance, but it is important that a trainer's dress does not distract or intimidate the students.

Intelligence is difficult to assess without testing. Obviously trainers have to be intelligent enough to understand the concepts they are teaching, and not to look foolish in front of the class. A secondary indicator of intelligence is knowledge and it is relatively easy to check this out during an interview.

Maturity and emotional stability are essential to gain respect and credibility. Again, achievement in the past can help. Pure gut-feelings will probably mislead.

Checking a trainer's willingness

A trainer's attitude to work answers the important question of whether the candidate *will* do the job as well as being *able* to do it. Probe the candidates' reasons for applying for the job, as well as their aims, intentions, and ambitions.

Make sure they understand what the job means in terms of carrying boxes, unsocial hours, travelling, and nights away from home. Watch for any hesitancy in their reactions as you describe the job. Don't fudge the issue of describing the demands of the job for fear of discouraging a 'good candidate'. It is far better for applicants to be put off at this stage rather than after they have been employed.

Training is the kind of job that can be hell if you don't thoroughly enjoy it and get some kind of buzz out of teaching people. In some ways this characteristic of training makes it easier for an interviewer to judge a candidate's willingness. If enthusiasm for training and the subject matter does not shine through at the interview it is unlikely that the applicant will be able to survive as a trainer.

You might say that all this comes down to personality, but what is personality? Psychologists say it is a range of relatively unchanging characteristics. So it is better to test or probe for specific characteristics that are needed for the job rather than talk about personality in vague and general terms.

Selection and the law

Every interviewer should be aware of how the law applies to recruitment. The following is based on UK law but you will find that it enshrines the policies and values of most multinational companies.

- It is unlawful, unless the job is covered by an exception, to discriminate on the grounds of a candidate belonging to a particular category (i.e., sex, marriage, race, religion, etc.).
- It is advisable to keep records of interviews, showing why applicants were rejected, for at least six months.
- Questions at interviews should relate to the requirements of the job. Questions about marriage plans or family intentions should not be asked, as they could be construed as showing a bias against women. Information for personnel records can be collected after a job offer has been made.
- Each individual job applicant should be assessed according to their personal capacity to meet the requirements of a given job. Applications from men and women, married and single (of whatever race or religion), should be treated in the same way. Where it is necessary to assess whether personal circumstances will affect the performance of the job (e.g. unsocial hours), this should be discussed objectively without detailed questions based on assumptions about marital status, children, and domestic obligations. Interview questions should probe the experience and skills necessary to carry out the job.
- Employers should give careful consideration to the selection criteria that they use (including age bars, mobility, and hours of work), and whether this would discriminate disproportionately against a particular category. Criteria which cannot be shown to be necessary for objective reasons should be withdrawn.
- Selection criteria (job description and person specification) should be determined before the recruitment process starts.
- There are very few exceptions where it is legal to select a person of a particular category while excluding people of other categories (e.g. sex or race). These are called genuine occupational qualifications (GOQs). Basically these are: authenticity, privacy, decency, and the laws regulating the employment of women. Be very cautious about using a GOQ as a reason for not employing a person. You need to be very sure of your ground, and you will need to have demonstrated that you were unable to make suitable alternative arrangements for the person concerned.

You should not assume that:

- women are less ambitious or committed than men,
- women put their family commitments before their careers,
- men put their careers before their families,
- women will work for pin money,
- men will not work for a woman,
- women with children cannot work long or unsociable hours, or attend residential training courses,
- women are not prepared to relocate to follow their careers,
- women are unsuited to certain kinds of work (e.g., scientific, technical, heavy manual, or senior management).

The treatment of employees which is influenced by any of these assumptions may result in acts of unlawful discrimination.

Developing trainers

Developing your trainers is a very important part of managing the training process. There are three areas of development:

- developing the skills required to run courses, identify needs and develop new courses (trainer training);
- continuous development (assessing trainer performance);
- finding career paths either within, or through, the training department (career development).

Training trainers

The exact process for introducing a new trainer into the training department depends on the trainer's experience and the type of training to be done.

The train-the-trainer process certifies trainers at two levels: Instructor and Training Officer. An instructor is a person who has the professional skills to deliver courses. Training officers also carry out needs analyses and develop courses.

The process given in Fig. 4.3 is for a management trainer.

```
┌─────────────────────────┐
│     Induction into      │
│   training department   │
└─────────────────────────┘
```

This step is used to introduce both new and experienced trainers into the department. It assumes that the person has attended the company's induction course and it includes:

- the mission of the training department (see Chapter 1 for an explanation of what a mission is),
- where the training department fits into the organization,
- roles and responsibilities of the training department's personnel,
- meeting members of the training department, clients, and suppliers,
- location of offices, training rooms, storage areas, photocopying, and other facilities,
- current issues, and
- future direction of the department.

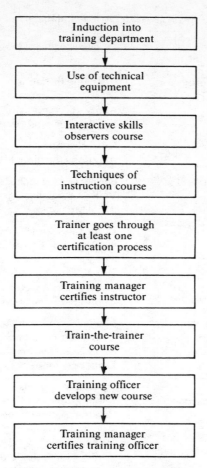

Figure 4.3 *Train-the-trainer process*

> Use of technical
> equipment

There are very few courses that are run without any technical equipment. An overhead projector seems to be the absolute minimum—even though it is perfectly possible to run a course without one. In addition, a trainer can be expected to deal with audio-cassette recorders, video recorders, video cameras, camcorders, computers, interactive video, satellite links, 35 mm slide projectors, and 16 mm film projectors.

Film and 35 mm slide projectors are becoming less common, which is just as well as they are notoriously unreliable. I would always try to avoid these 'technology traps' by having them transferred on to video.

Although all trainers cannot be expected to be technical experts and to fix every fault, they should at least have a minimum level of expertise. This will keep embarrassing equipment failure delays down to a minimum.

Table 4.2 shows the minimum technical knowledge that a trainer should have for each type of equipment.

Table 4.2 *Minimum knowledge of technical equipment*

Equipment	Minimum technical knowledge
Overhead projector	Changing the lamp Cleaning the optics Adjusting colour fringes Keystone effect (how to adjust for)
Audiocassette recorders	Head cleaning Azimuth adjustment
Video recorders	Formats and standards (VHS, Super-VHS, VHS-C, Betamax, U-matic, PAL, NTSC, SECAM) Colour, hue, brightness, sharpness, contrast, tracking and skew adjustments Cueing Head cleaning Leads and connectors Counter/time relationship
Video cameras Camcorders	Manual/auto iris, focusing, panning, tilting, zooming, tracking Sound and lighting Leads and connectors
Computers Interactive video	Operating systems Booting-up Random access memory Copying and deleting files Disk formats (5¼″, 3½″, single-sided, double-sided, single-density, double-density, hard disk) Word processing Databases Graphics Desk-top publishing
35 mm projectors	Loading Lamp changing Optics cleaning
Film projectors	Film threading Lamp changing Leaders and lead-in Sound leads and connectors Splicing broken film Rewinding

> Interactive skills
> observers course

The accurate observation of verbal behaviour is one of the key skills that are required by a management trainer. The system that we use is based on the work of Rackham and Morgan (1977). It provides an efficient method of giving feedback to students because the system has a common vocabulary and well-defined categories of verbal behaviour. Students can compare their perceptions with objective observations of their behaviour. Comparisons can also be made with standard profiles such as 'Expert Negotiators' or 'High Performing Managers'. Definitions of the categories are given in Table 4.3.

The standard of reliability required for interactive skills observations is 95 per cent agreement with an expert observer.

> Techniques of
> instruction course

There are many organizations that provide techniques of instruction courses and choosing one is the same process as for choosing any other course (see Chapter 3 'Training Courses'). I would recommend selecting a supplier who issues a recognized certificate or award as this sets the standard. A professional qualification is good for trainers' morale and the credibility of the training department. An example of this type of course is the City & Guilds' 7331 Trainer Training Foundation course.

More and more awarding bodies are aligning themselves to National Vocational Qualifications (NVQs). For example, the Institute of Training and Development's (ITD) 'Direct Trainer's Award', 'Certificate in Human Resource Development' and 'Diploma in Human Resource Development' are based on NVQ Levels 3, 4, and 5. The 'Direct Trainer's Award' would be a suitable qualification for a developing instructor. It is based on NVQ Level 3 with additional units.

It is important to understand that NVQs are not awarded on the basis of passing a training course. They are awarded on the basis of assessment of competence in the workplace. See Appendix 1 for more information on National Vocational Qualifications.

> Trainer goes through
> at least one
> certification process

The course certification process is the means by which an instructor or trainer becomes proficient to train a course without assistance. This process is described in detail on page 110.

> Training manager
> certifies instructor

At this point the training manager reviews the new instructor's progress. This should be no more than a formality if the process I have described

Table 4.3 Behaviour categories

Behaviour	Definition
Proposing	Puts forward a new concept or suggestion that is actionable.
Building	A special kind of proposal that extends or develops a proposal that has been made by another person.
Supporting	Involves a conscious, direct, and reasoned declaration of support or agreement with another person or concepts.
Disagreeing	Involves a conscious, direct, and reasoned declaration of difference of opinion, or criticism of another person's concepts.
Defend/attack	Attacks another person or defensively strengthens an individual's own position. These behaviours usually involve value judgements and often contain emotional overtones.
Testing understanding	Seeks to establish whether an earlier contribution has been understood.
Summarizing	Restates the content of previous discussions, or considerations, in a compact form.
Seeking information	Seeks facts and opinions from another person.
Giving information	Offers facts, opinions, or clarification to other individuals.
Shutting out	Excludes, or attempts to exclude, another group member (e.g., talking over, interrupting).
Bringing in	A direct and positive attempt to involve another group member.

Source: Rackham and Morgan, 1977

has been followed up to this point. If your trainers are following the NVQ path, you may want to delegate this step to the NVQ assessor.

```
┌─────────────────────────────────┐
│       Train-the-trainer         │
│            course               │
└─────────────────────────────────┘
```

Once an instructor has become proficient in delivering courses, a development discussion may reveal a desire to become a training officer. The first step is to attend a train-the-trainer course, followed by gaining a recognized qualification or award.

The Institute of Training and Development's Diploma in Human Resource Development is a suitable competency-based award. It is based on NVQ Level 4 with additional units.

```
┌─────────────────────────────────┐
│       Training officer          │
│      develops new course        │
└─────────────────────────────────┘
```

New training officers will now demonstrate what they have learnt on the train-the-trainer course by developing a new course. This should be done under supervision and using the process described in Chapter 3.

```
┌─────────────────────────────────┐
│       Training manager          │
│    certifies training officer   │
└─────────────────────────────────┘
```

The training manager reviews the training officer's progress and provides formal certification. Again, you may want to delegate this to the NVQ assessor.

Assessing trainer performance

Assessing trainer performance is a very important skill. Good assessment ensures the employment of suitable trainers, as well as maintaining and improving the quality of existing trainers. To be effective, an assessment must:

- provide the training manager with relevant data which enable appropriate development activities to be recommended;
- provide an opportunity for trainers to explore their performance strengths and weaknesses;
- motivate trainers to investigate new developments in instructional techniques.

How often should trainers be assessed?

There are no 'hard and fast' rules on how often a trainer should be assessed, but three to six-month intervals usually gives the maximum benefit. New trainers should be observed more often than experienced trainers. The final decision on how often assessment should be conducted also depends on the workload of the trainer and the availability of the observer.

How long should assessment take?

There is, however, much more to training than the mechanics of presenting information. Trainers work with individuals. They must be able observation. It is also unlikely that any meaningful feedback could take place in under 20 minutes.

How objective is assessment?

Although observation is more reliable than selection interviewing it is not entirely objective. If all students were influenced by trainer performance in the same way, to the same degree, and at the same time—then it might be possible to have objective assessments.

But it isn't that simple. Every trainee is an individual and each will respond differently to the trainer. An action which may have the desired effect on one trainee, may not have the same effect on another. What makes objectivity even more difficult is that it sometimes takes many hours to see the effects of that action. Sometimes it is impossible to assess the effects of a trainer's actions.

Similarly, observers' evaluations are influenced by their own subjective reactions. Sometimes observers confuse style with substance and will give a low rating simply because the trainer has a different style, and feels more comfortable with different jokes and anecdotes. While assessment should be designed to be as objective as possible, it is important to understand the influence of subjective factors.

Even though assessment may be influenced by subjective factors it is still vital to maintaining and improving the standard of training. Training managers must have a basis for evaluating what their trainers do and how well they do it. All trainers are entitled to an evaluation of their performance, and most trainers will actively request it.

Trainers will also have their own opinions of how well or how poorly they are performing their tasks. These opinions are extremely important to the trainer—and to the training manager. Yet the fullest benefit cannot be obtained from both the trainer's and the training manager's opinion, unless comparison and discussion takes place.

This means that training managers must base their opinions on what they actually see. They must observe trainers in the classroom and then set up a meeting where both the manager and the trainer can share their opinions and agree on appropriate follow-up activities.

What is assessed?

Trainers are sometimes regarded primarily as subject matter experts. Whatever other qualities they bring to the classroom they are, by definition, subject matter experts. Trainers tell, show, test, and then decide when a topic has been adequately covered.

There is, however, much more to training than the mechanics of presenting information. Trainers work with individuals. They must be able to deal with student motivation. They should try to remove the obstacles that prevent learning.

Trainers also need to pay attention to the fact that they are role models for the trainees. Their enthusiasm for a subject or their adherence to policies affects student behaviour. Although being a role model will not necessarily cause students to follow suit, its absence will almost certainly be copied by students: 'If the trainer doesn't care, why should I?'

How should assessment be handled?

Although there are many different views on how an assessment should be done, all workable systems have four elements in common:

• preparation,
• observation,
• feed-back, and
• follow-up.

As each of these elements involves both the trainer and the observer, planning the availability of suitable observers is essential.

Preparation (45 minutes)

Before any assessment takes place, training managers should discuss the process with the trainers. When everybody involved understands what is involved in the process individual observations can be scheduled. At least one week's notice should be given.

Observation (45 minutes)

The observer should be seated as unobtrusively as possible. The best position is off to one side and behind the students. Try not to sit in the middle of the back of the classroom as trainers will feel that they are being stared at all the time. The trainer should not be interrupted at any stage of the observation period.

During the observation the training manager should record the observations. If a new trainer is being observed an observation checklist (see Fig. 4.4) should be completed. If an experienced trainer is being certified on a new course notes can be made on a copy of the lesson plan.

Feedback (20 minutes)

Feedback should be given immediately, or as soon as possible, after the evaluation. Only the trainer and the observer should be present.

It is recommended that a counselling approach be taken. Counselling, in this situation, is an attempt by the observer to help the trainer explore strengths and weaknesses so that the strengths are reinforced, and suitable actions are taken to improve performance. Figure 4.5 gives the elements of counselling.

The observer should start off by *setting the climate*. This is to make sure that the trainer is relaxed. If the observer knows the trainer well, setting the climate will only take a few minutes. Always be sincere. Do not delay getting down to business any longer than necessary or tension will be unnecessarily increased.

The observer must take the time to *set expectations*. This means that the trainer understands the purpose and process of the session.

The next step is to *seek trainer's views of strengths and weaknesses*. Here the observer invites the trainer to express opinions on the trainer's own performance strengths and weaknesses. Appropriate use of questioning techniques should be used to ensure the trainer fully explores all of the

Trainer:	Date:
Session:	Observer:

Behaviours	Comments
Preparation —Rehearsed lesson —Administration —Classroom layout —Materials and equipment prepared —Arranged to be free from interruptions	
Presentation —Introduced subject —Communicated objectives —Communicated agenda —Followed logical sequence —Summarized —Checked students' understanding —Kept to time —Kept to subject	
Manner —Showed commitment —Showed enthusiasm —Create interest —Sensitive to group —Credible —Knowledgeable	
Technique —Voice —Questioning —Pace —Movement —Eye contact —Mannerisms —Use of audio-visual aids	

Figure 4.4 *Observation checklist*

1. Set climate
2. Set expectations
3. Seek trainer's views of strengths and weaknesses
4. Develop an action plan

Figure 4.5 *Elements of counselling*

1. IT IS NOT JUDGEMENTAL

    Making judgemental statements such as 'You really are a bad listener' are not very useful and they can cause the receiver to react defensively.

2. IT IS SPECIFIC

    A far better approach is to describe a specific incident: e.g. 'At the end of the lesson you interrupted Hazel before she could finish explaining her problem.'

3. ITS PURPOSE IS TO HELP THE RECEIVER

    Sometimes we give feedback to make ourselves feel better. It helps us to get things off our chests. This might be good for the giver but it does nothing for the receiver. Ensure that the only reason for giving feedback is to help the receiver improve performance.

4. IT IS ABOUT BEHAVIOUR THAT CAN BE CHANGED

    Frustration is only increased when a person is reminded of some shortcoming that cannot be controlled.

5. IT IS CLEAR

    One way of making sure that the feedback is clear is to have the receiver paraphrase the feedback.

6. IT IS TIMELY

    Generally, feedback is most effective immediately after the behaviour. The exception to this is when the receivers are not ready to hear the feedback such as when they are feeling depressed or are 'on a high'.

Figure 4.6 *Guidelines for giving constructive feedback*

observed strengths and weaknesses. Where opinions differ, evidence should be provided by the observer.

It is much better if trainers are able to identify their own strengths and weaknesses. They are more likely to want to do something about improving their performance. However, the trainers can be unaware of some of their performance strengths and weaknesses, so the observer should not be afraid of prompting and giving direct feedback. Guidelines for giving constructive feedback are given in Fig. 4.6.

> - Do not try to change too much at once. It is better to improve 1 or 2 aspects of performance than to make no progress on 20.
>
> - Always agree a completion date for each of the activities.
>
> - It is easier, and probably healthier, to do more of a new behaviour than suppress an existing behaviour. For example, if the trainer talks for too long it is better and more helpful for the trainers to use more visual aids and ask more questions than to simply suggest that they talk less.
>
> - Always summarize what is going to be done, by whom, and by when.

Figure 4.7   *Guidelines for improving performance*

Towards the end of the feedback session the observer should help the trainer *develop an action plan*. List the strengths and weaknesses on an development plan (see Fig. 2.8 in Chapter 2), and then invite the trainer to suggest appropriate activities that will maintain the strengths and minimize the weaknesses. Figure 4.7 gives guidelines for improving performance.

Follow-up (unspecified time)

After the session the observer should assess how well the feedback session went and what would be done differently during another feedback session.

The trainer's performance should be monitored and, if necessary, additional observations and feedback sessions planned.

Career development

There are two ways in which training can be part of a person's career development:

- training as a profession;
- training as part of a development plan.

Training as a profession

Many trainers consider themselves to be career trainers. They would like to develop their careers within the training profession. Although they enjoy training they don't want to spend the rest of their working lives doing wall-to-wall training. It is important to have a career path within the training department if these trainers are not to lose their motivation.

Figure 4.8 shows part of a career path within a management training department. The right-hand side shows the skills and education that are needed to perform at each level. The left-hand side of the diagram shows the activities that each job involves.

Notice that even the most senior trainers are still expected to do the basic activities. What does change is the proportion of time spent on these activities at each level. Figure 4.9 shows how this varies for the management training jobs.

If you do this kind of analysis for your own training jobs, your compensation and benefits manager will be able to assess the jobs, and fit them

Management training, job content and experience

Job content	Management training assistant	Management skills trainer	First level management trainer	Middle management trainer	Experience
Develop new courses				▒	Certified to run middle management training courses
Plan and influence training				▒	
Co-ord manag training				▒	Management or supervisory experience
MMP				▒	
Manager dev progs			▒	▒	Experienced trainer, or experienced manager with potential to be a trainer
Develop new trainers			▒	▒	
Plan skills/qual courses			▒	▒	Certified to run first level management training courses
Workshop development			▒	▒	Completion of 'Training Programme Design' course, or ability to develop skills training workshops
MIX			▒	▒	
MAF			▒	▒	
MSP			▒	▒	
Workshop revision		▒	▒	▒	Recognized Train-the-Trainer course
Quality training		▒	▒	▒	
Skills workshops		▒	▒	▒	
IAS feedback	▒	▒	▒	▒	IAS Observers Course. Set-up/operate audio/visual and computing equipment
IAS observation	▒	▒	▒	▒	
Assisting	▒	▒	▒	▒	
Administration	▒	▒	▒	▒	

Figure 4.8 *Part of a career path in a management training department*

into your company's existing grading structure. Figure 4.10 is an example of this kind of analysis.

Somebody, with no training experience, could 'learn the trade' by starting as a training administrator, progressing to a training assistant, and then to a management skills trainer. If the person has managerial experience, the person could also progress to the higher levels.

If trainers have insufficient experience, skills, or knowledge to progress from one level to the next, actions would be identified for their personal development plans. This might include leaving the training department for a year or two to gain managerial experience.

Training as part of a development plan

The career map shown in Fig. 4.8 is essentially a longitudinal progression with each step serving as an entry point. Training can also be used for development of people from other parts of the company. There is nothing like teaching for learning and forming contacts!

A secondment to the training department is particularly useful for managers and 'high fliers'. It also broadens the experience of people whose career paths have been within one department.

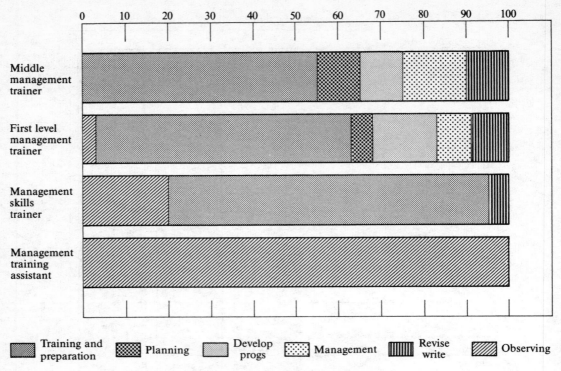

Figure 4.9 *Activity profile for different levels of trainer*

The benefit works both ways because secondment bring new ideas into training and helps keep the training in touch with reality.

Certifying trainers

The process of ensuring that a trainer is ready to train a new course is sometimes called 'accreditation' in Britain or 'certification' in the USA. Although it really does not matter what you call it, telling people that you have just had your trainers 'certified' can cause a chuckle in Britain where certifying a person means committing that person to a mental hospital.

The exact process that is used to accredit or certify trainers depends on the complexity of the course and the trainers' experience. The trainers' experience also affects the time it takes to go through the certification process.

- Are the trainers experienced trainers?
- Have they trained this type of course before?
- Do they already understand the underlying concepts?
- Have they practised the skills in the workplace?

Fig. 4.11 shows a process that is used for a complex five-day course:

JOB TITLE : Management Trainer   **DEPARTMENT** : Human Resources

PROGRESSION / APPOINTMENT MATRIX - 1

	MGT TRAINING ASSISTANT	MGT SKILLS TRAINER	FIRST LEVEL MGT TRAINER	MIDDLE MGT TRAINER
Experience/ qualifications Professional qualifications are preferred but not essential in cases where they are substituted by broad experience and proven achievement in the training field	• Minimum 2-3 years' experience in human resources or • Degree standard and 2 years' relevant work experience	• Minimum 4-5 years' experience in human resources or • Degree and minimum 3 years' related work experience or • 2 years relevant training experience • Part qualified IPM • Recognised Train-the-Trainer Certificate	• Minimum 6-7 years' experience in human resources or • Degree and minimum of 5 years' related work experience or • 4 years' relevant training experience • Part qualified IPM • Recognized Train-the-Trainer Certificate • Certified to run first level mgt training courses	• Minimum 8-9 years' wide ranging human resources experience or • Broad industrial experience including supervision/management or • 6 years' relevant training experience • Qualified IPM • Recognized Train-the-Trainer Certificate • Certified to run first level and middle mgt training courses
Skills/ knowledge	• Analytical ability • Communication skills • Interactive skills • Organizational ability • Presentation skills	• Ability to influence • Research/analytical ability • Ability to organize own work • Writing skills • Problem solving -making recommendations • Increased communication skills • Training skills	• Ability to develop, plan and organize major aspects of training work • Decision making skills • Supervisory skills • Ability to develop training materials	• Broad base of training knowledge and skill • Sound negotiating skills • Managerial skills
Accountability	• Assisting on management training courses • Providing interactive skills observation and feedback • Running mini-modules	• Running management skills workshops • Running LTQ training • Revision of skills workshops • Project work • Contribution to training policy	• Running of first level management courses • Development of new management skills workshops • Plan skills and quality courses • Develop new trainers • Initiate and implement manager development programmes	• Develop new training courses • Influence corporate training policy • Run middle management courses • Co-ordinate activities of skills trainers, and management trainers
Payroll costs of trainee population	$10 million	$30 million	$60 million	$60 million
Scoreline	DI+3 D3(29) C+3-C A1 200 57 66 323	D+11-3 D+3(33) D-3C A1 230 76 87 393	E11-3 E3+(38) D4-C A1 264 100 115 479	E+113 E4(43) E-4-C A1 350 152 175 677

Figure 4.10   An example of a grading analysis

```
┌─────────────────────────────┐
│     Trainer attends course  │
└─────────────────────────────┘
              │
              ▼
┌─────────────────────────────┐
│       Trainer observes      │
│            course           │
└─────────────────────────────┘
              │
              ▼
┌─────────────────────────────┐
│      Discussions with       │
│      certifying trainer     │
└─────────────────────────────┘
              │
              ▼
┌─────────────────────────────┐
│       Trainer trains        │
│      first half of course   │
└─────────────────────────────┘
              │
              ▼
┌─────────────────────────────┐
│       Trainer trains        │
│     second half of course   │
└─────────────────────────────┘
              │
              ▼
┌─────────────────────────────┐
│       Trainer trains        │
│        entire course        │
└─────────────────────────────┘
```

Figure 4.11   *Certification process for a complex five-day course*

```
┌─────────────────────────────┐
│     Trainer attends course  │
└─────────────────────────────┘
```

The first step is to have the trainer take the course as a student. This is very important for two reasons. The first reason is the obvious one. To have any credibility trainers need to have the knowledge and skills that they will be teaching. The second reason, although not so obvious, is just as important. Trainers who take a course under the same conditions and pressures as the student will be better able to appreciate their students' learning difficulties. This makes for greater empathy and a better student–trainer relationship.

```
┌─────────────────────────────┐
│       Trainer observes      │
│            course           │
└─────────────────────────────┘
```

After taking the course as a student the trainer is then given a lesson plan so that the next course can be observed and followed. The trainer is encouraged to make copious notes during this observation and to start considering which parts of the course should be tackled first.

```
┌─────────────────────────────┐
│      Discussions with       │
│      certifying trainer     │
└─────────────────────────────┘
```

Soon after the completion of this observation the trainer has a discussion with the certifying trainer. The certifying trainer should ideally be the course originator or a trainer who has extensive knowledge and experience of the course. The discussion should include any questions the trainer has and the final decision as to which modules should be practised first.

```
┌─────────────────────────────┐
│      Trainer trains         │
│    first half of course     │
└─────────────────────────────┘
```

On the third course the trainer co-trains with the experienced trainer. Usually half of the course is trained, but it may be advisable to train only a third of a very complex course.

The experienced trainer should observe and give feedback to the trainer throughout the course. It is important that this feedback be given as soon as practically possible for maximum effect. Trainers vary in the formality of the feedback they require. For some, a few words at the end of the session is all that is required; others may require a full-blown counselling session at the end of the day. It will all depend on their experience, confidence, and ability to teach this type of course.

```
┌─────────────────────────────┐
│      Trainer trains         │
│   second half of course     │
└─────────────────────────────┘
```

The other sessions should be practised on the fourth course. Again, this should be done under observation and with feedback.

```
┌─────────────────────────────┐
│      Trainer trains         │
│      entire course          │
└─────────────────────────────┘
```

With the feedback that has been received so far, the trainer should be able to teach the fifth course alone. So you can see that for a complex course, which is run only once a quarter, it can take over a year for a trainer to be brought up to speed.

At the other end of the scale it should be possible for a trainer to take a simple one-day course as a student and then, given a comprehensive lesson plan, be able to teach the next course alone.

Although it is possible for an experienced trainer to train straight from a lesson plan without having seen the course before, you should really try to avoid this as even the best lesson plans cannot capture all the details that are required to make the course a success.

Certifying the certifiers

Of course all this begs the question of who certifies the certifiers. Ideally, accreditation should be done by the people who originally developed the course. However, this is not always possible because of time, distance, and cost. These problems are further compounded in large multinational organizations because of language and cultural difficulties. Foreign subsidiaries of these multinational corporations do not always appreciate having to pay for the cost of flying somebody in from afar every time they need to have a new trainer accredited. In any case not all trainers have a sufficient expertise in the corporation's prime language that would enable them to train and be observed in that language. In fact it could be argued that a trainer's certification would not really be valid unless the trainer's performance is observed under the conditions it would be taught under.

The answer to this is to have some trainers developed to the point to where they would be able to certify their own trainers in their localities. Where language is an issue the local certifiers would have to be bilingual and would probably have to run a course at the corporation's own training centre. A certain amount of trust would have to be in place for this scheme to work, but the advantage is that the quality of the training is maintained at a level which meets the corporation's standards, while at the same time giving flexibility to the local organizations.

Figure 5.1   Training locations and resources

5 Training locations and resources

This chapter covers another step in the training process:

• identify location and resources.

By this stage you will have selected the courses and trainers. The next decision you have to make is where you are going to run the courses, what the best learning situation will be, and where you are going to obtain the equipment and materials.

If you run residential courses the accommodation costs can be the single biggest item in your training budget. Running courses on your own premises will allow you to keep your travel and accommodation costs low.

Identifying training locations and resources

Figure 5.2 illustrates the process I will be describing for identifying training locations and resources.

```
┌─────────────────────────┐
│    Obtain course        │
│    specification        │
└─────────────────────────┘
```

The course specification details the facilities, materials, and equipment that are needed to run the course. This information is essential for deciding the type of learning environment required for the course. It allows you to check whether a location meets your specification. The specification is also an excellent method for communicating your exact requirements to a training centre.

```
┌─────────────────────────┐
│   Determine type of     │
│   learning environment  │
└─────────────────────────┘
```

The factors that affect your choice of learning environment are the cost, the facilities you need, the type of instruction, and whether the students need to be separated from home and work pressures.

Don't assume all training has to take place in the classroom. 'Open learning' and 'distance learning' widen the choice of learning environments. (See Chapter 9 'Delivering the Course', for a discussion of open and distance learning.) Choices of learning environment can cover:

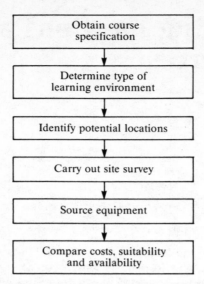

Figure 5.2 *Process for identifying training locations and resources*

- the home,
- the workplace,
- open learning centres,
- meeting rooms,
- dedicated training rooms,
- hotels,
- sports centres and social clubs, and
- residential training centres.

Home Home learning is suitable for programmed instruction, it is inexpensive, and many people would welcome the opportunity to learn at home.

The disadvantages are:

- possible distraction from home pressures,
- isolation from tutors, and
- lack of specialized equipment.

When we think of home learning we often think it is limited to text-based training. Home learning can be more creative if ways are found to overcome the disadvantages of isolation and access to equipment.

Isolation can be overcome by using the telephone or computer links. Videos can be broadcast from existing television stations—either during the day for large audiences or as a scrambled signal during the night for small, specialist audiences. The night programmes are automatically recorded by anyone who has a suitable decoder.

The Open University sends laboratory kits to their science and technology students by road. It is also possible for service engineers to learn how to repair small photocopiers on their kitchen tables!

In the workplace People do most of their learning outside the classroom, but most of it is random and unstructured. To make the most of experiential learning the student needs to have an experienced coach and a planned series of structured experiences.

Open learning centres Open learning centres are purpose-built rooms fitted with all the equipment and materials needed for private study. They provide flexibility of time, and students can learn at their own pace. Open learning centres are particularly useful in manufacturing areas because breaks in production are difficult to predict.

Meeting rooms Purpose-built meeting rooms are suitable for short training courses, but they are usually too small and the wrong shape for larger classes.

Dedicated training rooms Dedicated training rooms should be ideal if you were involved in their design and paid attention to the following:

- size and shape of training room,
- capacity of training room,
- heating and ventilation,
- lighting,
- light switches,
- acoustics, and
- equipment.

Further details of these aspects are given on page 120.

Distraction by work-related problems is the main disadvantage of an on-site training room. Raychem have a dedicated training room at their Swindon office, which means most people have to travel to their courses. This helps to minimize the disruptions. They also block-book bedrooms at a local hotel. This is cheaper than running courses at a commercial residential training centre, and avoids the problems and cost of running your own residential centre.

Hotels Many hotels are properly equipped to function as conference centres, but too many others see conferences and training courses only as a means of filling empty rooms. They often have to hire-in all the training equipment. Function rooms double as meeting rooms, and bedrooms have the beds removed to provide syndicate rooms. I have even seen instances of syndicate rooms not being ready until 11 a.m. because the hotel had rented them to guests the night before!

Sports centres and social clubs Much of what has been said about hotels also applies to sports centres and social clubs, except that the standard is even more variable. Don't automatically disregard these venues, however, because some of them provide excellent service and facilities at competitive prices. Always make sure you carry out a thorough site survey.

Residential training centres

Residential training centres are in the business of providing excellent training facilities in suitable surroundings. They are also very expensive. You would only use a residential training centre for the longer, more complex courses.

Identify potential locations

Once you have decided on the type of training location the next step is to identify a number of potential alternative training locations. You may already have a number in mind from past experience, but if you are new to the job or have just relocated to a new area you will need to look further afield.

Training magazines and *Yellow Pages* are useful sources of advertising. *The Training Directory*, published annually by Kogan Page, has sections listing conference centres and management training centres.

Many of the UK's largest companies run their own training centres and, although they do not always advertise, they are often willing to hire rooms to other companies to help their own utilization rates.

Finally, don't forget to ask your own colleagues—they may have attended training centres with other companies.

Carry out site survey

If you have never used a particular training centre before, it is imperative that you carry out a site survey to make sure the training location is suitable for your needs. It is worth taking a couple of hours to really get the feel of the place. The centre's management will be only too pleased to show you around—after all it could lead to a lot of business.

Talk to the staff, trainers, and students. Explore the buildings and the grounds. Use a checklist like the one shown in Figure 5.3.

Location

Most training centres are situated in remote areas. This is not usually a problem for residential courses but you will need to check the following.

- Is it accessible by public transport with, perhaps, just a short taxi journey at the end? (You would normally expect very remote training centres to provide a minibus service to and from the nearest train station, bus terminus, or airport.)
- Is there a reasonable connection to the motorway network?
- Will foreign students have enough time to get to the airport after the course has finished?
- Will students arriving by car have no more than a five-hour drive?

If the course is not residential, the training centre needs to be far more accessible.

Date:	Location:

Checkpoint	*Comments*
Location	
Parking	
Reception	
Contacts	
Delivery arrangements	
Staff	
Access to training room	
Size/shape of training room	
Capacity of training room	
Heating and ventilation	
Lighting	
Power sockets	
Light switches	
Acoustics	
Equipment	
Wall space and fixings	
Syndicate rooms	
Toilets	
Access for preparation	
Food	
Meal and break arrangements	
Bedrooms	
Leisure facilities	
Security	
Emergency procedures	

Figure 5.3   *Checklist for doing a site survey*

Parking

It is another of those universal laws that the number of cars expands to fill the available parking space. When you arrive to do the site survey you will soon see how easy it is to park your car. When you leave check to see if anybody is blocked in and whether cars are parked on the road outside.

Reception

The first impression you get of a training centre is of the reception area. It is at the reception where frustrations and inefficiencies surface. The receptionist should be expecting you and you should not have to wait too long to be seen. This will give you an indication of how well the place is being run. For a better indication you should try to be in the reception area when students are booking in and out.

Contacts

It is best to get the names of the staff you will need to contact if you decide to use the training centre. As well as making your life easier, this will also give you an indication of whether people have specific roles and responsibilities.

Delivery arrangements

If you need to have materials delivered to the training centre, check out the process for receiving the deliveries and getting them to the class-room. Again, get the name of a contact for this purpose.

Staff

The relationship you have with the training centre's staff can make all the difference between a smoothly-run course and a course that is a series of irritations. Make sure you talk to the staff to get a feeling for their attitude towards you and the training centre.

Access to training room

If your trainers intend to bring their own materials, see how close they can park their cars to the classroom, how many steps have to be climbed, and check the width of the passageways. Also see what help is available—either in the form of trolleys or willing hands.

Size and shape of training room

Generally speaking, training rooms tend to be rectangular and too narrow. This is especially true if you have a preference for a horseshoe layout of tables and chairs.

With a class of 15 then you would probably have 5 people down each of the sides and 5 people along the back.

Rule of thumb: allow 80 cm of desk space per person.

Allowing 80 cm per person you would need a horseshoe of tables 5 m long and 4 m across. The width of the room would need to be increased to about 7 m to allow space for the chairs and a passageway down the sides. To allow room at the front for the trainer and equip-ment, plus a space for movement round the back you would need a room that is 8 m long.

Obviously you can use a narrower room by having a longer horseshoe (with three or four people along the back) and less room for movement along the sides. This squeezes everyone in, but the people along the sides will have difficulty in seeing all the audio-visual equipment. This can be overcome but you will probably find that you will have to indulge in a bit of 'scene shifting' by moving the television monitor and flip chart stands. Building training rooms back-to-back permits a small room for audio-visual equipment to be built between them.

Rule of thumb: an ideal shape for a training room is a square. Try to keep the ratio of the length to the width to less than 4:3.

This might give the impression that the larger the training room, the better. However, there is a limit to the size of the room and this is determined by whether the students can read the visual aids. A person with good eyesight can usually read a flip chart up to 9 m.

Rule of thumb: try to limit the distance between the flip chart stand and the furthest student to 8 m.

Capacity of training room

Taking all the above into account you should be able to see whether or not the room is large enough for your course. The horseshoe layout takes more room than a theatre-style or traditional classroom layout.

The training centre brochure should give an indication of the capacity of the room in these configurations. However, these estimates are usually on the optimistic side.

Heating and ventilation

Check that the training room has adequate heating and ventilation. Students who are too hot, too cold, or too stuffy do not learn as well as those who are comfortable—but not *too* comfortable! In fact, students seem to be unable to concentrate if the temperature is more than 5°C above or below their comfort zone. For optimum learning it is probably better to have a slightly cool rather than a slightly warm temperature.

Rule of thumb: try setting the thermostat to 18°C.

Don't underestimate the value of having an air-conditioned training room—even in temperate countries like the UK!

Lighting

Many rooms have far too low a level of lighting. This is especially true if you use hotel function rooms. Here the lighting has been designed to provide a certain ambience.

It is also possible to have too much light, making it difficult to view videos and overhead transparencies. Check the efficiency and ease-of-use of blinds and curtains.

There is a tendency for some training rooms to be devoid of natural light and air. This seems to be particularly true in the USA where the low-rise building has been introduced as an extreme reaction to the disenchantment with the high-rise tower blocks. The result of this is that the building tends to sprawl like a pancake and very few rooms have access to an outside wall or a window.

When the question is asked why the training room does not have any windows the rationale is nearly always that a view would be distracting. Perhaps the students might occasionally look out of the window, but if they are constantly looking out of the window then I would question the effectiveness of the course and trainer. On balance the motivational benefits to be gained from having a pleasant environment and undisturbed body clocks far outweigh any potential distraction.

Power sockets Check the positioning of the power sockets and that the room has sufficient sockets for the equipment. It is surprising how many you need: one for the OHP; two for the video; three for the computer set-up . . .

Rule of thumb: have a minimum of four power sockets available at the front of the room.

Light switches Make sure the light sockets are conveniently placed. You don't want to rush from one side of the room to the other every time you start or stop a videotape. Dimmer switches are useful for getting the optimum light level and for getting people's eyes used to the light after showing a videotape.

Acoustics Acoustics are not usually a problem unless you are using a very large room. Make sure you test the acoustics when people are in the room, as an empty room sounds very different.

Check the sound insulation from the outside and from neighbouring classrooms. A raucous class or a lawnmower nearby can be very distracting.

Equipment You would normally expect a training or conference centre to supply flip chart stands, an overhead projector, and a screen. Some centres have their own video equipment, others have to hire it in. Check the positioning, ease-of-use, and the operation of the equipment.

Wall space and fixings Many courses need to have posters and flip chart sheets fixed to the walls, so it is surprising how little attention is given to the space and fixings required. Many training centres, especially the converted manor houses, abhor the use of Blu-tack or masking tape, but don't provide sufficient alternatives such as pin-boards or Pendastrip rails.

Syndicate rooms Check that the syndicate rooms are conveniently situated and are large enough to accommodate the number of people in each subgroup, plus any observers. Look out for other areas that can be used for paired, or triad, activities.

Toilets Check the number, position, and cleanliness of the toilets.

Access for preparation Depending on the complexity of the course you may spend anything from 30 minutes to 3 hours preparing the training room. Ideally, you should do this the night or the Friday before the course starts. You will need to check whether the training rooms are used during the evenings or over the weekends. Even if the rooms are not being used you will need to check whether you can gain access at the time you need to prepare.

Food   There can be a considerable variation in menus from one training centre to another. Some provide meals to gourmet standards! You will need to decide whether the standard of the food and service available is compatible with the type of course you are running. When you are doing a site survey you would normally expect to be provided with a meal so that you can judge the standard for yourself.

Meal and break arrangements   Check the times and the flexibility of the meal and coffee arrangements. Also, check to see how long it takes to serve a complete meal as this can be critical if you are running evening sessions.

Bedrooms   With the increase in the standard of living and holidays abroad most people expect a high standard of accommodation. Most training centres now provide:

- desk, chair, and reading light,
- bed,
- wardrobe (but never enough coat hangers!),
- separate bath/shower/toilet/washbasin,
- television,
- clock/radio/alarm, and
- coffee/tea-making facilities.

Look at the variations in standard and size between bedrooms. People do compare notes and it is any inconsistency in standards rather than the absolute standard that causes people to complain.

Leisure facilities   If the course is more than a couple of days long, the training centre should provide sport and leisure facilities. This is especially important if the centre is in a remote area.

Security   Check that the training and accommodation blocks are secure, and that the car park is supervised. Is it possible to open the windows in the bedrooms without providing access for an intruder? If the accommodation is separate from the training block, are the paths well-lit and supervised?

Emergency procedures   Ask what the procedures are in the case of a fire or bomb alert. Gathering locations should be identified and, in the case of a bomb alert, these should be over 800 m away and out of direct sight of the training centre.

Source equipment

If you are running courses in a commercial training centre all you need to do is to hand over a precise specification of your requirements, and the equipment will be provided as and when you need it. If you do a lot of training on your own premises it is worth while buying the equipment you need. This is especially true of overhead projectors and video players which are also needed for meetings.

Unless you make frequent use of the more expensive and specialist equipment such as computers and projection televisions, you will find it more economic to hire rather than buy.

> Compare costs, suitability
> and availability

The results of the site survey will allow you to compare the suitability of the alternative training venues. Comparing costs will prove to be a little more difficult. Most residential training centres will give you a day rate and a 24-hour rate, but these rates are not always directly comparable.

It is very important that you understand what the rate includes. Some rates include everything; others provide a minimum and make additional charges for anything else. The golden rule is to ask for a written summary of what is included in the price.

The following is a list of items which may, or may not, be included in a 24-hour rate:

- main classroom,
- syndicate rooms,
- pencils and paper,
- flip chart stands,
- flip chart pads and pens,
- food,
- coffee,
- audio-visual equipment,
- computers,
- special table arrangements in restaurant, and
- making use of empty rooms for short exercises.

The cost of telephone calls (often priced at hotel levels), photocopying, and faxes (sending and receiving) vary widely from centre to centre.

Running your own training centre

As the amount of training you do increases the question that will come up is whether it is worth having your own training centre. Your own training centre can vary from a dedicated room, to a separate building or a residential centre.

The disadvantage of having your own residential centre is that you have to worry about making sure it is full. If you cannot fill the centre yourself you will have to hire it out to external customers—and then you might find yourself in the hotel rather than the training business.

Many companies do not want to be in the hotel business, and they do not like to have their cash tied up in a training centre, so they get a specialist company to buy and run the establishment for them. These companies make an annual charge for running the centre. If this charge is independent of the number of students, you will again be faced with the problem of filling the place. Unless you have nearly 100 per cent utilization rates this option will be just as expensive as hiring a commercial training centre only when you need it.

Designing a new training centre is a skilled activity. Architects are not trainers and do not always come up with the most practical layout. However, if you follow the advice given in this book you should be able to work with the architect and design the rooms you need.

Another possibility is to go to one of the suppliers of audio-visual equipment and commission them to design the training rooms and also provide a project manager to oversee the installation. Of course the suspicion will always be whether the design will be more biased to the sale of their equipment rather than exactly what is required. The most common problem people have when training rooms are designed for them is over-specification.

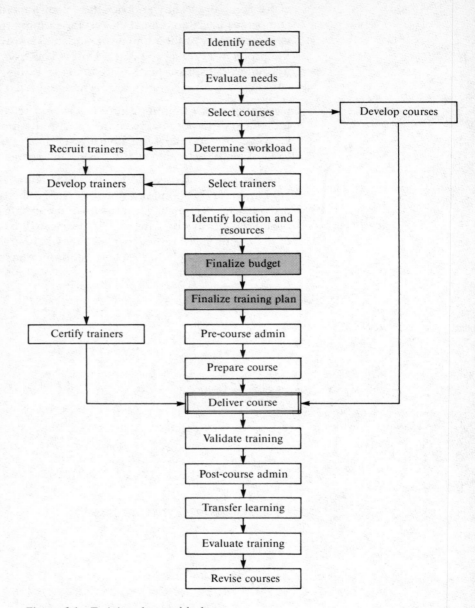

Figure 6.1 *Training plans and budgets*

6 Training plans and budgets

This chapter covers the content of a training plan and the preparation of a training budget, both of which are required to complete the next two steps of the training process:

- finalize training budget,
- finalize training plan.

In previous steps of the process we have covered the need, identified the courses to meet the need, and estimated the resource required to deliver the workload. Now we have to prepare a budget, match the desired level of training to the available resource, and prepare the finalized training plan.

Finalize training budget

One of the questions that has to be answered when a training plan is being put together is: 'How much will the training cost?' It is interesting to note that we are nearly always asked how much training will cost, rather than what is the size of our training investment. A better question might be: 'How much would it cost us if we don't do this training?'

Whatever question is asked, and no matter what we call it, working out the figures may not be quite as simple as it first appears. This is because of the difficulty of deciding what should be included in the costs. For example, should you include the trainers' salaries, the students' salaries, and the loss of production during training? You may end up doing a very detailed cost analysis or you may decide only to count what is normally deducted from your budget.

You may also have to decide whether your training department should be run as a profit centre. A profit centre means that you will sell your courses and training expertise in order to defray the expense of running your own training operation. This will involve you in preparing estimates and working agreements.

Whatever you include or exclude from your budget, the golden rule is to be consistent and to make your assumptions very clear. With all these parameters sorted out you will then be in a position to prepare a training budget.

The size of the budget is one of the main limiting factors when it comes to determining how much of the training demand will be delivered.

There are many ways of preparing a budget and the way you choose will depend on your company's accounting systems. What you include or exclude from the budget depends on these practices. The steps for finalizing the budget are shown in Fig. 6.2.

Figure 6.2 *Process for finalizing the training budget*

```
Determine whether to be a
        profit centre
```

This step will not be necessary for many training organizations—you are there to provide training only for your own organization or company. However, in a large company, you could be asked to run your training organization as a profit centre. In this case you will need to consider this step very carefully and include an estimate of your income in the budget.

Being a profit centre can mean many different things, so you will need to clarify the rules of the game. For example, it may simply mean you have to contribute to the budget by selling any excess training capacity. At the other end of the scale the intention might be for the training department to haven a 'zero-based' budget. This means that the training organization has to justify and completely maintain its existence by selling all its 'products' to other departments and perhaps to customers outside the company as well.

You will also need to understand the reasons for making the training department a profit centre. It might be to put a value on the training so that managers can make a business decision as to which training they buy. It might be to keep internal training competitive with external suppliers, or maybe a profit centre was the only way to justify the cost of a brand-new, purpose-built training centre.

Strictly speaking it might be impossible to have a true profit centre without making the training department a separate company. The reason for this is that it is extremely unlikely that any company would let its training department make its own decisions with regard to staffing levels, salaries, benefits, and capital investments. Even if the training organization were given this free hand you could imagine the amount of aggravation that would occur if you were busy recruiting trainers while in the rest of the company people are being made redundant.

The decision to form a separate company would be a very brave one, but it also has its advantages. One curious example of this is a measure called the 'direct to indirect ratio'. This ratio, of how many direct staff you have compared to the numbers of indirect staff, is one of the more popular measures of a company's efficiency. By direct staff we mean the people who touch the product or its design. That is, they are directly involved with the design, manufacture, or sales of a product. People who provide a service to an external, paying customer would also be considered to be direct staff.

Indirect staff are the people, such as managers and administrators, who support the direct staff. It is said that in the UK it takes 1 manager to supervise 10 production workers, whereas in Japan it takes only 1 manager to ensure that 200 workers go home on time. So you can see that in the interests of efficiency, the pressure will always be on to reduce the numbers of indirect staff.

All the staff in a training department would, without a moment's hesitation, be classified as indirect staff. Yet, if that department were made a separate company, the trainers would then be classified as direct staff even if they were doing exactly the same work for the same people.

There is another important consideration that must be taken into account before launching yourself into a profit centre mode of operation. This is the question of who the customer is.

In a large company the training department was probably formed to meet the training needs of one organization. This organization would probably expect to have first call on the services of its own trainers. Not an unreasonable request you might think. Now the paradox of the situation is that the more successful you are as a profit centre the less likely will you be able to meet the needs of your own organization because you will be too busy training other departments' staff. (You might even be asked which department you are working for.) This need not be a problem if your organization's needs analysis and planning have been done really well. In this case you will know how much spare capacity you have and you will be able to start taking bookings from other departments.

If you have spare capacity you might be asked why the training department needs to be as large as it is. On the other hand, if you do not have the capability to provide additional training, you cannot expect your potential customers to wait a year to get their training. They will simply go elsewhere. That lost business will be very hard to regain.

The real problem arises when circumstances change, such as an urgent need to train every manager on financial control. You are asked to provide additional training for your own organization at the same time as you have contracted to train other departments. Obviously the first thing you will do will be to try and renegotiate the contracts with your paying customers. You might be lucky and find their circumstances have changed as well. If this doesn't work then you are faced with the question of who is your customer. Is it your own organization? After all, supporting them is the very reason for your training department's existence. Or is it the paying customers? If you cancel their contracts you will not get any business from them again. Your reputation will be destroyed and it is unlikely that anyone else would use such an unreliable supplier. Perhaps the only way around this, if you are really serious about running the training department as a profit centre, is to take a loss on these contracts and bring in consultant trainers to take on some of the work load.

> Identify budget items

The following is a list of items that can find their way into a training budget:

- cost of external courses,
- purchase and hire of equipment, books, and videos,
- production of training materials,
- training staff wages/salaries,
- training staff overheads,
- hire of training venues,
- student accommodation costs,
- student travel costs, and
- student wages/salaries/overheads.

Rule of thumb: include everything that will be charged to the training department's budget during the financial year.

The aim of the exercise is to determine whether the cost of the training plan exceeds, falls below, or meets your allocated budget. Most budgets also show the expected spend by month so that you will be able to monitor the budget during the year.

If you are selling training to other departments you will also need to show the expected income for each month.

Be sure to find out what your company's financial year is. Some start in April, some start in November, while others are the same as the calendar year. Confusion can arise over financial years, especially if your suppliers or customers have a different financial year to your own, so be very careful about what should be in this year's budget and what should be in the following year.

> Identify cost of budget
> items

The costs of some of the budget items are fairly easy to determine. Others, like the cost of a trainer or the cost of a day of training, can get quite involved.

How much does a trainer cost?

The cost of employing anybody is not just the cost of the wages. There are other employment costs and overheads that have to be taken into account. Table 6.1 gives a fictitious example of the real cost of employing a trainer whose current salary is £22 000. I have assumed that the job involves a lot of travel, so a car will have to be provided.

Table 6.1   *Example annual employment cost of a trainer*

Item	Cost (£)
Trainer's salary	22 000
National insurance	1 000
Benefits	340
Car	5 500
Accommodation and facilities	2 700
Computer and information systems	1 000
Total	33 140

After taking away holidays a trainer is available for work for about 220 days a year. This means that this trainer costs about £150 a day to employ. If the trainer is working at a face-to-face ratio of 50 per cent, the trainer will cost about £300 per training day.

How much does a training course cost?

This is a reasonably easy question to answer for a commercial course. It is simply the advertised price, plus anything else such as travel, accommodation, and wages that would normally be charged to the training budget.

To answer the same question for an internal course is more difficult. It is the same class of question as 'How long is a piece of string?' It all depends on:

- the type of training,
- the number of delegates per course,
- whether you train off-site or on your own premises,
- whether you use your own or external trainers, and
- whether the course is residential or non-residential.

Not that you should let that daunt you. Your training plan should give you a good idea of the type and number of courses you need.

While I cannot give any definitive answers to how much a training course costs, I can give some examples of cost estimates for a number of different training courses. At least that will give you an approximate idea of how much training courses cost and it will certainly allow you to calculate your own costs.

In the following examples I have made the following assumptions.

- Neither the trainees' wages nor any costs due to lost production have been included.

- When training on your own premises I have not shown a direct cost for the training rooms, but have assumed that this is covered by the general overhead which has been included in the cost of the trainer. (This would only reflect part of the cost of the training rooms because every employee's overhead contributes to this cost.)
- When using your own trainers the costs shown are the trainers' wages, plus the general overhead, plus an allowance to cover the trainers' salaries when they are not training. The same figure is used when the trainers work off-site, because the overheads still have to be paid.
- Value added tax is not included.
- Travelling expenses are not included.

The cheapest classroom training that you can do is to use your own trainer on your own premises. Table 6.2 shows a one day, on-site workshop on decision making which is non-residential. The calculation has been made on the basis of 10 students. This is a fairly typical number for skills courses that are run to meet individual development needs.

- I have used the figure of £300 per day for the trainer cost. This was the figure that we estimated in the section on 'How much does a trainer cost?'
- The sum of £15 for 'Materials/student' is to cover things like copies of the training materials, binders, pens, pencils, and flip chart pads.
- No charges are shown for room hire as the cost of the room is covered by the general overhead.
- The £5 shown under 'Accommodation/student' only needs to cover coffee for breaks and sandwiches for lunch.
- Being a very straightforward course no equipment needs to be hired, and no expensive simulations are required. The cost per student turned out to be just over £50, but naturally this would change if the number of students is different.

This example, and the others that follow, were worked out using a spreadsheet on a small computer. The advantage of doing this is that once you have set up the parameters you can quickly work out the costs for a wide range of different courses.

A spreadsheet is also useful because you can 'experiment' with different numbers of trainers and students (but keeping the student to trainer ratio the same) to see which combination would be the most cost-effective. The formulae used for this spreadsheet are given in Appendix 2.

Table 6.3 is very similar to the previous example with the exception that a consultant trainer was used to run the course.

Costs for consultant trainers can vary wildly, depending on the type of training and whether the trainers are part of a large consultancy organization or just running their own show. These fees can range from £300 to over £1000 a day! The fee of £500 shown in this example is below the IPM average of £700 a day for management training, but you can still get some really excellent training for around £350.

Table 6.2 *Example of the cost of a decision making course*

Decision making course	
Type of training:	non-residential
Duration (days):	1
Number of students:	10
Number of trainers:	1
Type of trainer:	own
Location:	off-site
Additional rooms:	1
Trainer cost/day:	£300
Materials/student:	£15
Main room hire/day:	£0
Seminar room hire:	£0
Accommodation/student:	£5
Equipment hire/day:	£0
Simulation costs:	£0
TOTAL COST:	£505
COST/STUDENT:	£51
COST/STUDENT/DAY	£51

With this, as in all things, a higher price does not necessarily mean better training. You have to make your own decision on what you can afford, the type of training, the fees that the type of training normally commands, and your own assessment of the consultant.

The Quality training shown in Table 6.4 was part of the company's introduction of Total Quality Management. The decision was taken to use the company's own trainers where possible, and it was also decided to use an off-site training facility to avoid monopolizing the company's meeting rooms for the two years it would take to train every employee.

- The training centre did not make a direct charge for the main training room, but included it in the day charge of £49 per delegate.
- The trainer was counted as a delegate for the purposes of meals, etc.

Table 6.5 is a five-day residential course for first-time managers.

- The course runs with 15 to 20 students.
- Two trainers are needed to run the course.
- Four seminar rooms were required because of the number of subgroup exercises.

Table 6.3 *Example of costs for an assertiveness at work course*

Assertiveness at work	
Type of training:	non-residential
Duration (days):	1
Number of students:	10
Number of trainers:	1
Type of trainer:	consultant
Location:	on-site
Additional rooms:	1
Trainer cost/day:	£500
Materials/student:	£15
Main room hire/day:	£0
Seminar room hire:	£0
Accommodation/student:	£5
Equipment hire/day:	£0
Simulation costs:	£0
TOTAL COST:	£705
COST/STUDENT:	£71
COST/STUDENT/DAY:	£71

- The accommodation charge of £120 per student included the main lecture room and audio-visual equipment.
- A computer was hired for £50 per day to analyse the observation data collected during the day.

The final example (Table 6.6) is for a middle managers' course which involves a computer simulation and extensive behavioural observations of the participants. The simulation was specially commissioned by the American parent company to ensure that, as well as giving middle managers practice in running a large organization in coalition with other middle managers, the corporation's vision and values were clearly communicated to the participants.

- The simulation costs include licence fees for the simulation, air fare, and accommodation costs for the computer simulation consultant.
- The three trainers are the company's own middle management trainer and two facilitators who observe the teams and give feedback throughout the course.

Table 6.4 *Example of costs for a quality course*

Quality training	
Type of training:	non-residential
Duration (days):	3
Number of students:	12
Number of trainers:	1
Type of trainer:	own
Location:	off-site
Additional rooms:	1
Trainer cost/day:	£300
Materials/student:	£40
Main room hire/day:	£0
Seminar room hire:	£50
Accommodation/student:	£49
Equipment hire/day:	£50
Simulation costs:	£0
TOTAL COST:	£3591
COST/STUDENT:	£299
COST/STUDENT/DAY:	£100

- The equipment costs include the hire of five computers that are needed to run the simulation.

So, the cost of one day's training can vary from £50 to over £300, even when you are arranging the courses yourself. Although this sounds like a lot of money, it is still cheaper than sending everybody to public courses.

If you only have one or two people to train on a particular topic then sending people on public courses would be more cost-effective. Again, the cost of a day's training varies tremendously.

For example, sending someone to a course, similar to the 'Decision Making Workshop' in Table 6.2, at a local management training centre would probably cost something in the region of £150. A one-day non-residential course with one of the large London-based training organizations would work out at about £250 a day. Residential courses would add at least another £50 to the daily costs.

Table 6.5 *Example of costs for a basics of management course*

Basics of management	
Type of training:	residential
Duration (days):	5
Number of students:	20
Number of trainers:	2
Type of trainer:	own
Location:	off-site
Additional rooms:	4
Trainer cost/day:	£300
Materials/student:	£50
Main room hire/day:	£0
Seminar room hire:	£50
Accommodation/student:	£120
Equipment hire/day:	£50
Simulation costs:	£0
TOTAL COST:	£18 450
COST/STUDENT:	£923
COST/STUDENT/DAY:	£185

If a famous business 'guru' has come to town, you could easily sit in a room with a thousand other people and be entertained for the day for the princely sum of £300. Whether these seminars could be considered to be training as defined in this book is debatable. In any case you might well consider whether you would get a better deal by buying the book or the video.

Rule of thumb: if you want to get a 'wet-finger' estimate of the size of your training budget work on an average of £150 per student-day of training. This includes the trainer's employment costs, but excludes the trainee's employment costs.

> Negotiate and revise budget

You now know how much it will cost to deliver the training demand. I am willing to bet that this figure is larger than your allocated budget. In this case you will need to negotiate a larger budget or agree what training should be left out. Understanding what a reasonable training budget is can help enormously during these negotiations.

Table 6.6 *Example of costs for a middle manager's training course*

Middle manager's course	
Type of training	residential
Duration (days):	5
Number of students:	20
Number of trainers:	3
Type of trainer:	own
Location:	off-site
Additional rooms:	4
Trainer cost/day:	£300
Materials/student:	£50
Main room hire/day:	£0
Seminar room hire:	£50
Accommodation/student:	£120
Equipment hire/day:	£250
Simulation costs:	£9000
TOTAL COST:	£30 550
COST/STUDENT:	£1528
COST/STUDENT/DAY:	£306

How big should a training budget be?

The size of the training budget is one of those perennial questions which will always be difficult to answer. A way of approaching this is to use 'benchmarking'. Benchmarking is the process by which you compare yourself with the best of your competitors with the aim of exceeding or surpassing their performance in all aspects. So, if a company in your sector is doing better than you are, it would be reasonable to assume that their level of training contributed to their business success. Therefore it would be valid to compare their training investment with your own.

Getting to the figures can be difficult. This is not because of any reluctance to disclose the figures (many training managers are only too willing to share ideas and information), but because of a lack of systems available to retrieve the information. It will also take time to arrange and make these visits.

You may also find the figures were calculated on a different basis to your own. Differences occur over the inclusion or exclusion of items such as employment costs, overheads, and loss of production. You will find that most training managers exclude as many items from the cost of training as they can get away with. The most common difference is the inclusion or exclusion of trainees' wages. Not that this is an insuperable problem because it is possible to make an estimate.

Rule of thumb: inclusion of wages doubles the cost of training.

To give you an idea of a 'benchmark' for training budgets corporations like IBM and Xerox recommend that each employee should receive five days of training per year. Managers should receive a further five days of management training.

Another guideline given by these companies is that the training budget, exclusive of wages and other employment costs, should be about 2 per cent of the total labour cost.

Most companies fall far short of this recommendation. In his report, *Who Pays for Skills*, Henry McLeish MP revealed that the annual expenditure on training per employee varies from 0.4 per cent of total labour costs, in the construction and distribution industries, to 1.0 per cent in banking, finance, and insurance. If you assume the cheapest possible training this is a range from about half-a-day to three days' training for each employee per year.

These figures are averages and the actual figures vary wildly according to location, industry, and size of company. Investment per employee (including wages) was highest in Northern Ireland and lowest in Wales, representing 1.9 and 1.0 per cent of labour costs respectively.

The lowest training costs of just over 18p (excluding wages) a year per employee were in textile, footwear and clothing firms with fewer than 50 employees. Other typical spending levels were £4.73 a year in the food, drink, and tobacco industry, £3.66 in the timber and wooden furniture sector, and £31 in electrical and electronic engineering.

Office machinery companies came top of the smaller employers' league at £221 (excluding wages). They also came top, spending £286 a year, among companies with more than 1000 employees. Footwear and clothing came bottom of the league, spending only £12.26 a year.

For most sectors and industry types there is a direct relationship between the numbers of employees and level of training expenditure. Large employers have a consistently better record of training and have shown the greatest improvement over time.

Table 6.7 shows training costs (excluding wages) as a percentage of labour costs for different industries. 'Energy' includes water. 'Finance' includes banking and insurance.

The conclusion from this is that a training budget (excluding wages) of 1 per cent of labour costs is a reasonable figure given a poor financial climate, but this would need to be increased to nearer 2 per cent for the training revolution to begin in the UK.

Table 6.7   *Training cost as a percentage of total labour cost*

	Energy	Manufacturing	Construction	Distribution	Finance	Total
Wages	77.84	85.18	87.59	86.80	77.07	81.99
National insurance	5.91	7.02	7.57	6.82	5.68	6.49
Redundancy	3.40	1.59	0.40	0.56	0.60	1.45
Liability insurance	0.68	0.30	0.42	0.18	0.06	0.34
Social welfare	8.70	4.20	2.97	3.93	8.82	6.20
Benefits	0.88	0.12	0.14	0.20	0.63	0.45
Subsidies	1.94	1.15	0.60	1.18	6.18	2.49
Training	0.71	0.50	0.38	0.39	0.98	0.63
Government aid	−0.06	−0.04	−0.07	−0.06	−0.01	−0.05

Source: *Who Pays for Skills?*, Henry McLeish MP

Finalize training plan

When I was preparing my first training plan for presentation to the EITB (Engineering Industries Training Board), the EITB representative gave me an example of what a training plan should look like. Since that time I have always used a modified version of that plan for preparing training plans in my own organization. An example of this modified form is given in Fig. 6.3.

The kinds of information that you need on a training plan are as follows.

- Who is to be trained?
- Why are they to be trained?
- When are they to be trained?
- What course has been identified to meet the training requirement?
- What is/are the occupation(s) of the people who need to be trained?
- How long is the course?
- How much will the training cost?

The industry training boards which used to exist in the UK offered good advice on all aspects of training. For example, the Engineering Industry Training Board (EITB) set out the characteristics of a good training plan in their booklet *Guide to the Levy Exemption and Grant Scheme 1989/90* (see Fig. 6.4). The Engineering Training Authority (EnTra) now hold the copyright to EITB publications.

Up until the training year 1990/1 the EITB and a number of other training boards had the power to require companies, which did not hold a certificate of exemption, to pay a levy.

WHEN will training be done?	COURSE	WHO is to be trained?	No	CAT
88/12/13 – 88/12/15	Leadership through quality	Managers and supervisors engineers and clerical staff	9	1, 4 & 5
88/12/6 – 88/12/8	Leadership through quality	Managers and supervisors engineers and clerical staff	14	1, 3 & 5
88/12/8	EDO	2/3 level managers and supervisors	11	4
88/9/21 – 88/9/23	Leadership through quality	Adult operators	16	6
89/09/01 – 90/01/01	NEBSS	Shop floor	4	6
89/01/10 – 89/01/12	Leadership through quality	Adult operators	15	6
89/01/12 – 89/01/12	Noise sem.	Designers and engineers	17	5
89/01/16 – 89/01/16	Noise sem.	Designers and engineers	17	5
89/01/16 – 89/01/20	PLC-2 Family I	Electrical technicians	3	2
89/01/17 – 89/01/17	Understanding personnel	Fage	1	6

Figure 6.3 *An example training plan format*

The EITB's levy was 1 per cent of the total salary bill in 1989/90. To obtain a certificate of exemption companies had to satisfy the relevant training board that the employer had made adequate arrangements for the training and further education associated with the training of employees.

The White Paper, *Employment for the 1990s,* proposed fundamental changes to the way training is organized and undertaken. The Industry Training Boards ceased to exist as statutory bodies and were replaced in the training year 1991/2 by non-statutory Industry Training Organizations, funded by subscriptions and charges for services. The following

WHY are they to be trained?	HOW is training to be performed?	WHERE is training to take place?	TRAINER	HOW MUCH will it cost?
Qual. imp./co. strat. awareness	Classroom	Mitcheldean	(PH)	£465
Qual. imp./co. strat. awareness	Classroom	Mitcheldean	(PH)	465
Awareness training to comply with company policy	Class	Aylesbury	(KT)	1036
Qual. imp./co. strat. awareness	Classroom	Welwyn	(PH)	630
Business need	Class	Hereford College	(KJ)	1000
Qual. imp./co. strat. awareness	Classroom	Mitcheldean	(PH)	400
To increase job skills	Class	WGC Design Institute	(MB)	1659
To increase job skills	Class	WGC Design Institute	(MB)	1659
Support PLC controllers	Class	Sutton Coldfield	(MS)	3000
New appointment	Class	London	Industrial Society	408

Figure 6.3 *cont'd*

Industrial Training Boards have been completely wound up as statutory bodies:

- Clothing and Allied Products,
- Hotel and Catering,
- Offshore Petroleum,
- Plastics Processing,
- Road Transport.

The Construction ITB, the Agricultural Training Board, and part of the Engineering ITB remain, but with reduced scope.

> Employers will be required:
>
> - to have training plans based on identified needs to maintain and improve the business of the firm. The EITB will be particularly concerned with the process of planning that has taken place, with the resources which are proposed for implementation and with the evaluation of the effectiveness of the training . . .
>
> - to relate planned training activities to the known and anticipated manpower requirements for all categories of employee . . .
>
> - to anticipate significant skill shortages, (and) identify those which cannot be met by the employer alone . . .
>
> - to allocate responsibility and accountability for carrying out the necessary action at senior management level
>
> - training plans should indicate the main training procedures to be followed

Figure 6.4 *Characteristics of a good training plan*
Source: *Guide to the Levy Exemption and Grant Scheme 1989/90* © EnTra

During the recession of the early 'eighties the removal of the levy would have been a charter for many employers to cease training activities altogether. However, during the recession of the early 'nineties employers did seem more reluctant to reduce their training, but the removal of the levy will still make the training manager's job more difficult in two ways.

The first is that training budgets will be more difficult to justify. No longer will a training manager be able to say: 'Unless we do this minimum amount of training we will have to pay a levy of 1 per cent of our wages bill.' The second problem is that a source of 'free' consultancy will dry up. Strictly speaking the consultancy is not really free because even employers who gained exemption from the levy still had to make a contribution of 0.07 per cent of their wage bill towards the running costs of the EITB, but at least it was a guaranteed access to a relatively unlimited source of advice.

Figure 6.5 shows the overall process for finalizing the training plan.

> Assess capability to deliver

In some ways this step is just a summary of what you have done before. From 'Determining the Workload' you will know how many courses you will need to run, and you will have had the opportunity to 'lobby' for additional resources. You will also know what training locations are available and when they are available. From this information you can tell how much of the training demand you can deliver with your existing resource.

Figure 6.5 *Process for finalizing the training plan*

As a result of capability or budget restrictions you may find you are
unable to meet the training demand. In this case the students have to be
prioritized. Before you can finalize the training plan you need to
prioritise the list of candidates. Another reason for prioritizing candidates is to determine who should attend the early courses on the basis
of the urgency and importance of the training. Prioritizing also mini-
mizes the damage that would be done by a budget cut towards the end
of the financial year.

These priorities could be made by the training department but I feel the
organization should be responsible for its own priorities. A mechanism
for doing this is the human resource development committee (HRDC).

Human resource   An HRDC is a committee of peer managers who meet to make, review,
development   validate, or approve decisions which are related to the organization or
committees   development of people in their own areas.

The training department brings a list of people who have been nominated for the courses which are within the committee's responsibility.
As the training department has already validated the demand there
should not be many people on the list who obviously should not
receive the training. The committee makes a final check on the validity
of the list and then concentrates on prioritizing people for the limited
number of training places.

The timing of a course depends on when the skills are required and the
availability of training rooms, trainers, and trainees.

Public holidays are another complication. Some are easy to avoid
because they have a fixed date or because they are the first Monday

after a fixed date. Other public holidays are just too 'movable'. There has been a recent tendency for calendars and diaries not to show public holidays, and if they do, they only give the dates for the current year. This is not very useful if you are trying to put a training plan together six months in advance.

Easter is one of the trickiest holidays. It can catch out even the most wary. Originally Easter was associated by the early Church with the Jewish Passover but the exact date has been a matter of controversy for centuries. In AD 325 a method of determining the date was agreed at the Council of Nicaea. This definition, which is still used today is (wait for it): 'The first Sunday after the first full moon after or on the vernal equinox.'

This means Easter can fall on any Sunday between 22 March and 25 April. No wonder moves are being made to have Easter on a fixed date. In fact, on 15 June 1928, a Bill was passed by the House of Commons which would 'fix' Easter to be the Sunday after the second Saturday in April. This would have the effect of restricting Easter between 9 April and 15 April. However, this Bill can only take effect after it has been agreed by the World Council of Churches. Assuming that this agreement may be some time in coming Appendix 3 gives the expected dates for Easter Sunday well into the 21st century.

If you train abroad or if you have students coming from abroad then things are further complicated because of all the different holidays observed in other countries. Don't be too surprised if there are only three weeks in the year when you can avoid a public holiday. To reduce these complications for planning purposes I usually only recognize the public holidays of the country hosting the training course. This may mean that people miss their public holidays when they are travelling abroad, but this is usually far more acceptable than training when the rest of the country is having a day off.

> Revise training plan

Now that the budget has been agreed and the priorities have been made the final touches can be made to the plan in readiness to take its part in the company's business plan. The next phase of the training process is to implement the plan.

Responsibilities   It is very important that one person has overall responsibility for the training plan. This does not mean to say that all the training has to be delivered or arranged by this person. It means that somebody should be responsible for the quality, timely delivery, and cost of the training.

Will your plan be successful?   To a large extent the question of whether your training plan is successful will depend on how over or under-optimistic you have been about your training department's capability for delivering the plan. Over-optimism leads to rushed preparation, fire-fighting, and a general reduction in the quality of the training. Under-optimism means that your trainers will be under-utilized and the cost-effectiveness of the training will be diminished. If the under-utilization is extreme, low motivation and lethargy will set in. This also will lead to a reduction in quality.

In most planning there is usually a tendency to err on the side of over-optimism. This syndrome is sometimes known as 'planning for success'. What it really means is that absolutely everything in the plan will go right, there will be no setbacks, and it is assumed that all tasks will be completed in the shortest possible time. This, of course, is a recipe for failure. So, rather than 'planning for success' I prefer to 'plan to succeed'. This means that you take a realistic view of your department's capability, have contingency plans, and put the emphasis on preventing things from going wrong.

Having a realistic view of the capability of your training process will depend on your experience, but you should also collect data from previous years. This will give you the most accurate estimate of the department's capability. If you are new to managing the training department then the guidelines given in Chapter 4 on student-to-trainer ratios and trainer workload will give you a pretty good starting point.

Figure 7.1 *Training administration*

7 Training administration

Training administration is the 'glue' of the training process. This chapter covers two more steps of the training process:

- pre-course administration;
- post-course administration.

The chapter also considers the role of the computer in training administration.

Although training and development needs are becoming more complex you still have to get the right people, to the right courses, at the right time. This, as anyone who is involved in training administration will know, is much easier said than done. Just filling the course places, and keeping the drop-out rates low, are major challenges in themselves—let alone meeting the development needs of the individual and the business requirements of the organization.

In addition to all the work that was done in completing the training needs analysis, and training plan, there are still a myriad of details to be seen to:

- booking the trainers,
- booking the rooms,
- booking courses,
- booking accommodation,
- ordering materials, food, and coffee,
- notifying delegates of their course places,
- keeping cancelled places to a minimum,
- ensuring delegates are fully prepared,
- getting them to the right course, on the right day, and at the right time,
- keeping training records up to-date, and
- paying the bills.

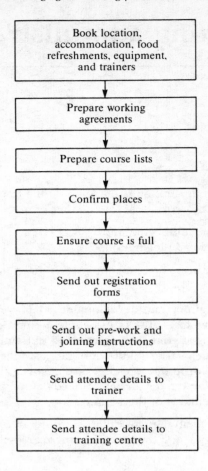

Figure 7.2   Pre-course administration process

Pre-course administration

Figure 7.2 shows the pre-course administration process.

> Book location,
> accommodation, food
> refreshments, equipment,
> and trainers

Once you have finalized the training plan you need to book specific dates at your selected training locations. You need to do this as early as you can. On-site meeting rooms need to be booked between two and three months ahead. Residential training centres often have their most popular dates booked a year ahead.

When you make the booking, make sure you have your preferred dates, plus several alternative dates, to hand. You should have previously made sure that the trainers are available on these dates. Confirm the booking in writing and be very specific about your requirements (you should already have the requirements listed on your course specification). Finally, confirm the dates with your trainers.

> Prepare working
> agreements

If you decide to set up as a profit centre it will be necessary to increase the administrative part of the process to keep track of what is being recharged to other departments.

- The trainers (or sales staff) let the training administrator know of any future rechargeable work.
- The training administrator draws up a numbered working agreement (see Fig. 7.3).
- Signatures to authorize the payment are obtained. A copy of the working agreement is given to the customer and the original is kept on file.

A working agreement is simply a contract between yourself and your paying customer. It should cover what work is going to be done, when it will be done, how much it is going to cost, when the charge is going to be made, and who will be paying for the work.

> Prepare course lists

The heart of an administration system is the course list. On receipt of the course dates and numbers, the administrator prepares a set of blank course lists. There should be a list for every course. When it is complete it should show:

- the title, date, and location of the course,
- the maximum number of places,
- the names and locations of the delegates,
- unfilled places, and
- reserve and 'wait-listed' delegates.

Reserves are people who:

- did not get a place on the prioritized list, or
- are on a later course, but are on standby for an earlier one.

If there are no 'wait-listed' people you can nominate students, who are on later courses, to be reserves. This also makes it easier for a student to change from one course to another.

There should be only one list for each course and only one person responsible for its maintenance. The list can be a sheet of paper in a book or it can be part of a computerized administration system. Although only one person should own the list, its information should be available to anyone who has a need to know.

WORK & RECHARGE
AGREEMENT

Work Agreement
No. 021

SUPPLIER
DOING THE WORK

CUSTOMER
PAYING FOR THE WORK

Division	Manufacturing Operations
Department	Management Training

Division	HQ
Department/Section	TRAINING DEPARTMENT

DESCRIPTION OF WORK TO BE UNDERTAKEN:

COURSE: MANAGEMENT STUDIES PROGRAMME   **DATES:** 15TH – 19TH JUNE, 1992

NUMBERS OF TRAINERS TO BE SUPPLIED: 2 **ADMINISTRATION CHARGE:** £160.00
@ **£160 PER TRAINER PER DAY**

RECHARGE DUE 3RD QUARTER, 1992

TOTAL AMOUNT RECHARGEABLE £1760.00

CHANGES: Changes to this Transfer Agreement can be made only with the joint approval of both parties. However, cancellations within a 6 week period of the course start date will incur cancellation charges equivalent to the full amount due per person.

APPROVALS

SUPPLIER

CUSTOMER

Name
Signature
Date

Name
Cost Centre to be Recharged
Signature
Date

Figure 7.3   An example of a working agreement

I believe in 'charts on walls' or, in this case, 'lists on walls'. Managers of the training process need to know the status of course bookings at any time. They need to do this quickly and without disturbing the course administrator. A wall display showing all the course bookings allows them to do this. The display could be hand-written charts, a computer printout, or a whiteboard.

A method that we have found very useful is the 'T-card system'. It is made up from a set of metal frames that have slits cut into them. 'T-shaped' cards fit into the slots. The 'ears' of the 'T' prevent the cards falling through the slots. The trunk of the 'T' is hidden when the card is in the frame. Each card has a space for the name and location of one student. Other, less frequently used information is shown on the hidden part of the card. Different colours represent the different courses. Details of the system are shown in Fig. 7.4.

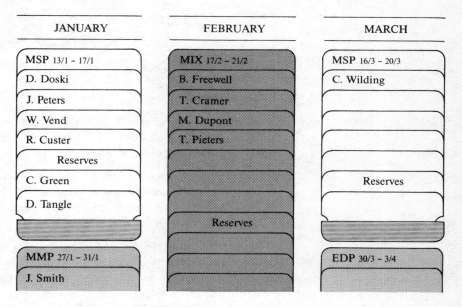

Figure 7.4 *'T-Card' system for displaying course places*

When the blank course lists have been drawn up the training administrator has to assign candidates to each course. This is most easily done from a priority list or on a first-come, first-served basis.

The system is more complicated than this in larger companies because the individual organizations will want to decide who goes on which course. In this case the training administrator allocates blocks of places to each organization.

The administrator determines the size of the block from the demand forecast. Figure 7.5 shows how the blocks would be reserved using the 'T-card system'. The allocations for the different organizations are identified by an abbreviation, e.g. MIT.

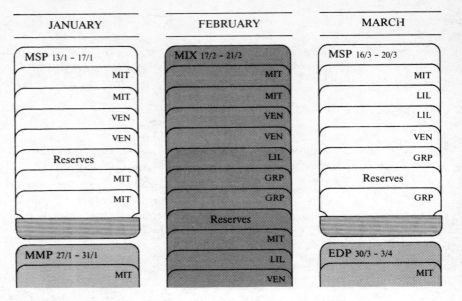

Figure 7.5 *Allocating training places to other parts of the organization*

Getting the names right

A customer's perception of quality depends on the care the supplier takes to get the details right. The details that matter are those which many suppliers would consider to be trivial.

Misspelling a student's name is a good example of this. Although it might be as trivial as spelling a name with a 'tt', instead of a 't', the student will form an immediate and unshakeable perception of the course's quality.

Getting the names right is not simple. Often we rely on the original training request for the correct spelling of the names. This is the first mistake. Training requests can pass through many hands before they reach the training department. It is also surprising how many managers do not know the correct spelling of their employees' names.

A good source of information is the internal telephone directory. Although not infallible, people do complain if their names are not correct in the directory. Often these directories will only have the initials of the forenames and this will make it difficult to discriminate between similarly spelt surnames. It is also difficult if the course is to be run on a first names basis.

Personnel records are the most accurate source. As these records deal with formal names, they are less useful when people prefer to use their middle names or nicknames.

The only foolproof way of getting a name right is to ask the people themselves. This need not be arduous if the administration process makes use of a registration form.

```
┌─────────────────────────────────┐
│        Confirm places           │
└─────────────────────────────────┘
```

The next step is to inform the candidates, and their managers, of the course dates. Also inform the local training representatives.

Inform candidates of their places as early as possible, so they can book the dates in their diaries. The reserves also should block out the dates in their diaries.

```
┌─────────────────────────────────┐
│       Ensure course is full     │
└─────────────────────────────────┘
```

The training administrator should keep a constant eye on how the course places are being taken up. If anybody drops out, the administrator informs the reserve that a place is now available.

Keeping cancellations to a minimum

The main cause of cancelled places is 'pressure of work'. A cancellation fee can help keep cancellations to a minimum. Some people think this is punitive, but this is not the idea behind the fee.

One of the reasons for charging a cancellation fee is that an unfilled place is a wasted opportunity. It reduces the amount of training that can be done because an empty place costs nearly as much as a filled place. At least a cancellation fee will pay for an additional place on another course.

Sometimes you have to cancel a course because there have been too many cancellations. Always consider a cancelled course as a failure because it is total loss of learning and resource. It might be worth recharging the entire cost of the cancelled course to the organizations that pulled their people off the course.

Another reason for introducing a cancellation fee is to allow managers to make a business decision as to whether they should withdraw their people from a course. For example, a manager might withdraw someone to write an important report. If there is no consequence, many managers would put the report before the course. However, if the cost of cancelling a place is £1500 then managers can make a business decision. Is getting the report written in the next five days worth an expenditure of £1500? If it is, then maybe the right business decision is to withdraw the person from the course.

Also have a good reserve system and let people know the dates well ahead of the course.

Then there is the question of double booking. The airlines favour this to make sure there are no empty seats. I am against this practice because we should never promise a customer something we cannot deliver. When I am told that the seat that I have booked and paid for has been taken by somebody else I am one very unhappy customer. I am not the slightest bit interested in the airline's problems or their utilization rates.

Double booking sets an expectation that cancellations will occur, and that we condone cancellations. We should set the expectation that the only reason for a cancellation is a personal emergency.

Always try to book the maximum number of students allowed by the course specification. If there are last-minute cancellations, you should still have the minimum number of students required to run the course successfully.

All the above suggestions for keeping cancellations to a minimum are no substitute for people, and their managers, really wanting the training to happen. People and organizations do what they believe to be important. This underlines the importance of getting the basics right and delivering the training that meets both the individual's and the organization's requirements.

```
┌─────────────────────────────┐
│     Send out registration   │
│            forms            │
└─────────────────────────────┘
```

The registration form reminds the students of their attendance. It also flushes out the people who are unable to attend. Send out the registration forms six weeks before the course is due to start. If you send the form much earlier there is a chance the course will be forgotten. Sending the forms much later will not leave enough time to find a replacement if somebody drops out.

An example of a registration form is given in Fig. 7.6.

The form should have the name of the course as well as the start and end dates of the course. It is always a good idea to put both the date and the day. This helps to identify mistakes and avoid misunderstandings.

Show charges and cancellation fees clearly on the registration form. This will keep future arguments to a minimum. Also, identify the person, or organization, responsible for paying the fee. A budget or cost centre number does this unambiguously.

Advising the student of the course venue at this stage allows them to plan their travel arrangements.

It is a good idea to ask for the students' full names as well as the names they would like to use during the course. It is surprising how different these can be. Don't forget to amend the course list if you discover any spelling differences here.

If certificates are awarded it is also a good idea to check how they would like their names to be spelt on the certificates.

It is better not to use the term 'Christian name' as this may cause irritation, if not offence, in multicultural societies. A better term would be 'first name' or 'given name'.

A staff number uniquely identifies a person's personnel or training record. This is the only way to ensure that the right person is coming

---

COURSE REGISTRATION FORM

PLEASE COMPLETE IN **BLOCK CAPITALS** AND RETURN TO:
The Training Administrator (IE16)

COURSE TITLE:

COURSE DATES:

COURSE FEE:

COURSE LOCATION:

NAME: (As you would like it to appear on
             a certificate. e.g. Bertram J Bloggs)

NAME: (As you would like to be called
             during the course, e.g. Bert Bloggs)

STAFF NUMBER:

JOB TITLE:

GRADE:

ORGANIZATION: (i.e. IHQ/ESC/EMO):

DEPARTMENT:

LOCATION ADDRESS:

ELECTRONIC MAIL ADDRESS:

INTERNAL TELEPHONE NO:

MANAGERS'S NAME:

MANAGER'S LOCATION ADDRESS:

MANAGER'S ELECTRONIC MAIL ADDRESS:

MANAGER'S INTERNAL EXTENSION NO.:

COST CENTRE NUMBER:
For course cancellation charge of £860
(Does not apply in a personal emergency)

MANAGER'S SIGNATURE: ....

Figure 7.6 *An example of a course registration form*

on the course. Having the staff number also makes it easier to update the training records. It also makes it more likely that changes to the training record will be made after the course.

The job title, grade, and organization provide a final opportunity to make a check on the course's suitability for the delegate. This information also allows the trainer to make better decisions about subgroup composition. Many courses work better with diverse subgroups. Other courses require homogeneous subgroups. Chapter 8 deals with the composition of subgroups in more detail.

The registration form should also ask whether the delegate has any special dietary, access, or other requirements.

```
Send out pre-work and
   joining instructions
```

Send out the pre-work and joining instructions no later than two weeks before the course. Increase this time if the students have to gather information, if there is a lot of reading, or if there is a holiday period before the course.

Keep pre-work to a minimum. Never issue pre-work that is not a prerequisite for the course. Similarly, do not go over the pre-work in class. This irritates the students and it also discourages them from completing the evening work.

Joining instructions should cover the following at a minimum:

- the course title,
- the start and finish dates of the course (mention the day as well as the date),
- the location,
- start and finishing times,
- directions to the venue,
- accommodation arrangements,
- dress code, and
- what they have to pay for (e.g. drinks in the bar).

An example of a joining instructions letter is given in Fig. 7.7.

Delegates also find it useful to have a booklet which gives additional details about the training centre. These details include:

- meal arrangements,
- message arrangements,
- sport and recreational facilities,
- smoking policy,
- emergency and security procedures, and
- local shops and banks.

Electronic mail, if it can handle graphics, is a convenient way of sending out pre-work and joining instructions. Sending large volumes of pre-work electronically gives some electronic mail systems a headache, so check with your systems expert before you do so.

```
Send attendee details to
         trainer
```

Memorandum

From: **A Traynor**   Location: **Aylesbury/432**   Division: **Human**
                            Extension: **2542**   **Resources**

To: **Attendees**   Location: Date: **25 May 1993**

Manager as Facilitator Workshop (Mining Group Gold)

Date: Wednesday June 16th – Thursday June 17th 1993
Location: Conference Room 1, 4th Floor, Hampden House, High Street,
            Aylesbury
Start: 8:30 am
Finish: 6:00 pm both days
Trainer: Andy Traynor

I am writing to confirm your place on the above workshop and to provide you with information on the following:

- The purpose, desired outcomes, and agenda of the Workshop
- Your Pre-Workshop assignment

Please find enclosed the above attachments and a copy of *Mining Group Gold*.

Notes on the Pre-Work:

- Please read *Mining Group Gold*
- After reading the *Mining Group Gold Manual*, develop responses on the enclosed pre-work sheets on chapters IV, V and VI.

My experience of this workshop is that completion of the pre-work is essential.

The time we have available for useful practical work is limited, and we will need to make good use of our time between 8:30 and 6:00.

A thorough understanding of the contents of *Mining Group Gold* will enable us to make the best use of this time. I estimate that the pre-work will take you at least 3 hours.

I look forward to seeing you on the June 16th. Please contact me if you have any questions or concerns.

Regards,

Andy Traynor

Figure 7.7   *An example of a joining instruction letter*

During the week before the course starts, the administrator should send the trainer the names of the attendees. This can either be a list or a copy of the registration forms. The advantage of using the registration form is that the information is supplied by the trainee and so is less likely to be wrong. It also has information which will help the trainer decide on seating plans and subgroup arrangements.

> Send attendee details to
> training centre

The week before the course, the administrator should send the hotel or training centre details of the attendees. This list includes the delegates' names, the nights they need accommodation, any special requirements, and whether they will be needing a meal the night before the course.

Figure 7.8   *Post-course administration process*

Post-course administration

Figure 7.8 shows the details of the post-course administration process.

> Trainer confirms students'
> attendance

After the course the trainer should give a list of the attendees to the training administrator. Copies of the course critique should also be sent to the administrator.

> Amend training records

Keeping the records accurate and up to date should be the responsibility of one, named person. In our organization the responsibility for the records lies with the training administrator. Training administrators can only keep control if they are the only people given authority to access and amend the training records. Even training managers should only be allowed to read the records!

The training records should be amended as soon as the training administrator receives the confirmed list of attendees from the trainer.

When a person goes on an external course extra precautions should be taken to ensure the training is recorded. The way to do this is to give the students a critique form to take with them. At end of the course the student returns the completed form to the administrator. If the students do not return the form, the administrator contacts them to check whether they attended the course. Using a critique form in this way helps to control the quality of external courses.

The risk of incomplete records increases when training has been organized from within another department. It is a good idea to have all training requests pass through the training department, and for the training department to hold the budget for all training.

The intention is not to control what functional training should be given to an individual. There is no way that anyone in the training department could have enough knowledge of all the professions to make any kind of sensible judgement. That decision is best left to the individual's manager. What the training department can do is to check whether good value for money is being obtained, co-ordinate separate demands for the same kind of training, and ensure that the amount of training received is not being under-reported.

Analyse course critiques

The course critiques are analysed for trends in the students' perception of the course. Details on how to do this are given in Chapter 10. Keep the analysis and the critique forms on file for at least three years.

Complete finances

After the course the administrator should pay the invoices that relate to the course. Recharges should also be made for unfunded places, cancellations, and work that has been completed for other organizations.

Controlling the budget
The amount you have spent needs to be checked at regular intervals, so you can detect deviations from your plan before they become an irreparable problem. How often the checks need to be done depends on the rate at which you are spending the money. It is unlikely to be more than monthly or less than quarterly. You will also need to check the accuracy of the invoices you receive.

If you do find you are overspending you will obviously need to determine what the causes were so that the problems can be avoided in the future. However, do not spend a lot of time beating yourself up. Those problems are in the past and you can do nothing more to prevent them. The problems that you can do something about are in the future and that is where you need to concentrate your efforts. Come up with solutions which will allow you to meet your targets with the budget you have left.

You need to be especially on the look-out for invoices that are received after the financial year has finished. You need to be able to carry forward an amount of money into the next year to cover these charges, otherwise you will find that either there will be no money to pay for them or that you will have less money to fund the training plan.

Computers and administration

One of the things you will notice as you get more involved in training administration is that the same information keeps on cropping up in different circumstances. This means that the administrator spends a lot of time typing, and perhaps correcting, the same information. It is precisely these circumstances which lend themselves to the use of computers.

Take the simple example of a student's name. This information appears in all of the following documents:

- course demand lists,
- course place notifications,
- course lists,
- registration forms,
- joining instructions,
- name cards,
- attendance sheets,
- drinks lists,
- subgroup composition,
- observation sheets, and
- course certificates.

Not only does the student's name have to be typed or written on every one of these documents, but the chances of getting the name wrong are very high.

If the students' names and other information were kept on a computer database, standard letters, and documents could be produced quickly and accurately.

There are several training administration training programs on the market, such as TCMS marketed by Fraser Williams and Training Administrator sold by Marlow Software.

You may find that some of the programs have been developed for a particular industry sector. This makes it even more important that you have a demonstration to make sure that the program is suitable for your application.

Facilities of a computerized administration system

To help you assess a particular system the following is a list of facilities that you would expect a computerized administration system to provide.

Programme planning

- Proposed course schedule
- Trainer allocations

- Locations
- Budget allocation
- Schedule revisions

Course booking
- Course place status
- Vacancy details
- Reserves
- Block bookings (without specified student names if required)
- Unconfirmed bookings
- Waiting lists
- Notification letters
- Joining instructions
- Pre-work enclosure list
- Invoicing
- Cancellation fees

Accommodation
- Room allocation
- Daily register of residents' details
- Registration
- Invoicing
- Visitors' accommodation

Course documentation
- Certificates
- Name cards
- Lapel badges
- Delegate lists
- Seating plan
- Groupings
- Drinks lists
- Contact lists

Charging
- Internal recharges
- Variable invoicing
- Separation of delegate incurred expenses

Statistics
- Profit/loss statements
- Numbers of delegates
- Number of delegates per course
- Drop-out rate
- Resource utilization
- Hours of training per employee
- Cost of training per employee
- Cost per course place

Training records
- Employee training record
- Record of bookings, transfers, cancellations, and fees
- Enquiry and report facilities
- Training records update

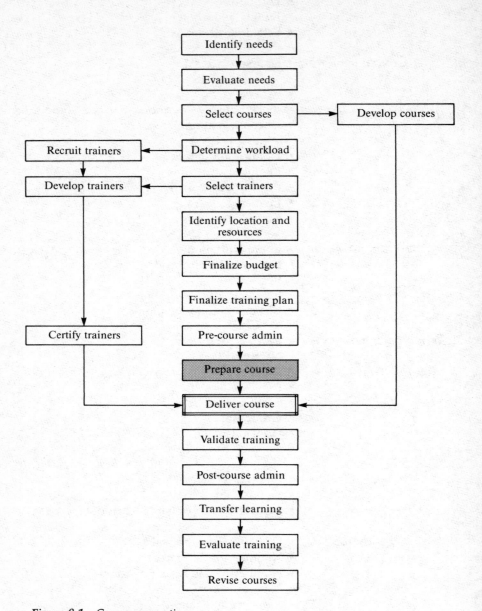

Figure 8.1 *Course preparation*

8 Course preparation

The more effort that is put into the preparation of a course, the more trouble-free that course will be. Always plan to prevent (or at least have a contingency for) what you know could go wrong. As Murphy's law says: they will go wrong, and at the worst possible time.

When you are dealing with these known emergencies you will be leaving no time for the hundreds of other gremlins that you didn't know about. Murphy's lesser-known second law—'Murphy's Law of Time Estimation'—also applies when you are preparing for a course. This law runs as follows: 'To determine the true time that a task will take, you should first make an estimate of the time. Double it and then move it up into the next time unit.'

For example, if you estimate that it will take five minutes to alter a document on your word processor, it will actually take 10 hours. If you estimate you can write a one-day workshop in three days it will most likely take you six weeks to complete.

There is a relationship between the amount of effort you put into preparation and the perceived difficulty of your job. The harder you work, the easier it seems. It is unfortunate that your strengths will always seem easy, simply because of smooth and professional execution. So don't be surprised when you are asked: 'When are you going to go back to doing a "real" job?'

Figure 8.2 shows that there are two parallel streams of preparation activity. Not only do trainers have to prepare, but students also have to prepare themselves for the course. For this reason this chapter has been divided into two parts: student preparation and trainer preparation.

Student preparation

> Students do pre-work

If you were to take a survey of how many students do their pre-work before arriving at the training centre, you would find the proportion to be less than 60 per cent. Of these, more than half would have left the pre-work to the last one or two days before the course.

Given these depressing statistics it has to be asked why we bother with sending out pre-work. The usual reason for doing pre-work is to

Figure 8.2 *Course preparation process*

shorten the time it takes to do the course. This, by itself, is not a good reason.

However, there are activities which do not make the best use of course time. Examples of these activities are:

- background reading,
- collecting data, and
- filling in questionnaires.

As students also vary widely in the time they take to complete these activities, it makes sense to set these tasks as pre-work.

The guidelines given in Fig. 8.3 will help to ensure that the pre-work is done in good time.

> Students meet their
> manager to discuss
> expectations for
> the course

An important part of ensuring that training is effective is to make sure that the participants know why they are on the course, and how they are going to use the training after the course.

You would be right in thinking that this is a bit late in the day for the

- Always make sure that the pre-work is essential to the running of the course.
- Give an accurate estimate of how long the pre-work will take.
- Prioritize the pre-work tasks.
- Let the students know why the pre-work is necessary.
- Let them know how the pre-work is to be used.
- Let them know when the pre-work will be used.

Figure 8.3 *Guidelines for setting pre-work*

participants to find out why they are going on a course, but if you need convincing that this step is necessary, try asking your next group of students why they think they are on the course.

A certain proportion will know the developmental reasons for their attendance, but a significant minority will, after a few seconds of stunned silence, come up with some serious, and some not so serious responses such as:

'I don't know.'
'I was told to come.'
'I came for the free lunch.'
'John couldn't attend, so I'm here as a substitute.'

The right time for people to know why they are on the course is at the time they are nominated. This is part of needs analysis and is dealt with in detail in Chapter 2.

Once the participants have a clear idea of why they are attending the course, they can discuss what their managers will expect them to do differently as a result of the course.

If the course is skills-based it is a good idea for the participants and their managers to select tasks that can be practised during, and used for application after, the course.

For example, depending on the course, you could select:

- tasks that need to be delegated,
- projects that need to be managed,
- reports that need to be written, and
- problems that need to be solved.

Not only does this concentrate the mind, but it also provides a final check as to whether a person needs to come on the course. It is very difficult for people to justify their need for a project management course when they are unable to find any projects they need to manage.

Trainer preparation

> Prepare print masters

Some years ago the idea of the paperless office was much put around. While there is a lot of merit in having visions of the future it will be a long time before people will feel comfortable without a piece of paper in their hands.

Undoubtedly computer technology has made tremendous strides already and will continue to do so. However, a computer's window on the world is still very small (about 200 words compared with an open book's 800). A computer prefers to act like a scroll rather than a book, and when it can be coaxed to turn pages it does so very slowly. It just cannot compete with leafing through a book. Surprisingly, even when super computers are used to simulate the speed and capacity of a book, people still found fewer errors in a proofreading experiment.

Computers do not like being folded up like a piece of paper and they always need more batteries and power than a book. Where computers do score is in their ability to search for a given word and their ability to present information in different orders, depending on the learning need.

So, it looks as if printed documents (also known as hardcopy) will be with us for some time to come. What is more likely to happen, and is beginning to happen now, is that the materials will be prepared electronically, but they will not be committed to paper until later in the process. One of the main advantages of having electronic masters is the ease of revision and modification.

There is no theoretical reason why the masters would be held in any form other than electronically. Practically, storing masters electronically is very expensive. There never seems to be enough room in the electronic files for all the documents that people want to store. Consequently, there is always pressure to transfer documents from the electronic 'network' to magnetic disks or paper.

Electronic storage of information is always susceptible to being lost or corrupted. Surprisingly, a flimsy sheet of paper can take a lot more damage than an electronic file before it is impossible to retrieve the information. This is why computer users are always being urged to make 'backups' (additional copies) of their work.

Unfortunately, this has the effect of doubling the cost of storing information, but it is still far cheaper than losing all your work. Because of the volatile nature of electronic storage I would always recommend having a printed copy of the latest version of your work.

If the worst comes to the worst you can always have the document scanned electronically. These optical character recognition devices (OCRs) work especially well if you use a simple typeface like Titan 12 or Courier 12.

In the future you could imagine a small terminal in the training room that prints the material as the students arrive, and produces the hand-outs only when they are needed. In this way there should be no wastage whatsoever.

Currently the best method of producing materials is to make copies of paper masters that you have produced electronically. With this approach you can still produce the materials, even if the whole of the computer system has 'gone down', because you can find a photocopier in nearly every office.

Another disadvantage of using electronic masters is that they are usually compatible with only one system. The chances of finding a similar system that could print them out for you are quite small. Most systems can read simple files on disks that are compatible with the MS-DOS format.

For this reason either keep a copy of your text files in the simplest format possible (usually called an ASCII file) or make sure you know how to convert your text to an ASCII file. Appendix 4 gives some tips on how to do this. Although this seriously restricts what can be done (the document will be unformatted and you will not be able to have combined text and graphics), it does mean you can access your text from a wide range of word processor programs.

> Obtain printed materials

Be sure you have enough copies of the training materials ordered, printed, or photocopied in time for the course. Ideally you would want the printed materials to arrive at the training venue on the day you set up the training room. This ideal is risky unless your suppliers are of the highest quality. You will probably arrange for the materials to arrive a couple of days before the course to allow for contingency. What you don't want to do is have your office or storage area cluttered up with training materials months before you need them.

How many copies should you make?

In an ideal world you would have exactly the same number of copies as you have students. Yes, I know that, in spite of all the administrative systems we have put in place, it is still almost impossible to ensure full attendance. I also know that on occasions more students than you expect turn up. Sometimes the materials have defects and you need spare copies to replace them.

Assume that you order a couple of extra sets of materials when you run a workshop for 10 people. This may not seem a lot but you are increasing the cost of the training materials by 20 per cent. This is a significant chunk out of your training budget. You may argue that having additional materials does not really matter as you can always use them on the next course. But when will the next course be? Where will you store the extra materials from this workshop and the materials from the other courses that you run? What happens if you revise the course? Will you have the time to 'rework' all the binders you have in the stores? Can you be certain that all your materials will have the same revision level? Can you ensure that the materials will not get dirty or be damaged while they are being stored? In fact, you might be better off throwing the spare materials away.

This might seem to fly in the face of today's emphasis on conservation and recycling, but it need not. First concentrate on ensuring that the right number of people turn up to the course. Then have a really close look at the materials. Check to see whether they have been printed simplex or duplex (single-sided or double-sided). If the materials can be printed double-sided, there will be a 40 to 50 per cent saving on paper usage and cost.

See if the materials can be printed on recycled paper. Rather than throwing excess materials in the bin, remove them from their binders and arrange for a recycling company to come and collect the waste paper. Return the binders to your printer or copy centre or hold on to them yourself if you must. At least you can reuse them quickly because they will hold the materials for any of your courses.

If you have the impression by now that I am not in favour of storing anything, you would be pretty close to the truth. This might seem counter-intuitive because trainers find a certain amount of comfort in having large stacks of materials. They also have difficulty in throwing anything away—you never know when you might need it.

The trouble with storage is that you can never have enough of it. The quantity of materials you have to store will always increase to exceed the amount of storage space you have available. Good systems have to be in place to help you find the items you require and there is always a danger of damage to the materials while they are in storage.

Storage is very expensive. Ask your financial director how much a square metre of space costs your company. This money is then locked up and doesn't earn a penny for your company. The stored materials do not add any value to the business until they are removed from the store and are either used or sold.

Just in time materials   This concept of stockless operation is called 'just in time' (JIT). It is one of the many ideas that have come over from Japan. The idea is that you train your suppliers to deliver the materials you need at the exact time you need to use them. So, in a supermarket, a new delivery of tooth-paste would arrive just as the last tube was being taken from the shelf. Not only do your suppliers have to be well disciplined but you also have to be able to use the materials immediately. If you don't you will be buried under a mountain of stock.

This mode of operation seems to be a little strange to some British suppliers . . .

Komatsu, the Japanese manufacturer of bulldozers, took over a factory that used to be owned by the Caterpillar company in the north of England. In keeping with the EC regulations the Japanese tried to use a proportion of locally manufactured parts in their bulldozers. One such part was the fuel tank. Komatsu asked the suppliers when they could supply the tanks.

'Next week,' came the reply.

'No, you don't understand', said the Japanese. 'Which day? Which hour?'

This does not mean to say this kind of approach cannot be transferred to a Western culture. Neither does it mean that everyone has to do exercises and sing the company song before starting work in the morning. There are many Marks & Spencer stores in England that now have a first-floor sales area where their stockrooms used to be.

Applying the just in time approach to training means you have the materials copied just before you run the training courses. In this way you will only have to find storage space for about four boxes at a time. The clever bit about this is it is your printer who has to find storage space for the paper and binder stocks.

Even if you copy the materials yourself it is still better to print off what you need, when you need it, because there is less money tied up in the raw materials than there would be in the final product.

There is always the temptation to order a whole year's worth of materials because you can get a better discount from the printer. Think very carefully before you do this. Are your training materials so good and your company so stable that the materials will need no revision during the coming year? It can be very expensive throwing away or reworking half-a-year's stock.

Also, compare the savings that you make with the discount with what you would have to pay for extra storage. Estimate the cost of stocktaking and damaged materials. Ask what else you do with the money that you have 'invested' in the stock.

Storing the masters

All this assumes that you have a superb system for storing, revising, and retrieving the masters for the course materials. One of the first decisions you are going to have to make is where the masters are going to be stored. The major options are: with the trainers, with the training administrator; or at the printers. The final choice of location depends on the security of the masters, and the stability of the course. If a course is stable and is run many times a year, it can be very convenient to store the masters at the printers and just make a phone call when you need some more copies printed.

Electronic storage of masters is becoming more practical although it is still expensive. Machines like the Xerox DocuTech Production Publisher

> Tab 7   *Visioning*
> —Single-sided
> —4-hole punched
> —White, recycled, A4

Figure 8.4   *Example of labelling a print master*

can even scan paper documents and turn them into 'digital masters' which can then be edited or enhanced electronically. When copies of the materials are required the 'digital masters' are retrieved and the materials are printed off complete with separator sheets, divider cards, and thermal binding.

It will also be possible to create a document on a personal computer and send it electronically to the DocuTech Publisher for printing and finishing. The machine will also be able to store the job, complete with its print specifications, ready for future reproduction.

Although the cost of this technology is likely to fall, it is reasonable to assume that for reasons of cost and security, paper print masters will be with us for some time to come. The masters should be kept in file boxes, and the file boxes should be in a locked cupboard or stored on shelves in a secure room.

Each handout or subsection of a student binder should be in its own plastic document wallet. The wallet should have a label that identifies the master and gives instructions to the printer on how the masters should be copied and bound (see Fig. 8.4).

This should be sufficient for relatively simple jobs. For more complex materials you should also provide a printer's dummy. A printer's dummy is an example of the finished materials so the printers can see exactly how they should produce the materials.

When you have the handouts printed, ask the printer to put them straight into the file you will be using during the course. It will not take the printer much longer, but it will save you a lot of time and bother.

Handouts v binder material

When I see a course that has many handouts, I start to suspect that the course is becoming out of date. (It is easier to produce another handout than to revise and reprint the student binder.) This suspicion becomes stronger if the trainer does not make full use of the materials that are in the binder.

> Review lesson plan

Make sure you have enough time to prepare yourself for teaching the course. If you are unfamiliar with a course this can take as much as a day of preparation for each hour of trainer presentation. A familiar five-day course may need no more than a hour to skim through the lesson plan.

No matter how familiar you are with the course, don't be tempted to miss out this step entirely. Familiarizing yourself with the course provides reminders of all the things you need to do before and during the course. Over-confidence leads to disaster.

```
┌─────────────────────────────┐
│      Obtain audio-visual     │
│      equipment and tapes     │
└─────────────────────────────┘
```

The course specification should have a complete list of all the audio-visual equipment required for the course such as:

- overhead projectors,
- flip chart stands,
- cassette recorders,
- video recorders and cameras, and
- computers and printers.

The technical specifications need to be very precise when you order or hire video equipment and computers. There are many different standards and, if the equipment supplied is not compatible with your tapes or software, you will not be able to use them.

The most common standards are VHS for video and IBM-PC for personal computers. I say standards, but even these popular 'standards' come with several different variations.

Overhead projectors Most training locations supply an overhead projector as standard. There is not a lot to choose between the different makes of overhead projector, although there are a couple of features you should look out for. The first is an internal spare bulb that can be changed quickly and easily by turning a handle. The second is the ability to 'tune' the optics so that blue and orange colour fringes can be eliminated. Some overhead projectors have a supplementary lens which flips over the lamp to increase the light intensity for computer display panels. Remember to move the lens out of the light path for normal use, otherwise the edges of the transparency will be too dark.

Check to make sure that your transparency frames do not foul the column that supports the optics head.

Flip chart stands Flip chart stands seem to be innocuous pieces of equipment, but like deckchairs they can be a trap for the unwary. Here are some pointers to look out for.

Height
Check that the stand can be adjusted for both your shortest and tallest trainer.

Weight

If you have to transport your own flip chart stands check the weight and bulk of the unextended stand.

Rigidity

Check that the stand does not move around or bend when you write on it.

Method for holding the paper

Look at the method for retaining the paper. This can be a spring-loaded jaw or a pair of pegs. Check that the pegs align with the holes in your flip chart paper. (Why on earth isn't there a standard for this?) Many of these stands have screw-on clamps which make it difficult to tear off sheets cleanly.

The jaw method of retaining the paper has the advantage of not needing a particular spacing for the holes, but it does not retain the pad so well. Some methods use a retaining bar and I have seen it take two people to insert the pad—one to hold the bar out of the way and the other to push the pad into the jaws!

Check to see whether the stand will retain single sheets—either by themselves or in addition to the pad. This feature is essential if you have subgroups reporting back to the main classroom.

Video recorders   VHS is the most popular format for video recorders but unfortunately it comes in three different standards: PAL, NTSC, and SECAM, depending on which country you happen to be in. (See the glossary at the end of this book for an explanation of these abbreviations.) Most European countries use PAL. France and what used to be the Soviet Union use SECAM, and the US uses NTSC.

Unless you can buy or hire a multistandard video recorder which will play PAL, SECAM, and NTSC, you will need to make sure that all your tapes are in the same format as the machine you are using. You can check this by looking at the label on the cassette or its case. If this doesn't give you a clue try playing the tape on your machine. A different standard usually runs the sound track at a different speed and produces horizontal lines on the screen.

If your tapes are in a different standard you will need to get them converted by one of the specialist video houses. A word of warning—if your tapes are commercially produced, you will be breaching the owner's copyright if you have the tape converted. So, when you buy a commercial tape make sure it is in the standard you will be using.

The introduction of camcorders, i.e., a portable video camera with a built-in video recorder, has introduced two new formats: VHS-C and 8 mm. This isn't a problem if you are using video feedback that will be played back during the course, but it will cause problems if you want to give the students their tapes to take away with them. The VHS-C cassette has to be either copied on to a standard tape or clipped into a special carrier before it can be viewed on a domestic video recorder. An 8-mm tape has to be copied on to a standard tape.

A more recent introduction is Super VHS. This has a cassette the same size as an ordinary VHS cassette. It has higher definition and picture quality. An ordinary VHS cassette can be played on a Super VHS machine, but a Super VHS cassette cannot be played on a standard VHS machine.

The other format of cassette that you can come across is 'Sony U-matic'. It was one of the first standards to be used for training purposes. The machines are bulkier and heavier than the VHS equivalent and this, coupled with the fact that they are not used domestically, make them less prone to being 'borrowed'.

Modern video recorders are very reliable and the most common problems are dirty recording heads and damaged connecting leads. The main symptom of a dirty recording head is a snowy type of interference. This problem can be easily solved using a head cleaning video cassette. Scotch™ make a version that has a prerecorded message and audio tone. The cassette is played until the tone is clear and the message is legible.

Audio-cassette recorders

Unlike video cassettes, the audio cassette is a universal standard. There is not a lot to choose between the different makes of recorder. It is convenient if the recorders have an internal microphone. A battery indicator light gives an early warning of flat batteries and helps you prevent spoilt recordings.

The most common problems you are likely to get with an audio-cassette recorder are:

- flat batteries,
- dirty recording head, or
- dirty pinch roller and capstan.

If you have poor sound quality always check the batteries first, and then use a head-cleaning cassette. If the problem persists refer to the user manual and clean the capstan and pinch roller. The capstan is a metal spindle that turns to drive the tape. The pinch roller is a rubber wheel that holds the tape against the capstan.

Computers and printers

The situation with computers is very similar to the video situation—different standards with many variations. Always check your computer matches the system requirements that are printed on the software's packaging or in the software manual. Appendix 5 explains computer specifications in more detail.

Obtain supplies

Supplies are consumables you need for every course, and have a habit of running out just when you need them. The trainer's checklists in

Appendix 6 suggests a selection of supplies that you will need during a course. It is a good idea to use the checklist before each course to ensure a sufficient stock of supplies.

Fixings　　It is almost certain that every course you run will involve displaying charts or posters on a wall. If you are working in a purpose-built training room, there should be rails or pin-boards on the wall for displaying posters and charts. It is an unwritten law of the universe that you will always need more display area than is provided.

Masking tape is the best all-round method for sticking charts to walls. If you are careful, it should not pull off paint and wallpaper when it is removed.

Sticky pads or Blu-tack, are less satisfactory as they can be difficult to remove without leaving a mark. A tip for removing Blu-tack is to roll up another piece of Blu-tack into a small ball, and then roll it over the wall so that it picks up the pieces like a snowball. Doing it this way decreases the likelihood of removing any paint.

Flip chart pads　　The holes in the flip chart pads should align with the pegs on your flip chart stand. Some pads are stapled together, which makes it difficult to tear off single sheets. One way to overcome this problem is to buy pads with perforations, but this leaves the holes behind which makes it difficult to put the sheets back on the stand. Another way around this problem is to buy pads which are held together by an adhesive rather like a note pad. A square grid printed faintly on the sheets helps you draw diagrams and keeps your writing on the level. Considering the amount of flip chart paper that is thrown away at the end of a course, it is a good idea to buy pads made from recycled paper.

Flip chart pens　　Flip chart pens or markers come in several different types: spirit-based, water-based, and dry-wipe. Black and blue are the best colours for reading from the back of the room, while red and orange are the worst. The pens' tips should have a minimum breadth of 5 mm.

White boards should only be written on with dry-wipe pens. Too many white boards have been spoilt by writing on them with permanent pens. If this should happen to you, all is not lost because there are several methods that you can use for removing the marks.

First there are the proprietary sprays. If you do not have any of these around when you need them, you can try 'Snopake' thinners. An effective but lengthy method is to scribble over the permanent marks with a dry-wipe pen. Then use a dry cloth to remove both marks together. As this method is also quite tiring it teaches you not to use the wrong pens on the board! You also could try using a plastic eraser to remove the marks.

The manufacturers of some water-based pens say that these pens can be used on white boards. This is true, but the marks have to be removed with a damp cloth. This can turn out to be a somewhat messy operation.

Some trainers take the preventive route by banning all pens except dry-wipe pens. The only problem with this is that dry-wipe pens are not very suitable for flip chart work. The lines they draw are not broad enough to be read from the back of the class, and the colours are not strong enough.

I prefer to use water-based pens for flip chart work. If you do accidentally use them on a white board, it is not too much hassle to remove the marks using a damp cloth. Another advantage of using water-based pens is that you do not spend all day breathing in fumes.

Throw flip chart pens away as soon as they dry out. Repeatedly picking up the same exhausted pen is a frequent source of frustration. No amount of shaking, or standing the pens on their heads, will get more than a few extra minutes of life out of them. It is advisable to bring your own flip chart pens with you as it is amazing how many training locations provide exhausted or unsuitable pens.

Overhead projector pens

There are two types of overhead projector pens: permanent, and water soluble. Pens with a medium tip are generally the most useful thickness, but you might find you will also need a set of fine pens. Red, blue, green, and black all stand out well on the slides.

Use permanent pens if you don't want them to rub off. Water-soluble pens are useful if you want to make corrections as you go along, or if you want to reuse the slide, but cleaning the slide can be a bit messy. Another option is to place a blank transparency on top and write on that with a permanent pen. I prefer to use this method even when I am using water-soluble pens because it is easier to throw the top sheet away than clean up the prepared transparency.

Whatever you do don't get the two types of pen mixed up. Buy pens that allow you to see easily which pens are which. For example, Staedtler make permanent pens with a black barrel, and water-soluble pens with a grey barrel. Permanent pens do not always write very well on some types of transparency material. If you have a problem, try a water-based pen instead.

> Check course logistics

Some courses are more complex than others when it comes to preparation. Scanning through the lesson plan will remind you of what you have to do.

Course specifications

When you provide many different courses it is always difficult to remember exactly what has to be prepared. The kind of details you need to remember are along these lines.

- How many syndicate rooms does this course need?
- At what time should we order the coffee for?
- What are the start and end times?
- What videos do we need to bring along?

**Project Control Workshop
Course Specification**

Venue
on-site

Duration
2 days

Times
8:30 am – 4:30 pm

Rooms
1 training room
1 breakout room

Dress
normal business

*Breaks**
coffee and biscuits 8:15 am,
10:00 am and 2:45 pm

Lunch
lunch at 12:30

Audio/visual equipment
OHP + screen*
VHS player* + monitor* + leads*
2 flipchart stands* (one in each room)
fresh flipchart pads*
fresh flipchart pens*

No. of Attendees
6–12 (min-max) †
8–10 optimum

Date
Wednesday and Thursday
October 14th and 15th 1992

Trainer
Andy Traynor

Pre-work (at least 1 week in advance)
Discussion with manager
Selection of suitable project
Completion of 'terms of reference'

Student materials
1 per student

Slides
1 set

Handouts
1 set

Charts
1 set

Video & Audio Tapes
'Managing Projects' video
(VHS format)

Course Description
Project Control is a two day workshop.

The first day concentrates on skill-building (including Critical Path Analysis and Gantt charting) and covers:

—What is a project?
—Video
—What is project management?
—Stages of a project
—An example project
—Team leading
—A case study

* To be arranged by local administrator
† Note: The course cannot run with fewer than the minimum number of students shown above.

Figure 8.5　*An example of a course specification*

This problem is compounded when you are training away from your home base. You may have to rely on somebody else to prepare the classroom and to make all the necessary arrangements.

As suggested above you could scan through the lesson plan to answer these questions, but you need to prepare the logistics long before you start in-depth preparation of your sessions.

The answer to this problem is to have a specification for every course you run. A course specification only needs to be two or three pages long at the most. Figure 8.5 gives an example of a course specification.

I usually send my customers a copy of the course specification as soon as the course dates have been confirmed. You will notice that I give a detailed specification for computer and video equipment. This is to avoid the embarrassment of not being able to play the tape, or run the software, on your customer's equipment.

I also make it clear what equipment I will be bringing, and what equipment needs to be supplied by the customer.

Fred's list

The course specification is sufficient for short, straightforward courses. Courses that have complex logistics need the equivalent of a course specification, or a checklist, for every module. This checklist details the items that you need to prepare or obtain for the module.

We call the complete set of checklists 'Fred's List' in honour of a colleague of ours whose lists helped us through the logistics of a particularly tricky course.

You will still need a course specification for the course's general requirements. 'Fred's Lists' are for trainers' eyes only—they are far too detailed to be shown to the customer.

Seating plans

When students ask me how I chose the seating plan, they are disappointed to learn the simplicity of the criteria. (They suspect that I use some complex psychological method.) There are two basic approaches for seating people on a course. The first is to have them sitting next to somebody they know, the second is have them sitting next to somebody they don't know.

One of the advantages of a residential course is the opportunity to meet people with different backgrounds. To foster this, I often arrange the seating so that students sit next to someone they do not know.

If the course intends to do team building I would have the participants sitting in their natural work groups. This situation is one of the few times that I would have managers and their people in the same group, since having a manager and one of the manager's people on the same course can make it difficult for both parties to act naturally.

Before you can make any decisions on the seating plan you have to have some data on the students. The registration forms have information which indicates whether the participants know each other. Look to see whether they work in the same location, are part of the same organization, or work for the same manager. Although this approach is no substitute for local knowledge, it does have a high success rate. In the absence of this data, a random seating plan is as good as any other. Having the students sit in subgroup order helps the logistics (and the trainer's memory) considerably.

If you know the students well enough, you may be able to avoid potentially explosive seating combinations. In practice, predicting the interactions of 20 people is just too difficult to get right. Having too many criteria makes it impossible to find a suitable seating plan.

Subgroup assignments

The guideline of keeping the criteria simple also applies to subgroup assignments.

The composition of the subgroups should match the objectives of the course. Diverse groups allow people to learn about other departments. Homogeneous groups permit delegates to share knowledge and experience.

Be careful if you use criteria of race, age, sex, religion, or nationality for creating diverse subgroups. You must have a good training reason for using these criteria. 'Let's split the girls up' is not a good reason. Giving people practice in managing diversity is a better reason. The safest selection criteria are: experience, location, and the delegate's job.

Mixing the subgroups

A good way to have a nervous breakdown is to change the subgroup composition for each exercise. For an even better nervous breakdown try arranging the groups so every student has worked with every other student by the end of the course.

After a few hours of brain-bashing, you will come to the conclusion that only certain combinations of course and group size provide a complete solution.

Set up the training room

Setting up a training room, checking the equipment, putting up posters, and laying out materials for 20 people can take up to 2 hours. If the training room is free the day or evening before, I would recommend that you set up the room then—you still have all night to sort out any problems. There is nothing worse than trying to get the video recorder to work as the students are walking in. Even better, get somebody you can trust to set up the room for you.

One of the training venues I had been using for many years understood my requirements so well that they would lay out the training room exactly as I would have done it myself.

This arrangement worked well for both parties. I did not have to book the room for the night before to lay out the materials, and the squash club could run profit-making functions into the early hours of the morning. All I had to do was to give the manager a copy of the course specification, a drawing of the room layout, and make sure that all the materials were on site.

To give you an idea of how well this worked, I was once delayed by a traffic jam on the dreaded M25 and arrived at the training venue just as a team-building event was due to start. Everybody had helped themselves to coffee, as indicated by a notice on the flip chart stand, and I was able to walk in, switch on the overhead projector and say, 'Good morning and welcome to . . .'

Of course, having somebody to set up the training room for you does not work this well every time. It takes several years to build up this kind of relationship with a supplier, and you would not normally want to cut things this fine—even with your most trusted supplier—but this episode does underline the importance of having the training room set up as early as possible.

Room layout

Check that the tables and chairs are positioned so everybody will get a clear view of you, the video monitor, and the overhead projection screen. Walk round the room and look at the layout from every student's viewpoint.

If you want to encourage discussion between the participants, avoid having students sitting with their backs to each other.

Arranging the tables in a 'U' shape is a good layout, but don't get stuck with only one kind of layout. Try out some more interesting variations. You could use groups of tables, or you could have gaps to allow for freedom of movement in the room.

Audio-visual equipment

Checking the audio-visual equipment should be one of the first things you do when you are setting up a classroom. This will give you the maximum time to have the equipment replaced, or repaired, in the event of a major malfunction.

Check the sound level of the video, but bear in mind that the soundtrack will appear louder than when the room is full of sound-absorbing students.

After you have checked the sound and picture wind the tape back to the beginning. Cue the tape by playing it up to where you want it to

> This basic mistrust of technology was once demonstrated to me when I lent a videotape to a group of senior managers.
>
> The video was in two parts, separated by a period when the screen faded to blue.
>
> When the first part had finished the managers assumed that the video recorder had gone wrong so they switched it off. Later I timed the interval between the two sections of the tape. It was six seconds!

start. You may have to experiment with the exact stopping point as some recorders do not restart at the same place they were stopped. This should help you avoid showing a blank screen and the copyright notice. The few seconds that it takes for the video recorder to get itself started will give you time to turn out the lights.

People do not have a great tolerance for video recorders that do not show a picture as soon as you press the play button. This must be due to a basic mistrust of technology.

If you are using audio-cassette recorders, make a test recording on every recorder to make sure the batteries aren't flat and that the recorders are recording properly.

Switch on the overhead projector and, using one of your own slides, check that the projector is in focus and the optics are clean.

I usually remove the clamp from the flip chart stand, remove the staples, and cover sheets from the flip chart pads to make it easier to tear off sheets. I also lightly attach short lengths of masking tape to the back of the stand so I have tape readily available when I want to stick sheets on the wall.

Student materials Lay the student binders, pens, pencils, and erasers on the tables. Use this opportunity to do a final quality check on the materials.

Locate the handouts where they are easily accessible. If you are training in your permanent location, consider investing in a wheeled set of hanging files. If portability is your first consideration then a card 'concertina' expanding file will be more convenient.

Name plates Name plates are essential for the first few hours of the course so that you can get to learn the students' names. There are several type of name plates. The simplest is a sheet of A4 card folded along its length. Other types use individual plastic letters. The letters have small pegs on the back so that you can press them into the holes on the name plate. Not only do these seem to take for ever to prepare, but they are also an irresistible temptation for the members of 'Anagrams Anonymous'. You will be amazed at their creativity. You will never catch them in the act because they strike when you least expect it.

A popular type of name plate has a shiny-white surface which can be written on with dry-wipe pens. These are quick to prepare, but the name can only be written on one side, and the lettering is easily smudged.

One of the best name plates that I have seen was made in-house by one of the major conference centres. The base was a piece of wooden moulding that had a groove cut into its length. A name card was held by a piece of perspex that had been bent in half along its length. The perspex fitted into the groove on the wooden moulding.

You can get the students to fill in their own names as part of the warm up. This helps if you are not confident of who is going to turn up. It also helps if you are not sure whether the names are spelt correctly.

My preference is to have the names already filled in on the name plate. This allows you to decide where the students will sit and it also makes the students feel expected when they walk in.

Consider having the names printed or written on both sides of the name plate. If you can withstand the jokes about students not knowing their own names, you will be able to see who the students are from any part of the room. This also helps the participants find their places when they first walk into the training room.

> There was one incident that convinced me that the names should be on both sides of the name plate. It was the course when some of the students knew everybody's names except those of the people they were sitting next to.

Prepare syndicate rooms
Visit each syndicate room to make sure that the correct wall charts have been put up. Check the lighting. See if there is enough flip chart paper. Test the felt-tip markers to make sure they have not dried out.

Check that there is sufficient supplies of other consumables such as masking tape, Post-its, and drawing pins.

Trainer materials
Finally, set out the trainer's guide and transparencies at the front of the room. Check that all the supplies you need are close to hand. Make sure you have the latest version of the student materials in front of you. In this way you will not have the embarrassment of referring to the wrong page or to an exercise that was removed three courses ago.

Final check
When you think you have finished setting up the room take a few moments to look round the room and check that everything is in place. Make sure that you know:

- where the keys are kept,
- where the light switches are,

- how to control the heating, and
- how to open and close the windows and the window blinds.

Then turn off all the equipment at the wall, turn off the lights and lock up the room.

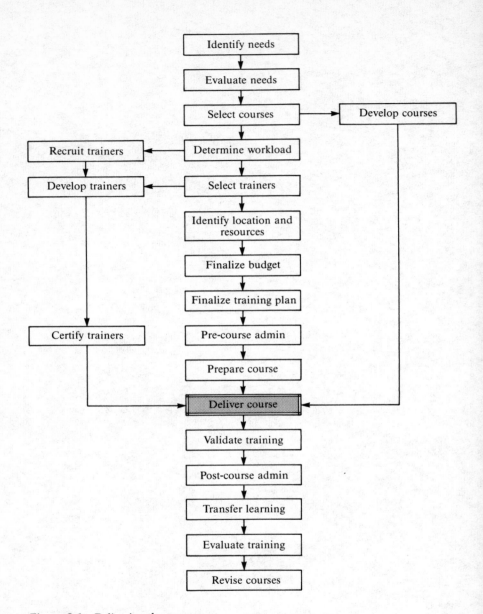

Figure 9.1　*Delivering the course*

9 Delivering the course

This chapter deals with the pivotal step of the training process:

- course delivery.

Because the thrust of this book is about managing the training process, rather than learning to be a trainer, the emphasis in this chapter is on the principles associated with the steps of the delivery process, plus consideration of the following three topics:

- open and distance learning;
- training in other languages and cultures;
- the use of computers in the classroom.

Course delivery process

The process for delivering a course is shown in Fig. 9.2.

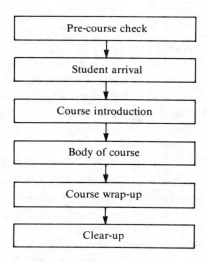

Figure 9.2 *Course delivery process*

Pre-course check

Although you should have already prepared for the course, it is worth taking a few minutes to check that the following are still in order:

- lights,
- materials,
- overhead projector, and
- video equipment.

The telephone   You will already have asked reception not to put calls through to the training room. As an extra precaution I would also recommend diverting the calls or disconnecting the telephone from the socket—it is amazing how persuasive some people can be in trying to contact their staff.

If you forget to disconnect the telephone and it rings while you are in the middle of a session, keep talking while you walk over and disconnect the phone. Ignore the gasps of amazement—some people are psychologically unable to resist the call of a ringing telephone.

Don't worry about the call being urgent—they seldom are—most things can wait for 45 minutes. If it was a matter of life or death you can be sure somebody will ring the alarm bells or run round to the classroom.

Spike Milligan once drew a cartoon of a person who was tied, head-to-toe, to a post. The only part of this person's anatomy you could see was an arm sticking out between the coils of rope.

A ringing telephone was placed on a pedestal that was just out of reach of the arm. The cartoon was entitled: 'Chinese Telephone Torture'.

Student arrival

The impression the students get within the first few minutes can make all the difference to the success of the course. If the course is residential it is essential that the registration goes smoothly, and the rooms are clean and available. If you are not able to meet them as they arrive, it is a good idea to leave a welcoming letter at reception. The letter can also include additional details about the course and its location.

Be in the classroom before the first student arrives so you are there to greet them. The important thing to remember about this step is that you want the student to feel comfortable about the training.

Coffee   One way to help students feel comfortable when they arrive is to have coffee available. This gives them a chance to relax and to get to know each other.

Dress code   The participants' joining instructions will have advised them on the level of dress that is expected to be worn on the course. The recommended level of clothing is part of the course design, and depends on where the course is being run and the training philosophy of the course.

Some training courses are designed to have a more informal atmosphere so students are asked to dress casually. No matter what is put in the joining instructions, it is another one of those unwritten laws of the universe that at least one of the students will turn up wearing a business suit, and will continue to wear a suit for the rest of the week. There is no problem with this as long as the person feels comfortable with what they are wearing.

Whatever the dress code, the cardinal rule is that trainers should not be dressed very differently from the students. If a trainer adopts a dress style which is the same as the most casually dressed student, the more smartly dressed may start to feel uncomfortable; and vice versa. The best approach is for trainers to try and adopt a level of dress that is at about the middle of the students' range.

As the students arrive you will get a feeling for the level of dress. If the level of dress is biased towards one end of the dress code, you can subtly amend your dress. This can be as simple as removing a jacket or rolling up your sleeves.

Late arrivals

Always insist that training courses start on time. I know there is always a temptation to wait for late arrivals, but there is no way of knowing how long they are going to be or whether they are going to turn up at all. Waiting punishes the people who have been punctual and destroys the momentum that is required at the start of a course. Five minutes lost at the start of a course often translates into an hour's loss by the end of the course.

When the latecomers arrive do not make any fuss and do not stop the course to bring them up to speed. Making a fuss just disrupts the course and could lead to strained relationships. Stopping to summarize communicates that it is all right to be late because the trainer will always bring you up to date.

Course introduction

The purpose of the course introduction is for:

- you to get to know the students,
- the students to get to know you,
- the students to get to know each other,
- communication of the course aims and structure,
- validating student expectations,
- understanding the reasons for them being on the course, and
- communicating course logistics.

If there are two trainers, consider having both trainers take part in the introduction as the co-trainer is often disadvantaged by having to sit at the back of the room.

Student introductions The standard course introduction is to go round the room and have the students give a brief autobiography to include:

- their name,
- job title,
- organization,
- how long they have been in the company, and
- hobbies and interests.

This method is a bit pedestrian and it often does not achieve what it sets out to achieve. People stop listening when they are thinking about what they are going to say. In a class of 20 this introduction can take up to an hour and each person is only directly involved for 5 per cent of the time. Here are some variations you might like to try.

Claim to fame
Most people have met somebody famous or have done something excitingly different. Most people like talking about it. So, instead of getting people to do the standard introduction you could get them to relate their claims to fame.

The best claims to fame don't always come out during the course introduction so have another session later in the course if you want to hear the juicier stories.

Paired interviews
Some people do not like talking about themselves in front of the class. In this type of introduction the students pair up with the person they know the least and interview each other. After about 15 minutes each person reports back with a brief biography of their partner.

A picture of my life
Provide coloured pens and sheets of A3 drawing paper. Ask the students to draw a picture of who they are and what they do—both at work and at home. You will find that people, despite initial reservations, really get into this exercise and disclose more about themselves.

Catch ball
Instead of going round the class in order, throw a ball (preferably a soft one) to one of the students who then does the first introduction. This student then throws the ball to someone else. Challenge the class to complete the introductions without throwing the ball to the same person twice. It is probably a good idea to clear the coffee cups before starting this exercise!

Mugshot
Ask the students to bring either a passport photograph or their identity badges to the course. Display the photographs on the wall along with an identifying letter (the identity badges should have the names taped over). Supply each student with a copy of the course list which has had

the names substituted with the identifying letters. The objective of the exercise is to write the names of the other students against their identifying letters on the course list. This involves matching the people in the room with the photographs on the wall. When approached, people should only give their name. They should not say which photograph is theirs. The worse the photographs, the better this exercise works.

Course logistics

Communicate the minimum of course logistics at the beginning of the course—very little is remembered of an information dump. Obviously emergency procedures need to be given at the beginning but coffee, lunch, and dinner arrangements, etc., can be communicated as they are needed.

Training course or assessment centre?

It is important to communicate whether a report will be sent back to the students' managers.

Unfortunately, some managers expect training courses to do the job of assessing how good their people are at doing their current job. Apart from the fact that this would be an abdication of one of the manager's prime responsibilities, training courses are not adept at and, for that matter, not designed for carrying out this task. The environment on a training course is very different to the work environment. If it were exactly the same, there would be no difference between formal training and on-the-job training. This difference in environment means that an observed behaviour on a training course would not necessarily be a good predictor of behaviour back at work. The ability of a trainer to accurately assess 20 individuals on a week's course would also have to be questioned. It can take up to two days to learn all the names!

If you assume each student participates equally and the exercises where behaviour could be assessed make up 60 per cent of the course, you would only have a maximum of one hour's data on each person. Not a very efficient assessment process.

If the students work in subgroups, it is the other members of the subgroup who are in the best position to make an assessment of an individual. I am not suggesting students should 'spy' on their fellow students, but feedback to an individual from other class members can, if handled sensitively, be very powerful.

At this point it is worth pointing out the difference between training courses and assessment centres. Training courses are for increasing knowledge and the development of new skills. Assessment centres are designed to measure or assess existing skills.

In the development of new skills it is essential for a person to be able to reveal their current deficiencies, and then to experiment and make mistakes without being punished. It follows that confidentiality is an essential part of a training course. If a person feels that everything they do is being reported back to the organization or their manager, they will be very reluctant to participate openly and the training will not be as effective.

With assessment centres the question of confidentiality does not arise because everybody knows and accepts that a report will be made.

It might be argued that it is essential for a person's manager to know whether that person has reached the desired standard in the skills that they were expected to learn. This is a reasonable request and complying with it need not be inconsistent with the principles outlined above.

With self-paced training a person could in theory remain on the course, receiving additional coaching until the desired level of expertise is attained. Thus, completion of the course itself would be the indicator of meeting the required standards.

Of course it would not be good business practice to allow everybody to stay on a course for an infinite period, so most courses would have an upper limit to the duration. Above this limit it would be uneconomic to continue the training to completion. It would also probably indicate that the student concerned would be very unlikely to make the grade under any circumstances.

You should consider any failure to complete a course as an error in the process and a waste of your limited training resources. The cause of this kind of error is usually in the selection of the student for the course or the selection of the course for the student.

With trainer-paced courses the completion of the course gives no indication of the standard reached unless a student is sent home early. So how can the organization be assured that individuals have attained the necessary standards without reducing the effectiveness of the training? The answer is to make a distinction between the parts of the course where learning is taking place and the parts of the course which are assessed.

You would have to make this distinction very clear at the beginning of the course and assure the students that no reports are being made during the teaching phase. Under no circumstances should you imply that there is confidentiality where in fact there is none. Not only would this breach professional etiquette, but would quickly lose you all trust and ruin your reputation.

Expectations and reasons for being on the course

Take some time to understand what people are expecting from the course and why they are attending it. You will find the course will meet most people's expectations but there will also be some expectations that the course was not designed to meet. Be open about the extent to which the course will meet your students' expectations.

Understand the reasons for the students being on the course—this will help you deal with any emotional issues that might arise during the course.

Course aims and structure

Describe the aims and structure of the course. Explain what will happen and when it will happen. Describe the linkages between the components. Take the opportunity to emphasize the parts of the course which best meet the students' expectations.

I like to have the course agenda displayed as a poster. (For a five-day course this could be as big as three sheets of flip chart paper.) The students can then refer to this at any time to check where they are, and you can use it to reinforce the course structure as you move between components.

Body of course

I believe that there are four main phases in teaching:

- presentation,
- assimilation,
- practice, and
- testing.

Presentation

In this context presentation has a broader meaning than is usually understood. It includes any method that presents the skills and facts to the students. So, in addition to the trainer standing up and making a presentation, it would also include videos, demonstrations, text, and self-discovery exercises.

We learn through all of our senses (the usual six, plus sense of movement and rhythm), yet training makes limited use of only two—auditory and visual. Try introducing more colour into your presentations. Have exercises that involve movement and people doing things with their hands. Try presenting a lesson to the accompaniment of baroque music.

Assimilation

After presenting the facts or demonstrating the skills the temptation is to go straight on to the next set of facts without allowing an opportunity for learning to take place. Even if the skills are practised and the knowledge tested the assimilation phase is often left out. By assimilation we mean the process by which the students are given 'space' to make sense of what they have just heard and seen. It also allows them to fit this new knowledge into their existing model of the world. If the training proceeds before they have had this opportunity, the course will be building on a very shaky foundation.

This opportunity can be given in several ways. You can give the students a couple of minutes to reflect, you can get them to jot down a few notes, and you can give them the opportunity to ask questions. If you presented the lesson to the accompaniment of music you can replay the music to help the assimilation.

Practice

The third phase is for the students to practise what they have been taught. Practice is an absolutely essential part of learning, so it is a pity that it is the first thing to go when the pressure is on to reduce the duration of a training course. The only circumstance under which you should permit the removal of practice from a course is when you can guarantee that supervised practice will occur immediately after the course has finished.

There is sometimes a debate on whether the skills should be practised on case studies or on real examples. The argument against case studies is that it is difficult to use the skills outside of the classroom because case studies are too simple and unrealistic. The argument against using real projects is that they are too complex and the students will spend far too much energy on the detail to the exclusion of learning the concepts. As with many 'either/or' arguments the answer is not 'either/or' but 'both'.

The process I prefer for courses where the appropriate teaching style is more 'directed' rather than 'discovery' is as follows.

- First give an 'overview' of the concept, principle, or process.
- Then demonstrate, using a simple example. Don't worry if the example seems trivial; this will allow some humour to creep in and will make the demonstration of the skills all the more memorable. For example, you could use a 'tea-making' example for teaching critical path analysis and have a heated discussion about whether the milk should be poured into the cup before or after the tea.
- After the simple example the students can then practise on a more complex case study.
- Finally, they can be coached on an example from their own work area. If they have any difficulties they can always refer back to the example and the case study.

Testing   Finally you should check the extent to which the students have learnt the skills and knowledge. This could be a formal pencil and paper test, but more effective, and incidentally less intimidating, is the observation of the student applying the learning to a project or their own work. This also increases the chances of the learning being transferred back into the business.

Another way of testing is for the trainer to ask questions in class. Even better, get the students to write the questions themselves.

Instead of using the 'pose then pounce' or 'pounce then pose' techniques try asking the question as you throw a ball to the student ('throw *and* pose' technique). Throwing the ball is not a gimmick; the idea is to distract the student's conscious attention so the answer can surface from the subconscious. Suitable balls for this exercise are either sponge balls or balls that have been constructed from strands of rubber in the fashion of a pompom.

> I had some reservations about the 'catch ball' technique until I used it to help teach a dozen theories of motivation and leadership.
>
> The lesson included a videotape which described all 12 theories in 40 minutes: obviously too much to take in at one go. I had already split up the tape with discussions about the theories, and I also had 'stills' from the video on display. Despite this it was still apparent that the students had little confidence that they could remember the theories. I decided it might be worth while trying the 'catch ball' technique.
>
> After showing the video I called a coffee break to allow the students to relax and to give some time for assimilation. When they returned I named one of the theories and threw the ball to one of the students. Immediately the student explained what the theory meant. The ball was thrown from student to student, each student explaining one theory and naming another. To our amazement all the theories were accurately recalled.

Accelerated learning

Some of the techniques described above were first developed in 1956 at the University of Sofia by the Bulgarian psychologist Dr Georgi Lozanov. Colin Rose's book *Accelerated Learning* describes these techniques in more detail.

Level of intervention

One of the things that is the most difficult to get right is the trainer's level of intervention with the students. If students have problems with a task it is best if they can sort the problems out for themselves. If they can't sort out the problems for themselves, and the trainer does not intervene, they begin to flounder and lose confidence. If the trainer intervenes too early the students become frustrated and learn little. In extreme cases the trainer ends up doing the task for the student.

The best way to find the correct level of intervention is to identify the parts of the course where students are likely to have a problem, monitor regularly and discreetly, and to err slightly towards intervening too late. (It is difficult to tell whether you intervened too early because they might have got on to the right track if you had not intervened.)

The pudding shift

The pudding shift, otherwise known as the graveyard shift, is the session that immediately follows the lunch break. It is difficult to get concentration and attention then because this is the time when we would rather be having a siesta. For this reason it is best to avoid presentations and have a participative exercise immediately after lunch.

Course wrap-up

During the course wrap-up you should:

- check whether the students' expectations have been met;
- have the students complete a course feedback form;

- thank the students for their participation and share your feelings about the course;
- if applicable, distribute certificates;
- stand near the door to say goodbye as they leave.

> At the end of every course, a colleague of mine used to say that this was the best course he had ever taught and that he loved them all!
>
> Now the amazing thing about this was that he really believed it—and, more amazingly, so did the class!

Clear-up

The end of a course can be a bit of an anticlimax, but you need to pack up the materials and to take a few minutes to think about how the course went.

- Ask yourself how you feel. If you feel down, consider what you could do better next time. If you're on a high, the course might have gone exceedingly well, but check to make sure you were not playing games with the class. Feeling quietly pleased is a good position to be in.
- Look through the feedback forms. You will find more on this in Chapter 10.
- Clear up the rubbish so the cleaners can distinguish between what should be thrown away and what should be kept.
- Pack up the materials that need to be sent back to store.
- Send a copy of the feedback and attendance sheets to the appropriate administrator.

Open and distance learning

In Chapter 5 we discussed the 'Identify Location and Resources' step of the training process. An important part of this step is to determine the type of learning environment. We usually think of the classroom when we talk about the learning environment. Although the classroom provides a controlled environment, it is usually more expensive and does not provide the flexibility of 'open learning' or 'distance learning'.

The terms 'open learning' and 'distance learning' are used interchangeably as this type of learning is usually 'open' to everyone (as with the Open University) and is carried out 'at a distance' from the creators of the material.

Learning can be at home, in the workplace, or in specially adapted rooms known as 'open learning centres'. These rooms are resource centres and usually come equipped with books, audiotapes, videotapes and computer programs—along with all the necessary equipment. The great advantage of open learning is that students can study at their own pace and at their own convenience.

The need, selection, development, administration, and delivery of open learning courses should be given the same attention as any other type of course. If this is not done the use of open learning will become haphazard and random, and will fall into disrepute. The training process described in this book applies to open learning as much as it does to any other kind of learning. The principles of managing the training process remain the same.

Training in foreign languages and cultures

Unfortunately the British tend not to be fluent in any language other than their own. When compared to other nationalities such as the Scandinavians and the Dutch we are truly put to shame. Yes, English is spoken widely, and few other countries speak Swedish or Dutch, which makes it easier for them and harder for us. However, this is not a good excuse for refusing to learn even a few words of another's language.

Whatever our level of linguistic expertise, most of us still have a problem when faced with a class of foreign students. Of course the problem is minimized if all your students speak excellent English. In this case you should be able to train the course in the same way as you do for English students.

It is often assumed that the course should be presented in the students' own language and that all the materials should be translated if the students' command of English is less than perfect. Luckily, there are several levels of translation that can be applied and this can be critical when time or cost is at a premium. Table 9.1 shows the relationship between the level of translation and the standard of English.

When the language ability is very high all the presentations, materials, and exercises can be in English.

Where the command of the language is not perfect, but still very good, the presentation and materials can still be in English but the participants should be allowed to complete the exercises in their own language. It is still possible to use English trainers. If a translator is not available they will have to rely on their knowledge of the course, body language, and tone of voice to understand what is going on. This is not as difficult as it might seem because a trainer who has an intimate knowledge of the exercises will soon be aware of any problems or difficulties. It is then just a matter of intervening and asking what is happening.

The next level is to have the course presented in the students' own language, but still have the written materials in English. Videotapes would have to over-dubbed. When producing videotapes that are to be used abroad make sure the master has two soundtracks. The first track should have the music and sound effects, and the second track should have all the language-sensitive material. This makes the dubbing of the foreign language very much easier.

As the language ability decreases, more and more of the materials will need to be translated. However, not all of the written materials will

Table 9.1 *Relationship between language ability and the level of translation*

	High	Good	Fair	Poor
Exercises	English	own language	own language	own language
Materials	English	English	translate	translate
Presentations	English	English	English	own language

need to be translated unless the language ability is very low. Articles and explanations of concepts would need to be translated, but simple instructions may not.

Some companies use a restricted vocabulary to write the service manuals for their engineers, so the time and cost of translation can be avoided. The author is asked to use only a vocabulary of about a thousand of the most commonly used words. The words in this vocabulary are carefully chosen and they are also defined to have only one meaning. If the user is taught the same vocabulary, the service manual can be understood by somebody with a minimal knowledge of the language.

The use of restricted vocabulary also makes computer-assisted translation easier. Computer translation has come a long way since the time when a computer's Russian translation of 'The spirit is strong, but the flesh is weak' as 'The vodka is good, but the meat is bad'. However, the best use of computer-assisted translation is still as a translator's tool, where the original and the computer's translation are shown 'side by side' on the screen. The translator is then able to make adjustments for grammar, idioms, and style.

Culture is a thin but very important veneer that you must be very careful not to scratch. People are basically the same and respond in the same way. Make sure you understand the basic customs, and show an interest and willingness to learn the differences between your cultures.

One of the most surprising things I have experienced is that there is often less difference between people of differing nationalities who share

---

The meaning of Chinese words changes with the pitch of the voice. A word spoken at a low pitch has a completely different meaning to the same word spoken at a higher pitch.

I was aware of this, but I was still caught out when I was teaching a class of Singaporeans.

I was asking Tng a question but I didn't seem to be getting his attention. To make matters worse the whole class burst out laughing.

When I asked what the problem was, they told me that I had been saying 'Tng' with a high, instead of low, pitch—I had been telling him to go home!

the same profession, than between people of the same nationality who work in different professions. The cultural differences between companies, between civilians and service people, and between sales, marketing, and manufacturing are fascinating, and can easily catch out the unwary.

The use of computers in the classroom

A computer is a tool—no more, no less. Computers are excellent for running business simulations and can be used to present instructional material. There is some very effective computer-based training around.

When it comes to training, a computer is just one media among many. Just like any other media it is appropriate in some situations and less appropriate in others. The most effective training is usually a skilful blend of differing media.

One of the most effective uses of computers is to use them as part of a simulation. In this way it is possible to give students very fast feedback on their decisions and actions.

A computer is not only a useful tool for training, but it can also bring large increases in course administration productivity. If you find yourself spending a lot of time on a repetitive task, consider whether a computer could give you a productivity increase.

Interactive skills observations involve categorizing people's verbal behaviour. Every time a person speaks the observer records the interaction as one of 11 types of behaviour.

After the observation the observer has to perform a series of calculations which involves working out each type of behaviour as a percentage of the person's total number of behaviours. With a class of 20 this would typically take two hours to complete—even with the assistance of a calculator. Not only did this take up a lot of the trainer's time, but it also meant that the students would often not get feedback until the following day.

This time was cut in half by using a computer with a spreadsheet program. After the observation, data was fed into the computer and the spreadsheet performed the calculations.

The time was cut even more dramatically by using a hand-held computer to record the observations directly. The hand-held computer was then connected to a printer and the students received a copy of their feedback within five minutes of the last observation being made!

The following is a checklist of activities where a computer can improve your productivity:

- preparing course materials,
- revising course materials,
- record keeping,
- presenting slides,

- making slides,
- course administration (delegate lists, subgroup composition, certificate lists, certificates),
- interactive skills observation and analysis,
- business simulations,
- analysis and presentation of course statistics,
- communication via electronic mail,
- access to centralized training records,
- computer-assisted learning,
- computer-assisted personality testing, and
- computer-assisted career counselling.

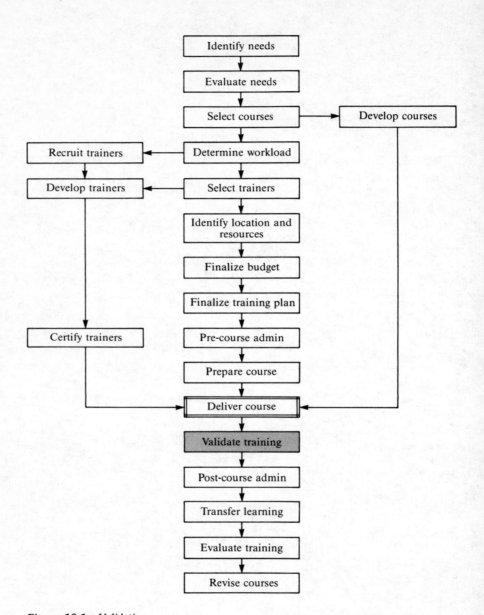

Figure 10.1   *Validation*

10 Validation

Validation ensures that the course meets, and continues to meet, the aims and objectives you set for it. Validation is an internal check on the course. The following is the definition of validation used in this book:

A systematic analysis of data and judgemental information, collected during a training course, which is designed to ascertain whether the course achieved its specified aims and objectives.

See Chapter 12 for a discussion of other definitions of validation and their origins.

Validation does not give you information on whether the students will use the skills and knowledge. It does not tell you whether those skills and knowledge contribute anything towards business effectiveness. Neither does it tell you whether the objectives were the right ones. I might have learned how to play 'Rachmaninov's third piano concerto', but will this help me manage a group of sales people when I get back to work? It is evaluation, the subject of Chapter 12, that deals with these questions.

Validation is critical because learning cannot be transferred to the business unless the course has met its objectives. Good validation systems show us not only what needs to be changed, but they also prevent us from changing a course for change's sake. They give an early warning of a drift in the course's standards before disaster occurs.

Validation tells us whether the course has had the desired effect. There are two perspectives from which this can be done:

- validating against student perceptions and comments, and
- validating against the course objectives.

Validating against student perceptions and comments

The first way of seeing whether the course meets its objectives is from the student's point of view. This is often done using end-of-course feedback sheets (sometimes called 'Happiness Sheets') comprising a questionnaire and a comments section. The questionnaire asks how much the students liked the course, whether they thought they met the objectives, and what they thought of the trainer. It also gives them an opportunity to make open-ended comments.

MANAGEMENT DEVELOPMENT PROGRAMME FEEDBACK

Directions: Please take a few minutes to respond to some of the statements about the course as a *whole*. Answer each statement by placing a tick in the appropriate box to the right of the statement. Space has been provided for any comments you might wish to add.

1. Relevance of workshop to your present job

    ☐ ☐ ☐ ☐ ☐
    Very Low   Very High

Comments : _____

_____

_____

2. Confidence in your ability to use the skills and knowledge

    ☐ ☐ ☐ ☐ ☐
    Very Low   Very High

Comments : _____

_____

_____

3. Usefulness of the pre-work

    ☐ ☐ ☐ ☐ ☐
    Not Useful   Very Useful

Comments : _____

_____

_____

4. Overall satisfaction with the course

    ☐ ☐ ☐ ☐ ☐
    Very Low   Very High

Comments : _____

_____

_____

5. One change you recommend for improving the workshop: _____

_____

_____

6. One aspect of the workshop that should be left as it is: _____

_____

_____

THANK YOU FOR YOUR ASSISTANCE

Figure 10.2 *An example of a course feedback sheet*

Figure 10.2 is an example of a typical feedback sheet. Most courses get the students to complete a feedback sheet at the end of the course.

Make sure that the sheet has a space for the student's name. Some people feel feedback should be anonymous, so the students do not feel restricted in the feedback they give. Unfortunately anonymous sheets prevent you from following up comments to get further clarification or to clear up confusion.

Explain why it is useful to have the names on the feedback sheet, but let them know that their feedback can be anonymous if they prefer. If you have established trust and credibility during the course, the students should not feel they need to withhold their names.

Feedback sheets give you data on how the students feel at the end of the course, but they do not tell you much about how they felt along the way. This interim information is essential for continually improving the training process. Avoid giving the students a questionnaire to complete after every course module. You might get away with this on a pilot course, but under other circumstances they will become rapidly frustrated.

A technique we use is to provide the students with some cards. They write their comments on one of the cards whenever they feel they have some feedback to give us. A 'postbox' is provided at the back of the class. Once a day we review the comments, give responses to the feedback, and, where necessary, clear up any misunderstandings.

Halo effect The danger with perceptions is that many different factors affect them. The halo effect occurs when a student judges a course in terms of a general feeling.

For example, some trainers are skilled performers, they have the class eating out of their hands, and they get amazingly good feedback regardless of how good or indifferent the course is. The students are judging the course in terms of how they feel about the trainer.

The halo effect also works in a negative direction. Students might give a course poor feedback because they had a bad experience on a previous course or because they have had problems with accommodation, or they might not feel too good because of a hangover.

Despite this weakness, student feedback is essential. Student perception is one of the major factors that determine a course's credibility and reputation. Student perceptions and comments are also essential for identifying unexpected effects of the training.

Validating against course objectives

The second way of looking at validation is to see whether the students met the course objectives. Checking whether the students have met the objectives can be either very difficult or very easy—it all depends on the quality of the objectives.

If the objectives meet the guidelines given in Chapter 3 you will know what behaviours to test, the conditions to test them under, and the standards that should be reached.

Testing or measuring is implicit in validating a course against its objectives. A test does not have to be a 'pencil and paper' examination. It can just as easily be an observed exercise where the trainer records the results on a check chart.

Reacting to validation data

Be careful how you respond to validation data. It is all too easy to either overreact or to rationalize problems away. Overreaction can make the course lurch from one extreme to the other.

For example, an exercise receives some negative feedback the first time you run a course, so you decide to remove the exercise. The next time you run the course you find that important objectives are not being met, so you reinstate the exercise. On the third course the exercise receives more negative feedback . . .

It's similar to the way some people adjust the thermostat on a radiator. The room is feeling a bit cold so they turn the control up to maximum. After a while they start feeling hot, so they turn the control down to minimum. When the temperature drops . . .

They end up spending all day adjusting the thermostat while the room temperature lurches from being too hot, to being too cold, and back again. What they should do is let the system settle down and then only make minor adjustments when necessary. What is needed is a light touch on the steering wheel.

Although one piece of feedback may not mean anything by itself, you shouldn't fall into the trap of ignoring obvious problems. Too often we avoid taking action because we don't have a 'statistically significant' sample.

How many plane crashes does it take for us to think that something is wrong? How many times does a coin have to come up heads before we suspect that something was wrong with the coin?

Deciding when to react to feedback or a deviation is a difficult judgement to make. After the course has run several times you will begin to get a feeling for what is normal, and what is significant variation. The decision then depends on the intuition and experience of the individual trainer.

The problem is similar to deciding when to adjust a machine on a manufacturing line. Until the introduction of Total Quality Management the decision was either left to the operator's experience, or nothing was done until the product drifted out of specification. The entire batch would then have to be inspected, and as much as 20 per cent of the production would have to be scrapped.

Statistical process control

Manufacturing's answer to the problem of when to react to deviations is statistical process control (SPC). The idea behind SPC is to collect data on a process and statistically determine what is abnormal variation. These data are displayed on a control chart. The chart has two lines, an upper control limit (UCL) and a lower control limit (LCL), drawn on it.

The operator takes no corrective action as long as the data remain between the two control limits. If the data go outside the limits, the operator knows the variation is significant and requires action before the process goes out of specification. This is similar to a driver turning the steering wheel before the car hits the kerb.

Figure 10.3 gives an example of a control chart for the manufacture of a 10 mm disc whose diameter should be a minimum of 9.90 mm and a maximum of 10.10 mm.

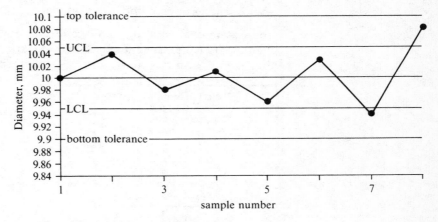

Figure 10.3 *An example of a control chart*

Applying SPC to training validation

When you are running the same course many times (such as when you are training every employee) it is possible to collect sufficient data to apply statistical process control to the validation results.

SPC allows you to detect changes in the course performance which are due to significant causes. It allows you to check whether different trainers are training to the same standard. It shows you whether the course, in its present form, is capable of meeting the objectives. Most importantly, it gives you an indication of when you should not make changes to a course.

Measurements versus targets

The very act of measurement has the effect of distorting the data. If we are sensitive in how we carry out validation, the distortion should not make a significant difference to the results. Measurements are essential for maintaining the quality of our courses and we should do everything to reduce distortion to a minimum.

A single measurement is not a complete description of a course's quality. At best it is a prime indicator. The number of measurements required to define a course's quality completely would be so large as to make any validation system unwieldy. This need not be a problem as long as we take care in choosing the measurements we use as prime indicators of quality.

However, the moment a measure is turned into a target the underlying weaknesses of using a few measures become apparent. (This is compounded when a trainer's pay increase is directly linked to measures such as student perception of 'trainer effectiveness'.)

Trainers will soon subconsciously realize which unmeasured indicators can be sacrificed to improve the measured ones. They will also learn which are the best times to make the measurements—such as just after telling the class they are the best students they have ever trained, or after breaking open a bottle of champagne!

The way to deal with this is not to dispense with measures, but to make the trainers responsible for their own quality. It is very unlikely that they would, even subconsciously, deceive themselves.

Figure 10.4   The validation process

The validation process

Figure 10.4 gives an overview of the validation process. First, the data have to be collected throughout the course. Student perceptions, comments, and test results are examples of validation data. A preliminary assessment is made at the end of the course, while the course and any incidents are still fresh in the trainer's mind.

Next the data have to be organized and displayed so you can see whether the feedback is significant or just due to natural variation.

Then the data have to be analysed and interpreted so you can determine the causes of the significant variations. Once you have understood the causes it is possible to make changes to the course. Always make the smallest adjustment consistent with solving the problem.

The next time you run the course you will need to go through the process of collecting and analysing the data again. This is to check that the changes have had the desired effect.

The remainder of this chapter looks at these steps of the validation process in detail.

```
Collect perceptions,
comments, test
results, and other
performance measures
```

When collecting perceptions, it is common practice to use feedback forms with five-point response scales. The responses can be numbered or labelled. These responses have different labels depending on the type of questions asked.

Table 10.1 summarizes some of the more common labels and relates them to the five-point scale. Figure 10.5 gives examples of the types of questions that are used with the different labels.

Table 10.1 *Relationship of different labels to a five-point response scale*

	1	2	3	4	5
A	Very poor	Poor	Fair	Good	Very good
B	Very unsatisfied	Unsatisfied	Fairly satisfied	Satisfied	Very satisfied
C	Very low	Low	Medium	High	Very high
D	Strongly disagree	Disagree	Neutral	Agree	Strongly agree
E	Much too short	Too short	Just right	Too long	Much too long

A	What opinion do you have of the course?
B	How satisfied are you with the course?
C	What is the probability of you using the skills when you go back to work?
D	The course is the best that I have been on.
E	The length of the course is . . .

Figure 10.5   *Types of question used with the different labels*

Deciding whether '1' represents 'Very Poor' or 'Very Good' is an arbitrary decision. I use the convention of 'higher equals better'. The exception to this is scale 'E' where the best score is '3'. Be careful when you are using this type of scale as it can lead to confusion.

I also have the numbers run from '1' on the left-hand side to '5' on the right-hand side. This corresponds to the way Western cultures read across the page. It also makes it easier to use graphical display programs because this is the convention used for graphs.

Always stick to the same convention, no matter which one you decide to choose. Always give a warning when the scale changes.

Although rating questions against a five-point scale is a very popular format, it has the disadvantage of driving inconsistent definitions for the responses. People have varying views of what 'Very Poor', 'Poor', 'Fair', 'Good', and 'Very Good' mean. You get better consistency when it is possible to frame the feedback questions in the form of opposites (see Fig. 10.6).

	1	2	3	4	5	
The trainer did not give satisfactory answers to any of my questions by the end of the course.				X		The trainer gave satisfactory answers to all of my questions by the end of the course.

Figure 10.6   *Using opposites as feedback questions*

This format produces a five-point continuum and the students put an 'X' in the column that best matches their perception.

The wording used in Fig. 10.6 can have the effect of grouping the responses around the middle because of the 'all or nothing' nature of the extremes. One way round this is to use a seven-point scale so there is more definition around the middle.

Another way to avoid the problem is to reword the questions. Don't make the wording too weak as this will reintroduce the problem of inconsistent definition. Figure 10.7 gives an example of weak wording. (Does 'most', mean 50, 60, or 80 per cent?) Figure 10.8 gives a better example.

	1	2	3	4	5	
The trainer gave unsatisfactory answers to most of my questions.			X			The trainer gave satisfactory answers to most of my questions.

Figure 10.7 *Example of weak wording for feedback questions*

	1	2	3	4	5	
I was very unsatisfied with the answers the trainer gave to my questions.				X		I was very satisfied with the answers the trainer gave to my questions.

Figure 10.8 *Example of stronger wording for feedback questions*

Make sure that the questions used are true opposites, otherwise this format becomes very confusing. Figure 10.9 gives an example of questions that are not true opposites.

	1	2	3	4	5	
The trainer did not seem to care about whether I learned.		?		?		The trainer was very enthusiastic about the course.

Figure 10.9 *Example of questions that are not true opposites*

Collecting comments Although feedback on a five-point scale is easy to display and analyse, it is restrictive because you will only get feedback on what you asked for. Neither does a cross on a one-to-five scale give many clues to the reasons for the response. To overcome this each question should have a comments space for the students to expand on their responses.

Also, leave space at the end of the questionnaire for general comments which will give you feedback on aspects you never dreamt about when you were designing the questionnaire. Good questions for stimulating a response are as follows:

- Is there anything that should be left out of the course?
- Is there anything that should be put into the course?
- What should be kept as it is?
- Is there anything that should be done differently?
- Any other comments?

Collecting test results

A test is a measure of whether the behavioural objectives of the course have been met. As tests should be based firmly on the objectives, your students should not be surprised by any of the test items.

The objectives should also give you the required standard as in: 'Given a list of 20 countries you will be able to name the capital cities of at least 17 of those countries.' Many objectives, like that one, lend themselves to written tests. Others are best tested through observations of practical exercises. The observations can then be compared to a checklist or a profile of behaviours.

Good trainers constantly validate their training by asking questions as they go along. Although you can get a feeling for the level of knowledge by noting how many students want to answer, you can only be sure that one person knows the correct answer. One way round this is to ask multi-choice questions. Each student is given a device which allows them to display their response to the question. A Cosford responder (see Fig. 10.10) is an example of such a device.

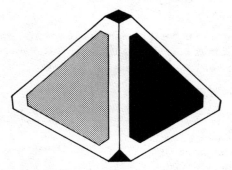

Figure 10.10   A Cosford responder

A Cosford responder is a cardboard tetrahedron which has a different colour on each of its faces. Each colour represents a different response to the question. In this way the trainer can easily see which students responded correctly.

Collecting other performance measures

Look out for other indicators which tell you how the course is progressing and whether you need to make any adjustments as you go along. Be as creative as you can. The following are some suggestions.

Room tidiness
A colleague of mine once said that the success of a course is inversely proportional to the tidiness of the room. At first I thought this was just

a clever remark, but the more I think about it the more I am convinced it has a relationship to the participants' energy level.

Smiley charts
A smiley chart is used to collect student perceptions during a course. The chart is drawn on flip chart paper and at the end of the day the students are asked how they feel. The trainer makes a mark or puts the student's initials in the appropriate square. These feelings are then explored by the trainer.

Figure 10.11 *Smiley chart*

Stress level chart
A stress level chart works in a similar way to a smiley chart, but it is based on the premise that everyone has an optimum stress level. If the stress level is too low, people become lethargic and are not motivated to learn. Too high a stress level interferes with learning. The stress level chart allows you to monitor the parts of the course which are too challenging and those parts which are too easy.

Working-on
A measure of student interest and motivation is whether groups continue working on projects after the 'official' end of the day. This does not mean they have to 'burn the midnight oil' every night.

	Mon	Tue	Wed	Thu	Fri
Stress too high					
Optimum stress					
Stress too low					

Figure 10.12   *Stress level chart*

Talking-on

On a residential course see whether your students make jokes or talk about the course content in the bar. This will give you a useful indication of interest and retention. It is even better if they impose cash penalties on each other for talking about the course.

Alertness

Note when the students start to drift off, start to be distracted, or their eyelids start to droop.

Quiz challenge

Asking questions is a good method of measuring learning. A variation on this is to split the class into three or four groups and ask them to write questions for each other. The number and quality of the questions will give you an additional measure.

> Make a preliminary
> assessment of
> feedback data

At the end of the course you should collect all the evaluation sheets and test results. Immediately count the feedback sheets to make sure you have received one from every person. Also check to see if there have been any omissions—sometimes people forget to complete part or some of the questions. It is much easier to collect the missing data now rather than after your students have returned to work.

Incidentally, you should initially suspect that omissions are caused by the feedback form rather than being a 'student problem'. For example, we should not blame the students for failing to complete the second side of a feedback sheet if we have not printed 'continued on other side . . .' on the first side of the sheet.

Scan through the sheets, and look for obvious patterns and messages. Don't delay doing this—even if it means spoiling your evening or weekend! Timely feedback is the most effective feedback. Some comments are difficult to understand at the best of times. By the time you get back to the office, you will have even more difficulty understanding the comments.

Preliminary assessment of comments

Read the comments and try to recall any incidents that might have triggered the comment. Look for the same comment coming from different people. Make a mental note of those comments that will need further clarification, and those people you will need to give additional explanation of the concepts.

Preliminary assessment of perceptions

Look at the scores that have been given for the feedback categories. You won't be able to make many conclusions without doing further analysis, but make a mental note of those scores which stand out as being very high or very low. Check to see if these scores have comments associated with them.

Preliminary assessment of test results

Look through the test results to see if the class was having the same type of difficulty throughout the course. (You should have already checked the individual test results immediately after each test to see what changes you needed to make during the course.) Detailed analysis of the test results can wait until you get back to the office.

Organize and display data

It is difficult to draw conclusions about data when the information is spread over 12 or more evaluation sheets. The raw data need to be organized and, where possible, displayed graphically.

Organizing and displaying perceptions

The usual way of organizing these types of data is with a frequency table. Table 10.2 gives an example of a frequency table.

Table 10.2 *Using a frequency table to organize student feedback*

Question	Low 1	2	3	4	High 5	Total	Average
(a) Relevance		2		9	5	16	4.1
(b) Ability to apply			4	9	3	16	3.9
(c) Probability of using		1	8	6	1	16	3.4
(d) Overall satisfaction				10	6	16	4.4
(e) Trainer effectiveness				6	10	16	4.6

The process for constructing a frequency table is as follows.

• Work through the evaluation forms and count the number of students who gave the course a relevance score of 1 (i.e., very low relevance).

- Enter this number (if any) in the '1' (*Low*) column on the relevance row.
- Count the number of relevance scores of 2, 3, 4, and 5.
- Enter these numbers in the '2', '3', '4', and '5' columns.
- Add up the number of responses to make sure you have not missed any out. This number is put in the Total (*Tot*) column.
- Calculate the average relevance score and put it in the Average (*Ave*) column. For the example given in Table 10.2 the calculation is:

$$\frac{(2\times2) + (9\times4) + (5\times5)}{16}$$

- Follow a similar procedure for each of the response questions.

A computer with a spreadsheet program such as Lotus 1-2-3 allows you to make the calculations quickly and easily. Appendix 2 gives instructions for constructing this spreadsheet.

Although it is possible to draw conclusions directly from the frequency tables, it is a lot easier when the data are displayed graphically. The best tool for displaying distributed data is the histogram. A histogram is a set of vertical bars which represent the number of responses for each category of feedback. Figure 10.13 is a histogram for item (c) 'Probability of using'.

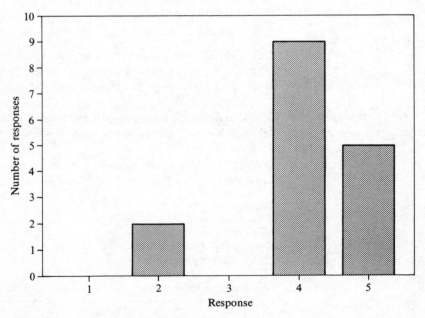

Figure 10.13 *Histogram of relevance scores*

Organizing and displaying comments

Qualitative data, like the feedback comments, are the most difficult to organize and display. The simplest way of organizing comments is to list them by question. Figure 10.14 gives an example of this. This is better than having the comments spread between all the evaluation sheets, but it is still difficult to detect patterns in the feedback.

COMMENTS

1. Relevance of workshop to your present job
    —Very relevant having recently acquired the responsibility for tracking projects within C&SE.
    —Not for most day-to-day activities, but useful for two projects just starting.
    —Useful reminding—will be able to use positively in the future!

2. Confidence in your ability to use the skills and knowledge
    —My only doubt is retaining the correct level of skills for when I have a specific project to work on.
    —Useful reminder/revision of work previously covered at college.
    —Having learnt how to implement CPA, etc., when setting up and running a project, would like to practise these skills.
    —This, I believe, will increase as I use these skills and knowledge.

3. Usefulness of the pre-work
    —Due to having no project to work on this was not completed.
    —Not relevant on this occasion.
    —Useful to have a project in mind to relate skills to, increasing relevance and learning ability.
    —Would have helped if Manager had given me proper terms of reference, information of what he actually wanted.
    —I received no pre-work.

4. Overall satisfaction with the workshop
    —An excellent workshop especially with the introduction of monitoring and working through a related project.

Figure 10.14   Organizing student feedback comments

Be careful when you group similar comments because there is a temptation to interpret the comments to fit into one of the existing groups. This has the effect of moving away from the original intent of the comments.

Where the same or similar comments are shared by more than one person it is possible to display this graphically as shown in Fig. 10.15.

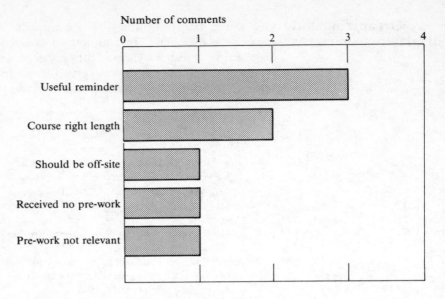

Figure 10.15   *Displaying student comments graphically*

Organizing and displaying test results

Much of what has been said about organizing and displaying perception data can be applied to test results. As with the student comments, a histogram gives a good display that assists interpretation.

The histogram takes a long time to produce so the temptation is to use the straight average. The problem with an average is that it does not give any information on the variability of the result. A good compromise is to display the average along with the lowest and highest scores (see Fig. 10.16). The distance between the highest and lowest score gives an indication of the variability, and the position of the average indicates how the results are skewed. As the results are displayed in a compact format this method is ideal for showing trends over a number of courses (see Fig. 10.17).

> Check whether
> deviations are
> significant or due to
> normal variation

It is essential that you make a judgement about whether deviations are significant and need action to be taken, or whether the deviations are due to normal variation and can be safely ignored.

Checking comments for significant variation

When you read the comments there will be some feedback that 'rings true'. You know it reflects a real problem, and you won't need a lot more data before you do something about it. There will be other comments that are not so clear-cut—others will be totally confusing. When

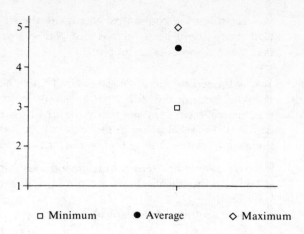

□ Minimum   ● Average   ◇ Maximum

Figure 10.16 *An average displayed with maximum and minimum scores*

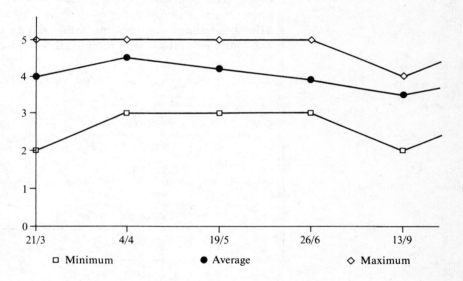

□ Minimum   ● Average   ◇ Maximum

Figure 10.17 *Tracking the results over a period*

I once received this puzzling comment on an evaluation for one of the courses I had been running: 'Keep the "brown-throaters" away from normal people.'

Being confused by this comment, I contacted the student who made it and asked for clarification.

'Oh! I meant separate the smokers from the non-smokers,' came the slightly embarrassed reply.

you get confusing comments, go back to the students and ask for clarification. They might be surprised, but you will be demonstrating that you take their comments seriously.

Checking perception scores for significant variation

You will need to run a course several times before you can definitely tell what are normal, and what are abnormal responses for the perception scores. As it can take many months to gather statistically significant data, I use the following guidelines to give a preliminary assessment of their significance. The guidelines are based on a five-point scale.

- Many people are reluctant to give a very high or a very low score. They do this on the basis that nothing is perfect and nothing is totally useless.
- People are more reluctant to give a '1' (very low) than a '5' (very high).
- The score of '3' is a neutral one. It means that this aspect of the course had little effect on the person. Always consider a '3' to be a defect if you are aiming for your courses to have high reputations.
- Taking the above into account, Table 10.3 indicates the significance that should be attached to individual responses.

Table 10.3 *Significance and acceptability of individual scores*

Score	Significance	Acceptability
1	Very poor score	Totally unacceptable
2	Poor score	Unacceptable
3	Neutral score	Not acceptable
4	Fair or good score	Acceptable
5	Good or very good score	Very acceptable

- The average score gives an indication of how the course performed. It also allows you to track how course performance changes from course to course. Table 10.4 gives you an indication of the significance and acceptability of average scores.
- Do not use the average by itself. The average smooths out the scores and hides problems. A person might be sitting on a block of ice and have their hair on fire, but on average their temperature would be just right.
- Always check the spread (range) of the scores as well as the average. The range is the lowest score subtracted from the highest. It shows how closely the students agree on their perceptions of the course. A small range indicates a stable learning process. A large range indicates an unstable process. Table 10.5 gives an interpretation for all the possible ranges on a five-point scale.

Table 10.4 *Significance and acceptability of averaged scores*

Score	Significance	Acceptability
1.0–1.9	Very poor score	Totally unacceptable
2.0–2.4	Poor score	Unacceptable
2.5–3.4	Neutral score	Not acceptable
3.5–3.9	Fair score	Fairly acceptable
4.0–4.4	Good score	Acceptable
4.5–5.0	Very good score	Very acceptable

Table 10.5 *Interpretation of a score's range*

Range	Agreement	Training process stability
0	Extremely high	Extremely stable
1	High	Very stable
2	Good	Normally expected level
3	Low	Getting unstable
4	Very low	Unstable

Note: a course can be stable at the low end of the scale as well as at the high end. This is why the range should be taken into consideration along with the average.

- 'Overall satisfaction' and 'Trainer effectiveness' usually score higher than other questionnaire items.
- 'Relevance' and 'Probability of using' often score lower than the other items. 'Relevance' scores lower than other items because of poor needs analysis and student selection. 'Probability of using' often has a low score because we do not pay enough attention to learning transfer.

The above guidelines reflect what are generally regarded to be normal responses. We shouldn't be content with these. We should aim for zero defects (i.e., every student giving every feedback item a score of 4 or 5).

Checking test results for significant variation

Every test should have a standard attached to it. Any failure to meet that standard should be considered to be a defect. At this stage we are not assigning causes to the deviation. The cause might be that the student was not able to reach a sufficient standard or there might be a defect in the teaching of the course. We are simply noting that a significant deviation has occurred.

> Analyse and interpret the
> data

Analysing and
interpreting comments

It is always difficult to receive negative feedback about one of your courses—doubly so if you wrote the course. A course is part of you. Feedback can feel like personal criticism.

These feelings are natural but misguided. You should seek and welcome feedback. Students are your customers. Like other customers, they are reluctant to complain. Instead, they usually stop using your services, and then loudly let their friends and neighbours know about it. You are the last person to find out. Often this is too late to save the business from damage.

When people complain, it is for one of two reasons. The first is when their frustration with the product or service overcomes their reluctance to complain. The second is when they respect you enough to want to help. You should always pay attention when people take the trouble to give you feedback. Good feedback is very rare.

Reacting positively to a problem enhances your reputation. Customers are impressed by suppliers who correct mistakes quickly. Curiously, suppliers who never make a mistake are thought less of. Don't let this tempt you into making deliberate mistakes! There should be sufficient real mistakes to give you enough practice.

Always consider negative feedback as a symptom of a problem you need to solve. Remember, no matter how trivial *you* think a problem is, it is always significant to your customer.

Guard against rationalizing the feedback away. 'He shouldn't have been on this course anyway' is a typical rationalization. Even if this were true, it's not the student's fault—it is a failure of our process. I find the principle of 'guilty until proven innocent' helps me rationalize less.

When I receive a piece of criticism I make the assumption that something is wrong with the course, or the way it was run. This doesn't mean I will change the course every time I receive criticism. This would throw the course into confusion and cause even more problems. Instead, I keep the feedback in mind and collect more evidence until I can reach a clear verdict.

Criticism often comes in the form of a solution. An example of this is: 'I think you should scrap the session on company objectives.' Taking this at its face value will lead to a poor training decision. Removing the session from the course will stop the negative feedback, but the course will fail to meet its design objectives.

There was obviously something wrong with the session on company objectives. You need to investigate further and find out what is causing the negative reaction. Could it be that they sit, without a break, for two hours listening to a presentation? Is the presenter unprepared? Perhaps the session makes no link between the company objectives and their own objectives.

The shapes of the perception histograms are useful in analysing and interpreting student perceptions. The following is a discussion of what the different shapes indicate.

The most common shape is the normal distribution which is symmetrical and bell-shaped (see Fig. 10.18). Most of the results are close to one value. Providing the histogram does not have a large spread it indicates a consistency in student perceptions.

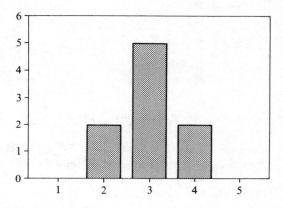

Figure 10.18 *Normal distribution*

A negatively skewed distribution (see Fig. 10.19) shows that the feedback is positive from the majority of the students. (I know this sounds contradictory but you'll have to argue that one with a statistician.) The trainer or training has had a significantly positive effect on the students.

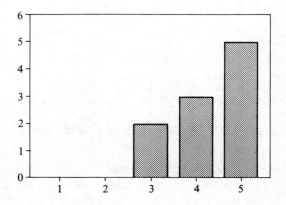

Figure 10.19 *Negatively skewed distribution*

A positively skewed distribution (see Fig. 10.20) shows that the feed-back is negative from the majority of the students. (Again, have a word with the statisticians about the apparent inconsistency.) The trainer or training has had a detrimental effect on the students.

Figure 10.20   Positively skewed distribution

A negatively skewed distribution with a wide spread (see Fig. 10.21) is often seen as a reaction to a trainer who has charisma but whose style is not liked by some of the population. We find that videos starring Tom Peters, the American business evangelist have this effect. The majority of the class is carried along with the energy of the presentation, but some are 'switched off' by being shouted at.

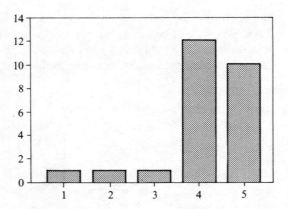

Figure 10.21   Negative skew with wide distribution

An isolated peak distribution (see Fig. 10.22) indicates the inclusion of a small number of people from a separate population. For example, if Fig. 10.22 represents a relevance score this would indicate the problem is more likely with the process for selecting students than with the course itself.

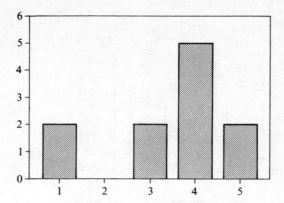

Figure 10.22 *Isolated peak distribution*

The twin peak distribution occurs when the results of two distinctly different populations are mixed together. For example, you might get this result when a course, originally designed for sales people, is given to a mixed sales and engineering class.

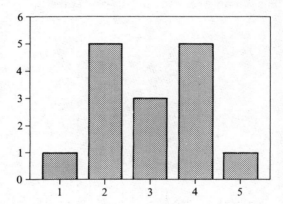

Figure 10.23 *Twin peak distribution*

This interpretation can be checked out by stratifying the data. Stratifying the data involves displaying the data so the two different populations can be easily identified. Figure 10.24 shows one way of doing this.

Figure 10.24 *Stratified twin peak distribution*

A flat distribution usually results from a mixed reaction to the course. It can also mean there are several different populations of students in the class. This is not a problem if you believe that the advantages of having a diverse group of students outweigh the disadvantages, and if the histogram does not have a wide spread.

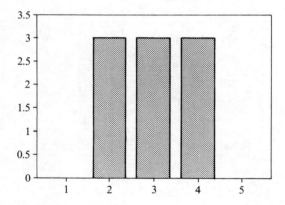

Figure 10.25 *A flat distribution*

Analysing and interpreting test results

A normal distribution means just what it says. It is the kind of distribution you would normally expect when things are left to themselves. If we get a normal distribution it may mean that our training has little effect on the students. Some examination results force the results into a normal distribution so 50 per cent of the students pass, 25 per cent get credits, and 25 per cent fail. As trainers we should be aiming for all our students to pass and to get the highest possible score. We want the distribution of our results to be skewed towards the top end. See Fig. 10.26.

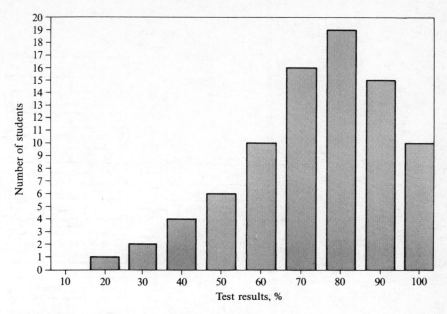

Figure 10.26 *An example of a positive effect on test results*

> Make minor
> adjustments to the
> course

After you have assessed all the validation data you will be in a position to know what alterations to make the next time you run the course. Don't try to change too many things at once, otherwise you won't know what changes caused which results.

Corrections to printed materials

Many of the minor adjustments will involve making revisions to the printed materials. These could be typographical errors, changes to exercises, or minor rewording of the text. You should correct these errors immediately or as soon as the course is finished.

If the materials are held electronically, make the corrections and then make sure you replace the affected pages in the print masters. All this sounds obvious but failure to make revisions while they are still fresh in your mind is one of the major reasons for the same mistakes turning up on every course.

> Check that
> adjustments have had
> desired effect

When you run the course the next time you should collect exactly the same data as the data which led you to make the change. This will give you confidence as to whether the changes have had the desired effect. You should also check the other validation data to make sure your changes have had no unexpected side-effects. (It has been said that the biggest cause of problems are solutions.)

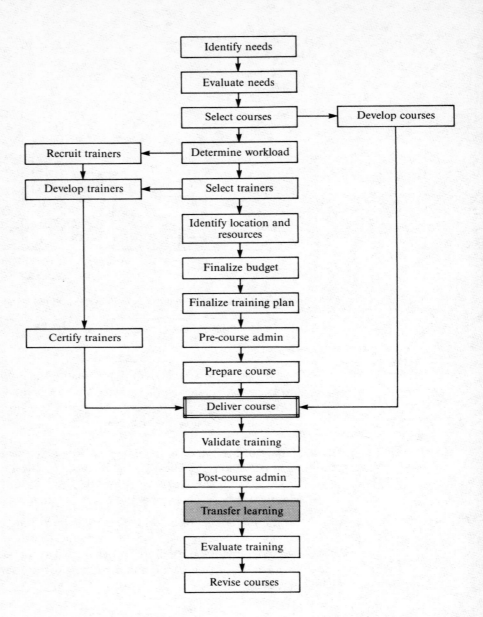

Figure 11.1 *Learning transfer*

11 Learning transfer

Training, no matter how good, is a waste of time if it does not help improve the business. Training will have no impact on the business unless the skills are used back at the workplace. Unused skills are skills soon forgotten. Within six months it will be almost as if the training had never taken place.

As learning transfer is so important you would think that companies would put considerable effort into making it happen. Yet, surprisingly, few training organizations give learning transfer the priority it requires. Perhaps they think that learning transfer is a natural outcome of training and, as such, does not need nurturing.

Nothing could be further from the truth. New learning is a fragile flower; it withers without constant attention. Unless considerable effort is put into learning transfer the effect on the business will be, at best, random and haphazard. Even companies that are aware of the importance of learning transfer find difficulty in making it happen.

In this chapter we will look at:

- the definition of learning transfer;
- what prevents learning transfer from taking place;
- what assists learning transfer;
- putting learning transfer into practice.

What is learning transfer?

The definition of learning transfer that I use is: 'The post-training application of the newly acquired knowledge and skills to improve the business.' You may think this definition too lenient because the skills and knowledge could be used once and then promptly forgotten. You might also argue that transfer is complete only when the students use the new skills and knowledge naturally, skilfully, and automatically.

This stiffer definition should always be the ideal to aim for, even though it is much more difficult to measure and attain.

What prevents transfer from taking place?

Given that learning is not efficiently transferred from the classroom to the business, the next step is to understand the causes of the problem. Assuming the students are not bothering to use the skills over-simplifies the problem. It just leaves us imploring them to use the skills. Unless we understand why the students are not using the skills, we will make very little progress towards solving the problem. Only understanding the root causes will allow us to remove the barriers.

The following is a selection of potential causes for poor learning transfer. You will need to check whether they apply in your situation, and whether there are any additional causes.

Poor needs analysis

Curiously enough, the seeds of this problem are sown long before the training ever takes place. If there is to be any chance of the students using what they have learnt, there must be a need for the skills and knowledge.

This takes us right back to the beginning of the training process—needs identification and analysis. Far too many people are put on to the wrong course, for the wrong reason, at the wrong time. Typical of these misguided reasons are: 'It's a long time since he's been on a course'; 'It's the next course in the series'; and 'We had a few spare places to fill'. If the training has little or no relevance, it should come as no great surprise that the training is not used.

Skills not used immediately after the course

If the needs analysis has been done correctly, the next aspect to look at is the initial use of the learning after the course. There should be an opportunity to use the skills.

Ideally the students should use the skills and knowledge immediately after the course. However, significant transfer still occurs if the skills are used within three weeks. If this were to happen after every course, there would be a lasting impact on the business.

The workplace environment

There is an aspect of the environment that 'punishes' the people who use the skills when they get back to work. This is known as the 'charm school effect'. This effect is particularly prevalent in management and behaviour training.

A person returns to the workplace, experiments with the skills, and uses a new vocabulary. The work group, faced with strange and new behaviours, starts to feel uncomfortable. Although they didn't like the old behaviours, at least they knew what to expect. This nervousness prompts them to make jokes like: 'Look who just got back from charm school!' In this way people get taught not to use the new knowledge.

Even if the returning trainee does not suffer verbal abuse, the work group's lack of training in the skills still provides an impediment. Many skills need a critical mass of people using them before they can take root in an organization. If this critical mass is not reached, the skill becomes extinct. Once the critical mass has been exceeded, even those who were sceptical about the skills will be swept along with the rest.

The culture of the company often reinforces the behaviours we are trying to change. We take people out of this environment, train them to use new behaviours, and then put them back into the environment that caused the problems in the first place. We then wonder why the learning hasn't transferred.

Little control over the transfer process

Another reason for poor learning transfer is the loss of control over the process. When the students are in the classroom they are a captive audience. You can monitor and give feedback; you can coach and counsel. But once the course is over that responsibility passes over to the delegates' managers.

One way to gain more control over learning transfer is to spread the learning experiences. For example, in the BBC's 'Managing Change' course the delegates meet a few days before the course. They do the introductions and get to know each other. The course then runs for five days. At the end of the course the students are given projects to do when they return to work. Three months later the delegates meet again to review how their projects are proceeding.

This approach goes a long way towards enhancing learning transfer. However, waiting three months to check a project is too long. It does not allow for the monitoring, feedback, and coaching that are required in the early days of learning transfer. Another problem with projects is that the students see them as additional work and a burden that gets in the way of their priority tasks. Consequently, it is put off and the bulk of the project work is done in a rush, just before it is due to be checked.

Using a trainer to coach a student through the early stages of learning transfer is an effective but expensive method. It also has the disadvantage that it is usurping the manager's role. Managers can only fulfil their role if they have coaching skills and they become partners in the training process.

Skills not learnt on course

No transfer can occur unless the students develop the skills in the first place. Some training is of the 'hosepipe' variety. The trainer sprays knowledge and experiences in the hope that all the students will grow.

Ideally, we should measure each student's performance, give feedback, and coach until every student reaches the required standard. As we will never have the time and resources to do this, we need to understand what can be done with the resources we have.

Courses that intend to teach a specific skill, or set of skills, range from half-a-day to two days. Although the length of a course depends on the skill and knowledge complexity, the following guidelines will give you some idea of what can be done in a fixed time.

Rule of thumb

Course length	*What can be done*
½ day	You can teach some basic concepts, models and terminology. There will be little or no time for practice. Unless the students practise the skills very soon after the course, there is little chance that the learning will

be transferred. However, half-a-day of theory in the classroom, combined with coached practice in the workplace is a powerful combination.

1 day
A full day's course allows time for some practice, but not enough time for a significant amount of learning to take place. As there is only enough time for one practice session, the students end the course on a low note. The practice will give them feedback on what they cannot do. They will not have the confidence they can perform the skills correctly.

1½ days
An extra half-day sees significant skill improvement, so the chances of effective learning transfer are greatly enhanced. The intervening evening also helps because the students can reflect on what happened during the day. Learning still goes on even after the practice has stopped.

2 days
Two days of training also allow the students to start a post-course project or to rehearse an application.

Complex skills need to be taught in stages. When there is time pressure on a course there is a temptation to move on before the basics are thoroughly understood. Students who are confused early on in a course get and remain hopelessly lost. They will neither hear nor understand anything that follows.

Longer courses have modules which cover different subject areas. Again, time pressure forces us to move on before the students have had time to breathe.

Assimilation time is important for both learning and its transfer. The students need to check whether they have understood the information, and how it fits into what they already know. They need to consider how they would use the learning back at work. Figure 11.2 gives an example of an assimilation aid.

Time also has to be given for the trainer to summarize what has gone before, and to introduce what is coming next. There also needs to be constant reinforcement of where the modules fit into the overall scheme of the course.

Difference between work and classroom environments

Another reason for poor learning transfer is the difference, and sudden transition, between the classroom and work environment. The classroom can be compared to a gymnasium; its purpose is to develop skills. Work is like the sporting event; the skills have to be used, in a complex environment, to produce results.

An athlete works out in the gym, practises on the field, and then enters a competition. No athlete would go straight from the gym to the Olympics. Yet this is what we do with our students. We give them the skills, send them back to work, and expect them to perform like champions.

Learning assimilation aid

1. What do you consider to be the main learning points of the module?

2. How do you currently behave when you find yourself in the situation described in the module?

3. Given what you have learnt from the module, as well as what you have learnt about yourself, what will you do differently in the future?

Figure 11.2 *An example of an assimilation aid*

We need to manage the transition from the classroom to the workplace. We need to create a transition environment that is more challenging than the classroom, and safer than the workplace.

The transition between the two environments is not helped by the common perception that training is not work, and work is not training. Training and learning need to be seen as a continuous process; an unending journey. The type of organization where the distinction between learning and work becomes blurred is called a learning organization.

Trying to do too much

The journey of a thousand miles starts with a single step. It should not start with a giant leap. Trying to cover too much ground too soon risks injury and exhaustion.

The same is true for learning transfer. Too many people return to their workplace and try to change the world overnight. Not only does this contribute to the 'charm school effect', but it is also a recipe for failure.

The first application of the skills and knowledge should be chosen very carefully. People need to succeed and to see the value of what they are doing.

> The European design managers of a large multinational organization were to be trained on counselling.
>
> The training started with a four-hour introduction to counselling and its techniques. Soon after the course each manager had a meeting with a facilitator to prepare for a real counselling session.
>
> Facilitators observed the managers carrying out their first counselling session. The facilitators explained to the counsellees that they were there solely to observe the managers.
>
> After the session the facilitators gave the managers feedback and, where necessary, further coaching in counselling techniques.
>
> One of the benefits of this training was that more appraisals were completed on time than ever before.

> Major Jeremy Moore, commander of the British land forces during the Falklands War, was asked what should be the first objective for a newly arriving battalion of paratroopers. 'A battle you are going to win,' he replied. The result of this advice was that Goose Green was recaptured on 28 May 1982.

What assists learning transfer?

The lessons to be learnt from what hinders learning transfer help us understand what assists the transfer of learning. The lessons are these.

- Training people, from the same work group, together aids learning transfer.
- Post-course project work assists learning transfer, but it is only effective if it is suitably supported and controlled.
- Some skills can only be transferred successfully if there is a cultural change in the company.
- Involve the managers before, after, and, in some cases, during the training.
- Ensure that managers have the necessary coaching skills to assist learning transfer.
- Ensure that competence is demonstrated at one level of difficulty or complexity before proceeding to the next.
- Ensure there is enough time to practise the skills on the course.
- Have at least two practice sessions. Complex skills need up to five practice sessions over a week's course.
- Allow time for assimilation between different subjects.
- Advise the students to be selective about what they apply the training to when they get back to work. Advise them against trying to do too much too soon.
- Manage the transition from the classroom to the work place.
- Reduce the perception that training is not work, and work is not training.

National vocational qualifications

NVQs (national vocational qualifications) can be used to help both learning transfer and the evaluation of the course. NVQs measure a person's effectiveness in the workplace rather than in the artificial environment of the classroom. A person will not be awarded an NVQ for passing a course. A course provides the background skills and knowledge that allow a person to demonstrate competence in the workplace.

If you design a course so it is consistent with NVQs you have an automatic link with the workplace. The skills are practised, managers function as mentors, and competence is assessed.

Putting learning transfer into practice

As you can see, transferring the training into the business can be both difficult and complex. Figure 11.3 shows a process for putting learning transfer into practice.

Figure 11.3 A process for putting learning transfer into practice

> Train managers, coaches,
> and assessors

The essence of learning transfer is support for the student before, during, and after the training course. You would normally expect the trainer to provide the support during the course. Support before and after the course is often a chance occurrence.

A process has to be installed, and a support network has to be established and trained. Coaching and counselling are essential skills for managers and coaches. If you are linking your training with NVQs, you will also need to have assessors trained and accredited.

> Student/trainer select
> skills and knowledge for
> initial application

Time is given during the course for the student to decide which skills and knowledge they should use during the initial application of the training.

> Student identifies initial
> application opportunities

Students should have a clear idea of the situations where they can use the skills and knowledge. The initial application will not happen unless they have a vivid mental picture of the situation. They should be able to imagine what it will look like and how it will feel.

For this reason a student should not leave the course without being sure of when the application will happen and who will be involved. Do not accept a fictitious or a generalized situation.

> Student discusses practice
> opportunities with
> manager

For learning transfer to be successful the manager must support the skills and knowledge application. This step of the process happens more than once. Potential application opportunities should be identified before the course as part of the student's preparation.

The discussion that occurs after the course is to let the manager know what is going on and to enlist the manager's help and support.

```
┌─────────────────────────────┐
│      Student rehearses the  │
│         application         │
└─────────────────────────────┘
```

Rehearsing the application in a simulated but safe environment is a powerful way to make a bridge between the classroom and the workplace. It allows the new skills and knowledge to be tried out, mistakes to be made, and feedback to be given.

```
┌─────────────────────────────┐
│    Student applies skills and│
│          knowledge          │
└─────────────────────────────┘
```

By this time the students should be fully prepared for their first application of their training. Where possible a coach should observe this initial application. The coach can be the person's manager or someone from a specially trained network of coaches. An alternative is the 'buddy system' where the students pair up and provide support, coaching, and feedback to each other.

```
┌─────────────────────────────┐
│     Student counselled and  │
│        given feedback       │
└─────────────────────────────┘
```

As soon as the students have completed their first application, they should review their own performance. They should ask themselves 'What they did well' and 'What they could have done better'. Give them feedback to cover what they might have missed. Then provide any additional coaching and practice that they might require.

```
┌─────────────────────────────┐
│      Assess student's       │
│         competence          │
└─────────────────────────────┘
```

When the student and coach feel the correct standard has been reached the student's competence should be assessed. If you have been following the NVQ path the job will done by the NVQ assessor.

An alternative method is to give the student a project book to complete after the course. The project book would have questions and exercises which allow the trainer to assess the extent to which the skills were applied after the course.

Figure 12.1   *Evaluation and revision*

12 Evaluation

This chapter covers the two final steps of the training process:

- evaluate training,
- revise courses.

Chapter 11 described a process for facilitating the transfer of learning from the classroom to the business. Evaluation checks whether transfer has occurred and ensures the training has had the desired effect.

While validation (Chapter 10) is an internal check, evaluation is about determining the effect of the course after the students return to the workplace. Validation assesses whether the students have reached the required standard before they leave the course.

A course might have an objective of being able to ice a cake. Validation would show that the students were able to ice a cake before they left the course. You would have no idea of whether the students would continue to ice cakes to the same standard or whether icing cakes is a skill that enhances the business.

Not only will we be covering the evaluation of training programmes, but we will also consider how to evaluate our training process. An outcome of evaluation is the identification of changes and additions to the training courses and process.

Evaluation versus validation

In my research for this book I came across many different definitions for both evaluation and validation. None of these definitions seemed to be satisfactory for the practical purpose of managing the training process.

The *Glossary of Training Terms* (Department of Employment, 1991) defines evaluation as:

The assessment of the total value of a training system, training course or programme in social as well as financial terms. Evaluation differs from validation in that it attempts to measure the overall cost-benefit of the course or programme and not just the achievement of laid down objectives. The term is also used in the general judgemental sense of the continual monitoring of a programme or of the training function as a whole.

The two problems with this definition are to do with 'the total value in social terms' and 'overall cost-benefit'.

From a practical point of view I have absolutely no idea of how to measure the total value of a course in social terms. Even if I did, I have a feeling it could be a lifetime's work.

It is not always possible to translate all the benefits of a training programme into financial terms. Even benefits which lend themselves to mathematical analysis involve complex calculations and the validity of the conclusions are nearly always suspect. Every outcome has more than one cause, so it is very difficult to apportion financial benefit to one activity rather than another. I have a suspicion that if you were to add up all the cost-benefits claimed for training and other activities in a company, the total would exceed the annual revenue!

The *Glossary of Training Terms* defines two types of validation: 'internal validation' and 'external validation'. Internal validation is defined as:

A series of tests and assessments designed to ascertain whether a training programme has achieved the behavioural objectives specified.

The definition of external validation is given as:

A series of tests and assessments designed to ascertain whether the behavioural objectives of an internally valid training programme were realistically based on an accurate initial identification of training needs in relation to the criteria of effectiveness adopted by the organisation.

Many writers reject these definitions as being too narrow. Validation also needs to reflect the perceptions of the participants and consider other, perhaps unintended, effects of the training. From a practical perspective, I have great difficulty in drawing the line between where external validation ends and evaluation begins.

Peter Bramley, in *Evaluation of Training* (BACIE, 1986), suggests it is better to take evaluation as a general term to cover the whole area rather than split it into three parts. He offers Goldstein (1980) as a broad definition:

Evaluation is the systematic collection of descriptive and judgemental information necessary to make effective training decisions related to the selection, adoption, value and modification of various instructional activities. (p 237)

This approach certainly simplifies the business of defining evaluation. However, I feel there is a world of difference between checking whether a course does what you expect it to do on the day, and the long-term effects of training on the individual, the department, and the organization.

For the practical purposes of this book I define validation as:

A systematic analysis of data and judgemental information, collected during a training course, which is designed to ascertain whether the course achieved its specified aims and objectives.

This definition corresponds most closely to the definition of internal validation given in the *Glossary of Training Terms,* but it also covers the participants' perceptions of the course. Validation is primarily at the

Table 12.1 *Quantitative and qualitative measures for each evaluation level*

Level	Quantitative	Qualitative
Individual	Do the individuals still have the knowledge they gained on the course? Are they still able to perform the skills?	Do the individuals still believe the training to have been worthwhile?
Departmental	Have the desired improvements or changes occurred at the departmental level?	Does the training have a good reputation in the participants' departments?
Organizational	Has the organizational aim been achieved? (e.g., profitability, productivity, flexibility, morale, commitment, achievement of business plan)	What is the organization's attitude towards training?

individual level—individual performance and reaction to the course. My working definition of evaluation is:

A series of tests, assessments, and investigations designed to ascertain whether training has had the desired effect at individual, departmental, and organizational levels.

Each of these three levels of evaluation can be further divided into quantitative and qualitative measures. See Table 12.1 for the types of quantitative and qualitative questions that can be asked at each of the three levels of evaluation.

Figure 12.2 is a simplified diagram showing the relationship of evaluation to the rest of the training process. It shows evaluation taking a 'helicopter view' of the process. An evaluation strategy needs to take account of:

- the original aims of the course as identified in the needs analysis,
- the behavioural objectives as identified during course development,
- the validation data collected during and at the end of the course, and
- assessment data taken during and after learning transfer.

Our definition of evaluation covers the effect of training as a whole and includes two broad areas:

- evaluation of training programmes, and
- evaluation of the training process.

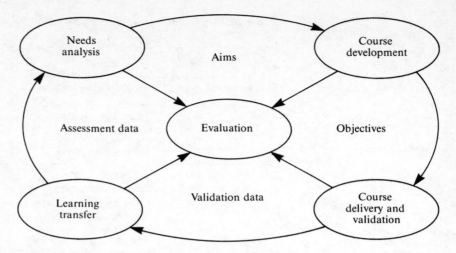

Figure 12.2 *Evaluation and its relationship to the training process*

Evaluating training programmes

When should training be evaluated?

Evaluation, by the definition given in this book, is carried out after the end of the course. The question is how long after the course this should be.

Evaluation would not be done after every course. With a new course you would want to make a check three to six months after the first course. When a course is established there is little need to do evaluation. Validation is normally sufficient to let you know that the course has not wandered off track and is still delivering to the required standard.

Another time evaluation is required is when there has been a significant change in the organization, or when the course is due to be revised or replaced by a new course.

Ideally evaluation of training should also occur annually when the organization is assessing the success of its business plan.

How should training be evaluated?

The way evaluation usually works is to go into the workplace, see the problems and successes that the organization, departments, and individuals are having, question whether training has helped them and then determine what additional training would be required.

This type of evaluation is usually qualitative and also involves sending out questionnaires. The questionnaires and their analysis follow a similar format to that used for validation (see Chapter 10).

I prefer interviews to questionnaires. With questionnaires people can only answer the questions they have been asked. Questionnaires assume the originator already has a good idea of what the problems with the course might be.

The problem with free-form interviews is that they do not have a structure. This raises questions about the validity of the data because different people would be answering different questions. It certainly makes analysis of the data very difficult.

Structured interviews give the best of both worlds. In essence it is an interview based on a questionnaire that includes all the basic questions that need to be covered. A sensitive interviewer will also be able to pick up on and probe for any other feedback on the course.

A half-way house between free-form and structured interviews is to start the interview with a series of open questions such as: 'Tell me about any problems you have in doing your current job.'

Evaluation is not only done with the students. The students' managers should also be asked if the course met the objectives from their point of view. With large-scale programmes feedback should also be sought from organizational and divisional heads. This ensures the training is evaluated at all three levels of evaluation. Different techniques are used depending on the level and whether a quantitative or qualitative investigation is being used. Table 12.2 shows some of the techniques that can be used.

Table 12.2 *Techniques for use at different levels of evaluation*

Level	Quantitative techniques	Qualitative techniques
Individual	Tests Observations NVQ assessment	Interviews Questionnaires
Departmental	Production indices Quality indices Staff turnover	Interviews Questionnaires Attitude surveys
Organizational	Assessment and diagnosis of business results Financial results	Interviews Questionnaires Customer satisfaction surveys

A process for evaluating training

The intuitive way of evaluating training programmes is to start at the first level of evaluation (individual level) and then proceed to the other two levels (departmental and organizational). This is the way that most evaluation is carried out, except that few investigations get beyond the first level.

If you start evaluating at the lowest level, the process becomes training-centred rather than business-centred. It becomes difficult to assess whether the course's objectives are the right ones because you are *actively* looking for examples of the course objectives being met in the workplace.

Starting at Level 1 also makes it difficult to prove that training is an essential contributor to the business because this narrow focus does not allow you to identify and isolate the other contributory factors.

Starting at Level 3, the organizational level, is more difficult, but it is the only way to prove whether training has contributed to the business. Figure 12.3 shows a process which, when used with this 'tops-down' approach, is an effective method for evaluating training.

> Review aims

In Chapter 1 we talked about the importance of training being aligned with the business. All training should support the maintenance or improvement of the business. When we evaluate at the organizational level (Level 3) we need to look at the original business aims the training was meant to support.

> Have aims
> been met?

Evaluating whether business aims have been met is not something that can, or should, be done by the training department alone. Well-run businesses assess the success of their strategies regularly—certainly at least once a year.

The assessment should be carried out by representatives of the company's main functions. Traditionally, the training function is not involved in these assessments. If we are serious about training being an integral part of the business, this is a critical omission.

> Determine how

If the answer to 'Have aims been met?' is yes, we should understand how we met our aims. A good result without understanding is just luck. There is no guarantee that we will be able to repeat our success. This step is often missed out because we are so pleased and amazed by our success.

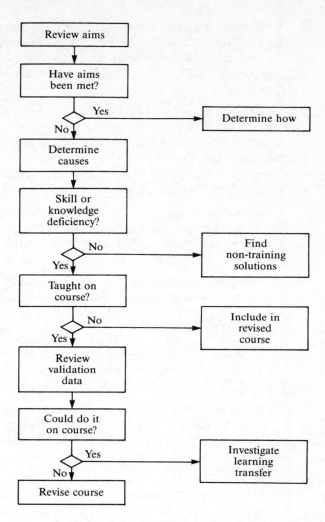

Figure 12.3 *A process for evaluating training contribution to the business*

Determining how the aims were met is really a type of problem solving. Instead of determining the causes of why something went wrong, we identify the factors which contribute to success; instead of implementing a solution to correct a problem, we carry out an action plan to capitalize on our success.

```
Determine
causes
```

If the aims were not met, we need to carry out an investigation to determine the causes. This is straightforward problem solving. Notice that we are still starting at the organizational level. The causes at this level are likely to be either strategic problems, or widespread deficiencies such as skill, knowledge, or motivation.

With any complex problem there are likely to be several causes. The root causes will often be found further down the organization. Tracing the problems down to their root causes is easier if the process of policy deployment (see Chapter 1) is followed when the business plan is put together.

Policy deployment is the process of cascading and translating corporate visions and directions throughout the organization. For each corporate direction, there are a series of supporting goals and strategies at the next level down. This process is repeated until we get down to objectives and work processes at the departmental and individual levels. You can see how policy deployment lends itself to our model of evaluation.

If an important corporate aim has not been met, we can see which of the supporting goals are contributing to the problem. We can look at the supporting goals we have not achieved and see which work processes are not meeting expectations.

Providing the training plan was put together as part of the original policy deployment, this process gives us a method of evaluating training's contribution to the business. It also allows us to evaluate the training process, as well as the individual courses.

```
┌─────────────────┐
│ Skill or        │
│ knowledge       │
│ deficiency?     │
└─────────────────┘
```

Skill and knowledge deficiencies can be in terms of quantity as well as quality. If qualified individuals are not meeting the course objectives, the course needs to be revised. If we have not trained the numbers of people we said we would train, the training process needs to be investigated.

Skill and knowledge deficiencies need to be investigated at all three levels of evaluation. Deficiencies in the number of people trained are first investigated at the organizational level. We then need to determine the extent of the deficiency across the departments. Finally, we should identify the individuals who have not been trained and ensure they are included in the next revision of the training plan. Deficiencies in the quality of skills and knowledge are dealt with in a similar manner.

```
┌─────────────────┐
│ Find            │
│ non-training    │
│ solutions       │
└─────────────────┘
```

If the causes of a problem cannot be attributed to a skills or knowledge deficiency, we have to look elsewhere for solutions. Figures 2.10 and 2.11 in Chapter 2 describe a process for finding alternatives to training. This process was designed for use during needs analysis, but it can also be used at all levels of evaluation.

```
┌─────────────────┐
│    Taught on    │
│     course?     │
└─────────────────┘
```

If one of the contributing factors to a business problem is a skill or knowledge deficiency, the next step is to check whether it was included in the course. This can be done by either looking at the minimum competency statement (see the section on 'Structure Course Content' in Chapter 3) or reviewing the course objectives.

```
┌─────────────────┐
│   Include in    │
│    revised      │
│    course       │
└─────────────────┘
```

If the deficient skills and knowledge were not taught in the original course, we need to make sure they are included when we revise the course.

```
┌─────────────────┐
│     Review      │
│   validation    │
│      data       │
└─────────────────┘
```

The next step is to review the validation data collected at the end of each course. These data should already have been analysed and displayed graphically as described in Chapter 10. It is during evaluation that you realize the benefits of having a good filing and retrieval system for your validation data.

```
┌─────────────────┐
│   Could do it   │
│   on course?    │
└─────────────────┘
```

The purpose of reviewing the validation data is to see whether the students were able to demonstrate the skills and knowledge while they were on the course.

```
┌─────────────────┐
│   Investigate   │
│    learning     │
│    transfer     │
└─────────────────┘
```

If the students were performing to the required level on the course, their performance must have deteriorated after the training. The next step is to look at the output of learning transfer.

Chapter 1 recommended that every job should have a description of the competencies needed to perform the job. It also recommended that everyone should have their competence assessed before being allowed to do the job by themselves.

Chapter 11 showed how national vocational qualifications could be used to carry out this assessment. Without job certification evaluation becomes a time-consuming and costly additional exercise.

If you do not have access to assessment data, you will need to retest a selection of students to see whether they are still able to meet the course objectives in the workplace. This underlines the importance of having objectives that are meaningful, both in the classroom and the workplace. For example, an objective that states: 'By the end of the course you will have participated in three simulations', is not useful because it cannot be measured in the workplace. It is more a description of the training content than an objective.

If your objectives are meaningful, you can use exactly the same approach as described in Chapter 10. In this case the only difference between validation and evaluation is when you carry out the investigation.

If your investigation or assessment data show there has not been a successful transfer of learning, you will need to find the causes for this and modify the learning transfer process. Chapter 11 considers the most common causes for poor learning transfer.

The assessment data may show that learning was transferred successfully, but waned after a period of use in the business. In this case it is unlikely that you will need to modify the original course. The usual response in these cases is a demand for refresher training.

Be cautious about making an immediate response to demands for refresher training. First look for environmental or cultural reasons for the decline in skills. If an environmental or cultural cause is prevalent, no amount of refresher training will overcome these factors.

If refresher training is appropriate, don't put people through the same course again. You will only be 'telling them what you told them' and it is unlikely you will get better learning transfer. As a colleague of mine says: 'If you always do what you did, you'll always get what you got!'

The answer to running the same course again is to run a different course which covers the same skill and knowledge from a different angle or at a different level. Another approach is to run a simulation which requires skilful application of the skills and knowledge.

> Revise course

If the students were not able to do it on the course, the course will need revising. Though it should be said that if you reach this step as part of evaluation, you should also look at the other parts of the training process.

Poor performance on the course should be picked up during validation. If the needs analysis and course development had been done properly, you should need to make only minor adjustments between courses.

As an example of how this process works in practice consider a company whose customer satisfaction ratings are disappointingly low.

The managing director calls a meeting to assess and diagnose the problem. The data suggest there is a widespread lack of skill in dealing with customers. Customer satisfaction training is not given to any of the people who have direct contact with the customer.

This evaluation at the organizational level led to customer satisfaction training being included in training of sales people, customer representatives, service engineers, telephone operators, and receptionists.

Further investigation of the data showed that manufacturing defects, administration errors, and service engineer response time all contributed to customer dissatisfaction.

Investigations continued by looking at each of these departments in detail. For example, in the manufacturing area most of the defects were attributed to materials problems. Only a few defects were attributable to workmanship. These workmanship defects were eliminated by minor modifications to the training.

Evaluating the training process

In the discussion on evaluating training programmes we saw how it is necessary to have a robust training process as well as excellent training courses to deliver training at the required quality, quantity, cost, and time.

One of the best ways to evaluate the training process is to decide which are the important indicators you wish to measure yourself against.

Once you have decided on these measures the next step is to go out and benchmark yourself against companies who have a known reputation for their training.

Quantitative training measures can be grouped into three headings:

- financial,
- utilization, and
- time.

Financial measures

The two types of financial measures are costs and earnings.

Costs

The following are some examples of training cost measures:

- total annual budget for providing training,
- training investment per employee per year,
- training investment per manager per year,
- cost of providing a day's non-residential training,
- cost of providing a day's residential training,
- cost of employing a trainer per day,
- cost of hiring a consultant per day,

- annual training budget expressed as a percentage of the company's total employment costs, and
- annual training budget expressed as a percentage of the company's revenue.

The annual cost of providing training can include or exclude the students' wages while they are being trained, depending on the convention used in the benchmark company.

Earnings If you are running your training organization as a budget centre, you will also be interested in measurements which will allow you to compare your earnings with those of similar organizations. The following is a selection of measurements you can use:

- earnings per trainer per year,
- earnings per trainer per day,
- earnings as a percentage of the training budget,
- earnings per day of developed course, and
- earnings per square metre of training space.

Utilization measures

The main two areas of utilization are trainer utilization and training room utilization.

Trainer utilization
- *Face-to-face ratio* (time spent in front of a class divided by the trainer's total available time). Often expressed as a percentage.
- *Preparation and delivery ratio* (time spent preparing and delivering existing courses divided by the trainer's total available time). Often expressed as a percentage.
- *Delivery to preparation ratio* (time spent delivering divided by the time spent preparing for existing courses).
- *Development ratio* (time spent developing new training materials divided by the trainer's total available time). Often expressed as a percentage.

Training room utilization Training room utilization is simply the percentage of time that the training rooms are in use. If you have an open learning centre, you will need to express the utilization as a percentage of time that the learning stations are in use.

Time measures

Time measurements fall into three categories:

- hours of training received,
- timeliness of training delivery, and
- course development times.

Hours of training received
- Hours of training per employee per year.
- Hours of training per manager per year.
- Hours of training per contractor per year.

Timeliness of training delivery

- *Lead time* (time between identification of training need and delivery of the training).
- *Timeliness* (percentage of training completed within agreed time limits). For example, 60 per cent of new starters trained on total quality management within three months. The target for timeliness would always be 100 per cent.

Course development times

- *Hours of development per page* (for text-based courses).
- *Development to course length ratio* (total time to develop the course divided by the duration of the course).

13 Appendices

Appendix 1 National vocational qualifications (NVQs)

For many years there has been concern about the fragmented nature of vocational qualifications in the UK. In 1986 the government established the National Council for Vocational Qualifications (NCVQ), whose mandate was to establish vocational qualifications based on competencies actually required in employment.

The NCVQ does not award qualifications itself but works through Industry Lead Bodies for Training and Development, and established examining and awarding bodies.

The Industry Lead Bodies are responsible for the development of occupational competencies. They also approve all new NVQs in their industry before they are submitted to the National Council for Vocational Qualifications for final approval.

Most lead bodies are industry-specific. For example, the British Marine Industries Federation is responsible for qualifications in the boat-building industry. Some lead bodies are general in their scope:

- the TDLB Secretariat looks after training and development;
- the Personnel Lead Body Secretariat develops competencies for the personnel profession;
- managers and supervisors are looked after by the National Forum for Management Education and Development, whose operating name is the Management Charter Initiative (MCI).

Competencies have to be assessed in the workplace. This means companies either have to have their own assessor trained or pay for a consultant assessor.

There are five levels of NVQ which indicate the level of the competence attained. This allows the comparison of competence between industries. Table A1.1 gives definitions for the five levels of NVQ, as well as comparisons between the Management Charter Initiative (MCI) and Institute of Training and Development (ITD) awards.

The Scottish equivalent of the NVQs are the Scottish vocational qualifications (SVQs).

General national vocational qualifications (GNVQs), the vocational equivalent of A levels, are currently being developed.

Table A1.1 *Definition and comparison of NVQ levels*

NVQ level	Definition	ITD Awards	MCI
1	Competence in the performance of a range of varied work activities		
2	Competence in a broader range of work activities involving greater individual responsibility		
3	Competence in skilled activities which are complex and non-routine including supervisory activities	Direct Trainer's Award (T&D Level 3 plus 2 additional units)	M1S Supervisory
4	Competence in the performance of complex, technical and professional activities, including supervision and management	Certificate in HRD (T&D Level 4 plus 7 additional units)	M1 First level management
5	Application of a significant range of fundamental principles and complex techniques. Extensive knowledge and understanding of the field; substantial personal autonomy; accountability for analysis, diagnosis, design, planning, execution, and evaluation	Diploma in HRD (under development)	M2 Middle management
. . .		Masters in HRD (under development)	Senior management (under development)

Appendix 2 Spreadsheet examples

The following examples of spreadsheets are provided so that you can use them as a basis for programming your own spreadsheets. The formulae are Lotus 1-2-3 compatible, but you should have no difficulty in converting them for use on your own spreadsheet.

1. Course cost calculations

This spreadsheet shows how Table 6.6 in Chapter 6 was put together.

- Set Default Currency to £
- Set Width of column A to 20
- Set Width of column B to 16
- Set Range B11..B21 to Currency Format, 0 decimal places
- Type the following into the cells indicated:

A1: 'Middle Manager's Course

A3: 'Type of Training:
B3: "Residential

A4: 'Duration (days):
B4: 5

A5: 'Number of Students:
B5: 20

A6: 'Number of Trainers:
B6: 3

A7: 'Type of Trainer:
B7: "Own

A8: 'Location:
B8: "Off-site

A9: 'Additional rooms:
B9: 4

A11: 'Trainer cost/day:
B11: 300

A12: 'Materials/student:
B12: 50

A13: 'Main room hire/day:
B13: 0

A14: 'Seminar room hire:
B14: 50

A15: 'Accomm/student:
B15: 120

A16: 'Equip hire/day:
B16: 250

A17: 'Simulation costs:
B17: 9000

A19: 'TOTAL COST:
B19: +(B11*B4*B6)+(B12*B5)+(B13*B4)+(B14*B4*B9)
       +(B15*(B5+B6)*B4)+(B16*B4)+B17

A20: 'COST/STUDENT:
B20: +(B19/B5)

A21: 'COST/STUDENT/DAY:
B21: +(B20/B4)

2. Spreadsheet for analysing student feedback

Constructing the spreadsheet

- Set range H4 . . . H8 to Format, Fixed, 1 decimal place
- Set the width of column A to 27
- Set the widths of columns B, C, D, E and F to 4
- Set the width of column G to 6
- Set the width of column H to 5
- Type the following into the cells indicated:

A1: \ –	A2: ' Question	A3: \ –
B1: \ –	B2: "1	B3: \ –
C1: \ –	C2: "2	C3: \ –
D1: \ –	D2: "3	D3: \ –
E1: \ –	E2: "4	E3: \ –
F1: \ –	F2: "5	F3: \ –
G1: \ –	G2: "Tot	G3: \ –
H1: \ –	H2: "Ave	H3: \ –

A9: \ –	A4: ' (a) Relevance
B9: \ –	A5: ' (b) Ability to apply
C9: \ –	A6: ' (c) Probability of using
D9: \ –	A7: ' (d) Overall Satisfaction
E9: \ –	A8: ' (e) Trainer Effectiveness
F9: \ –	
G9: \ –	
H9: \ –	

G4: @SUM(B4..F4)
H4: (B4+(C4*2)+(D4*3)+(E4*4)+(F4*5))/G4

G5: @SUM(B5..F5)
H5: (B5+(C5*2)+(D5*3)+(E5*4)+(F5*5))/G5

G6: @SUM(B6..F6)
H6: (B6+(C6*2)+(D6*3)+(E6*4)+(F6*5))/G6

G7: @SUM(B7..F7)
H7: (B7+(C7*2)+(D7*3)+(E7*4)+(F7*5))/G7

G8: @SUM(B8..F8)
H8: (B8+(C8*2)+(D8*3)+(E8*4)+(F8*5))/G8

	A	B	C	D	E	F	G	H
1	--							
2	Question	1	2	3	4	5	Tot	Ave
3	--							
4	(a) Relevance						0	ERR
5	(b) Ability to apply						0	ERR
6	(c) Probability of using						0	ERR
7	(d) Overall Satisfaction						0	ERR
8	(e) Trainer Effectiveness						0	ERR
9	--							

Figure A2.1   *Spreadsheet for analysing student feedback before data entry*

You can save time on entering the formulae by:

- Copying cell A1 to range (B1..H1)
- Copying cell A3 to range (B3..H3)
- Copying cell A9 to range (B9..H9)
- Copying cell G4 to range (G5..G8)
- Copying cell H4 to range (H5..H8)

Using the spreadsheet   This spreadsheet is used to analyse the end of course evaluation forms. The ERR in the '*Ave*' (Average) column stands for ERROR. The error is caused by the spreadsheet dividing something by zero. The ERRs will disappear as soon as data is entered on each line.

- Working through the evaluation forms, count the number of students who gave the course a relevance score of 1 (i.e., very low relevance).
- Enter this number in cell B4.
- Then count the number of relevance scores of 2, 3, 4, and 5.
- Enter these numbers in cells C4, D4, E4, and F4.

The '*Tot*' column will show you the total number of responses that you received for course relevance. This number is used as a check on the counting. The average score is shown in the '*Ave*' column.
Follow a similar procedure for each of the response questions.

Appendix 3
Public holidays

These dates are only given as a guide to help you identify when your training dates would coincide with a public holiday in the UK. The government has the final say on when public holidays occur each year. This is especially so when a public holiday falls on a Saturday or Sunday. Typically they would be held over until the following Monday.

Fixed holidays

New Year's Day   1 January. Scotland also has a holiday on 2 January.

Saint Patrick's Day	17 March. Northern Ireland only.
May Day	The first Monday after 1 May. (There are proposals to have a holiday in October instead of this May Day holiday).
Spring Bank Holiday	The last Monday in May.
Orangeman's Day	12 July (Northern Ireland only).
Summer Bank Holiday	The first Monday in August (Scotland only).
Late Summer Bank Holiday	The last Monday in August (not Scotland).
Christmas Day	25 December. If Christmas Day falls on Sunday, an additional holiday would normally be given on the Tuesday.
Boxing Day	26 December. If Christmas Day falls on a Saturday, Boxing Day is usually moved to the Monday, and an additional holiday is given on the Tuesday.

Movable holidays

Good Friday	The Friday before Easter Sunday. Falls between 20 March and 23 April.
Easter Sunday	The first Sunday after the first full moon on or after the vernal equinox. Falls between 22 March and 25 April. The following is a list of dates for Easter Sunday that will take you up to the 21st century:

1993	11 April	2002	31 March
1994	3 April	2003	20 April
1995	16 April	2004	11 April
1996	7 April	2005	27 March
1997	30 March	2006	16 April
1998	12 April	2007	8 April
1999	4 April	2008	23 March
2000	23 April	2009	12 April
2001	15 April	2010	4 April

Easter Monday	UK but not Scotland.
Easter Tuesday	Customary holiday for industry and trade in Northern Ireland only.
Ascension Day	Celebrated in some continental countries. Falls 40 days after Easter, counting Easter Sunday as the first day. Between 30 April and 3 May.
Whit Monday	Celebrated in some continental countries. The Monday following the seventh Sunday after Easter. Falls between 11 May and 14 June.

Appendix 4
Hints for converting a word processor file to ASCII format

Hint 1: Check to see if your word processor has a facility to convert documents to standard ASCII text files. If your word processor has such a facility, use it to create an ASCII text file.

Hint 2: If this doesn't work, see if your word processor will allow you to create a print file on a floppy disk. Use this option to create a print file from your original document.

Hint 3: Many word processors have a facility for creating and editing computer programs. If you use this facility to create your text files, you can usually use the normal word processing mode to edit the files and add formatting commands.

Appendix 5
Computer specifications

When you buy software to use on a course or for training administration it is important to make sure that it will work on the computers that you are using. If possible, try to see the software working on a computer system that is exactly the same as yours. Failing that, check the system requirements shown on the software's packaging or in its manual conform to the specification in the computer's manual. Figure A5.1 shows an example of a typical set of system requirements.

The things that you have to look out for are:

- the type of machine that the software runs on;
- the type of disk that the computer accepts;
- the amount of memory the program needs;
- the type of display it requires;
- the type of pointing device, if any, it requires;
- the operating system required.

Type of computer

There are many types of computer such as: IBM PCs, IBM compatibles, Macintoshes, Atari STs. Software written for one type of computer will not work on a different type of computer.

The software shown in Figure A5.1 requires an IBM PC/XT/AT/PS2 or compatible computer. Your computer's manual will tell you whether your machine is a PC, XT, AT, or PS2. The glossary at the end of this book gives an explanation of all these abbreviations.

Disks

When you buy a computer program it usually comes on flexible magnetic disks called 'floppy' disks. These disks are either 3.5" or 5.25" in diameter. It is essential that you buy the program on a disk that your computer will accept. A hard disk is a magnetic disk that is permanently installed inside the computer. If a program requires a hard disk, you will need to transfer the program from the floppy disks to the hard disk as part of the installation procedure.

Memory

This is known as RAM (random access memory) and is measured in kilobytes: 1 K (1 kilobyte) is approximately the memory it would take to store a thousand characters. Letters, digits, and spaces are all characters. A standard amount of memory for an IBM compatible is 640 K.

System Requirements

- IBM PC/XT/AT/PS2 or compatible

- Hard disk and 3.5'' or 5.25'' disk drive

- 640 K RAM

- CGA, EGA, MCGA, VGA, or Hercules graphics

- Microsoft, IBM, Logitech, or compatible mouse pointing device

- MS-DOS 3.3 or higher

Figure A5.1   *Typical computer system requirements*

Type of display   A computer's display looks like a television screen and is called a VDU (video display unit). Early computers were unable to display pictures (graphics) and were only able to display text. Today computers can display graphics in full colour and high definition. The development of graphics displays evolved over a number of years and, consequently, the number of different displays that a computer can have is quite bewildering.

Always check your computer manual to make sure that your 'graphics adaptor' is one of those supported by the software. The software shown in Figure A5.1 needs a CGA, EGA, MCGA, VGA, or Hercules type of display. See the glossary for an explanation of these abbreviations.

Pointing devices   Many programs need a pointing device to work properly. A pointing device allows you to access any part of a computer's screen faster than you can with the cursor (arrow) keys.

The most popular type of pointing device is called a mouse, so called because its plastic body approximates to the shape of a mouse and the lead looks like a tail.

Operating systems   When a computer is switched on it is like a newborn baby: all the wiring is in place and it can carry out basic functions, but it needs to be 'educated' to carry out more complex functions. This 'education' is carried out by a program called an operating system.

The most popular operating system for IBM compatibles is Microsoft's MS-DOS. It is essential that the software you are using has been written not only for the right operating system, but also for the correct version of the operating system. The version is indicated by a decimal number: e.g., 2.0, 3.3, 5.0. A program that has been written for an early version will normally work on a later (higher-numbered) version, but it is unlikely that a program written for a later version will work on an earlier version.

Appendix 6 Trainers' checklists

1. Trainer's kit and supplies for the session

- Bulldog clips
- Paper clips
- Drawing pins
- Packing tape
- Masking tape (25 mm width)
- Sellotape
- Blu-Tack
- Flip chart marker pens (water-based)
- Overhead projector pens (water-soluble and permanent)
- Spare overhead projector bulb
- Lens cleaner
- Cloths
- Overhead transparencies (blank)
- Pencils (H)
- Erasers
- Rulers
- Ring binders
- Folders
- A4 note pads
- Name cards
- Flip chart pads
- Post-it pads
- Self-adhesive labels
- Calculators
- Pencil sharpener(s)
- 2, 3, 4-hole punch
- Snopake
- Stapler
- Staples
- Staple remover
- Scissors
- Glue stick
- Hammer
- Extension lead (with two sockets)
- Batteries
- Screwdriver
- Penknife/scalpel
- Videotapes
- Audiocassettes
- Audio and video leads and adapters

2. Training location survey
- Size, shape, and capacity
- Location
- Heating, lighting, and ventilation
- Power sockets, light switches
- Toilets
- Doors, windows, emergency exits
- Parking
- Access for preparation
- Contact established
- Acoustics
- Wall space for flip chart pages
- Meal and break arrangements
- Bedrooms

3. Before the course
- Printed materials obtained
- Lesson plan reviewed
- Audio-visual equipment and tapes obtained
- Stationery and other supplies obtained
- Course logistics checked

4. Just before the course
- Room layout checked
- Ashtrays, waste bins, glasses, water, etc., checked
- Participant materials, pencils, pads, name cards laid out
- Visibility of screens, charts, etc., checked
- Felt-tip and dry-wipe pens tested
- Lighting, ventilation, and heating checked
- Direction signs displayed
- Telephone disconnected
- Check process for handling messages and phone calls

5. After the course
- Course feedback forms collected and analysed
- Room cleared up
- Equipment transported back
- Bills paid
- Keys, etc., returned
- Training records completed

Bibliography

BACIE/ITD (1992) *The Training Directory*, Kogan Page, London.

Bentley, Trevor (1990) *The Business of Training*, McGraw-Hill (UK).

Bramley, Peter (1991) *Evaluation of Training*, McGraw-Hill (UK).

Bramley, Peter (1986) *Evaluating Training Effectiveness*, BACIE, London.

Buzan, Tony (1975) *Use Your Head*, BBC Publications (UK).

Crosby, Philip B. (1980) *Quality is Free*, New American Library, New York.

Department of Employment (1971) *Glossary of Training Terms*, HMSO, London.

EITB (1989) *Guide to the Levy Exemption and Grant Scheme 1989/90*, EnTra, Watford.

Gleick, James (1988) *Chaos*, Cardinal, Sphere Books, London.

Goldstein, I. L. (1980), 'Training in Work Organisations', *Annual Review of Psychology*, 229–72.

Harrison, Rosemary (1988) *Training and Development*, Institute of Personnel Management, London.

Heron, John (1975) *Six Category Intervention Analysis*, Human Potential Research Project, University of Surrey.

Imai, Masaaki (1986) *Kaizen*, Random House, New York.

Kenney, John and Margaret A. Reid (1986) *Training Interventions*, Institute of Personnel Management, London.

Mager, R. F. (1962) *Preparing Objectives for Programmed Instruction*, Fearon, San Francisco.

Mager, R. F. and P. Pipe (1984) *Analysing Performance Problems*, Lake Publishing, California.

McLeish MP, Henry (1990) *Who Pays for Skills?* Labour Market Briefing.

Peters, T. and R. H. Waterman Jr. (1982) *In Search of Excellence*, Random House.

Rackham, N. and T. Rackham (1977) *Behavioural Analysis in Training*, McGraw-Hill (UK).

Rose, C. (1985) *Accelerated Learning*, Accelerated Learning Systems Ltd (UK).

Glossary

8 mm   A videocassette format used in camcorders. The tape is 8 millimetres wide.

A4   Standard paper size (210 mm × 297 mm).

Alignment   The process of ensuring that all parts of a company are pulling in the same direction.

Artificial intelligence   Apparent computer intelligence which allows a computer to solve problems.

ASCII   American Standard Code for Information Interchange. A code which uses numbers to represent digits, upper and lower case letters, punctuation, and additional characters such as RETURN.

Assessment   The process of determining the company's or organization's current situation.

AT   Advanced technology. IBM PCs or compatibles which are more advanced than the standard PC or XT.

Authoring tool   Software used to create instructional material delivered on a computer system.

Azimuth adjustment   The process of adjusting the angle of the recording/play-back head of a tape recorder with respect to the tape.

Camcorder   A portable video camera with a built-in video recorder.

CBT   Computer based training. Uses a computer to present and control the sequence of instructional information.

CGA   Colour graphics adaptor. A standard for a computer's display which has a definition of 640 × 200 dots (pixels) in monochrome and 320 × 200 in four colours from a choice of 16.

Check chart   A chart that is used for collecting and organizing data.

Control chart   A chart that displays statistical process control data.

Cycle time   The time it takes to go from the beginning to the end of a process.

Database   A large store of information.

Disk   A magnetic disc that a computer uses for storing information. There are two types of disk: a hard disk which is rigid, and a floppy disk which is flexible.

Displays   Devices which allow users to see the computer's output on a monitor. PC displays have developed over the years yielding greater definition and more colours. Starting with the least sophisticated, the current standards are: MDA, Hercules, CGA, MCGA, EGA, and VGA.

DVI   Digital video interactive. Technology that allows real time compression and decompression of graphics and animated displays.

Duplex   Printing on both sides of a sheet of paper.

EGA   Extended graphics adaptor. A standard for a computer's display which has a definition of 640 × 350 dots (pixels) in 16 colours from a choice of 64.

EPSS   Electronic performance support system. Software that helps users perform their jobs more effectively while they work.

Expert system   A computer system that stores expert knowledge in the form of rules. It is a tool that can be used by non-experts to make decisions.

Face-to-face ratio   The percentage of a trainer's available time that is spent teaching in front of a class.

Floppy disk   *see* 'Disk'.

Formatting (1)   The process of defining what a document will look like. For example, margins, top and bottom spaces, page length, tabs, and font types. (2)   The process of preparing a disk so that it can be used by a computer.

GOQs   Genuine occupational qualifications. Qualifications which make it legal to select a person of a particular category while excluding people of other categories (e.g., sex or race). Basically these are authenticity, privacy, decency, and the laws regulating the employment of women.

Goals   Quantitative figures that are established by top management.

GUI   Graphical user interface. A screen design employing graphics and colour in a consistent manner so that menus and other system features are easy for users to understand and use.

Hard disk   *see* 'Disk'.

Hardware   Computer equipment such as computers, printers, and plotters.

Hercules   A graphics standard for a monochrome computer display giving a definition of 720 × 348 dots (pixels).

Histogram   A graph in which frequency distribution is shown by means of vertical bars.

HRD   Human resource development. Used to be known as personnel.

HRDC   Human resource development committee. A committee of peer managers who meet to make, review, or approve decisions related to the organization and development of people in their areas.

HRM   Human resource management or human resource manager. Used to be personnel or personnel manager.

Hypertext   Electronic information that is linked so that users can easily move from one topic to another.

ITD   Institute of Training and Development.

IVD   Interactive video disk. Video images stored on an optical disk so that a companion computer can control their presentation, based on user responses.

Kaizen   The Japanese for 'continous improvement'.

Kilobyte A measure of a computer's memory. One kilobyte of memory will store approximately a thousand characters—about two-and-a-half pages of A4.

MBO Managing by objectives. An objective-setting process which increases commitment by involving employees in setting their own objectives.

MCGA Multicolour graphics array. A standard for a computer's display which has a definition of up to 640 × 200 dots (pixels) in monochrome and 320 × 200 in 256 colours from a choice of 262 144.

MCI Management Charter Initiative

MDA Monochrome display adaptor. The original standard for a computer's display. It can only display text in 25 lines of 80 characters.

Mission A statement of what the company or organization exists to do today.

Mouse A hand-operated device for selecting text and objects on a computer screen. Moving the mouse over a flat surface causes a corresponding movement to a pointer (usually an arrow shape) on the computer screen. Pressing a button on the mouse selects the text or object to which the arrow is pointing.

MS-DOS Microsoft disk operating system. The standard, single-user system for IBM, and IBM-compatible, computers.

NTSC National television system committee. An American television standard.

NVQs National vocational qualifications.

OCR Optical character recognition. The ability of a computer to scan a paper document and 'read' the text into its memory.

On-line reference Reference information presented on a computer screen. Often employs hypertext technology.

Operating system A piece of software which carries out a computer's basic functions. A computer has to have an operating system installed before it can run other programs.

Panning The side-to-side rotation of a film or video camera.

PAL Phase alternation by line. A televison standard used mainly in Europe.

PC Personal computer.

Philosophy A statement of a company's values and beliefs.

Pixels Picture elements—the individual dots of a computer screen's image.

Policy A medium to long-term course of action comprising a goal and a strategy.

Policy deployment The process for ensuring that a company's policies are understood from the highest to the lowest levels in the company.

QCD Quality, cost, and delivery.

Quality Conformance to customer requirements. Usually spelt with a capital 'Q' to differentiate from the everyday meaning of quality.

RAM Random access memory. A computer's internal memory—measured in kilobytes.

Read only access   A restriction on a computerized records system that allows a person to read the records, but does allow the person to amend, add, or remove a record.

SECAM   *Séquential à mémoire.* A French television standard. Also used in the former Soviet Union.

Simplex   Printing on only one side of a sheet of paper.

SME   Subject matter expert. People who support training development by providing expertise on specific topics to be covered in the training.

Software   The programs that are used by computers. Software is to a computer what a compact disc is to a compact disc player.

Stakeholder   A person who has a vested interest in the outcome of an event. Stakeholders usually have the power to positively or negatively influence the outcome, even though they may not take any direct part in the event.

Statistical process control   A method used to determine whether variation in a process is normal or abnormal. A decision can then be made whether to adjust the process.

Strategy   The means of achieving a goal.

TDLB   Training and Development Lead Body

Tilting   The up and down rotation of a film or video camera.

Tracking   Physically moving a film or video camera either parallel or at right angles to the subject.

Training philosophy   A statement of a company's or organization's attitude towards training.

Trainee-centred learning   A form of training where a student's progress (and hence pace) through a course depends on the student's readiness to move on to the next learning stage. Usually involves a form of programmed instruction. Also called self-paced learning.

Triad   A group of three students working together on an exercise.

U-matic   A semi-professional video format. It used to be the standard for training videos, but it is now being replaced by VHS.

UNIX   A computer operating system that supports multitasking and is ideally suited to multiuser applications.

VDU   Visual display unit. The 'box' which houses a computer's screen.

VGA   Video graphics array. A standard for a computer's display which has a definition of 640 × 480 dots (pixels) in 16 colours and 320 × 200 in 256 colours from a choice of 262 144. Super VGA and EVGA are extensions of VGA with definitions of up to 1024 × 768 pixels.

VHS   Video home standard. A domestic video standard. Now increasingly being used as the standard format for training videos. *See also* 'U-matic'.

VHS-C   A video cassette standard that is used in camcorders. It can be clipped into a carrier which allows it to be viewed on a domestic video recorder.

Vision   An inspiring 'picture' of where the company or organization wants to be in the future.

XT eXtended Technology. A more sophisticated version of the original IBM PC.

Zooming Adjusting the lens of a film or video camera so that the subject appears to get larger or smaller.

Index

Further titles in the McGraw-Hill Training Series